Healing Power

Ten Steps To
Pain Management and
Spiritual Evolution

by
Philip Shapiro, M.D.

authorHOUSE™

1663 LIBERTY DRIVE, SUITE 200
BLOOMINGTON, INDIANA 47403
(800) 839-8640
WWW.AUTHORHOUSE.COM

First published by AuthorHouse 07/20/05

ISBN: 1-4208-5726-6 (sc)

Library of Congress Control Number: 2005904569

Printed in the United States of America
Bloomington, Indiana

This book is printed on acid-free paper.

For my courageous sister, Suzanne

TABLE OF CONTENTS

PART SIX
SPIRITUAL QUALITIES / 225

PART SEVEN
CONCLUSION / 325

ACKNOWLEDGMENTS

I have been blessed with profound support from family, friends, teachers, patients, and editors. I would like to express my deepest gratitude to the following. Without their help, there would be no book. I thank:

My beloved parents, Edward and Dorothy Shapiro. My father teaches goodness. My mother embodies empathy. My sister, Suzanne, who showed me purity of heart. My grandparents, aunts, uncles, and cousins for their continuous love and support.

My patients, who teach me courage, forbearance, and humility every day.

All of my teachers.

The lineage of spiritual masters in Self-Realization Fellowship, for their boundless wisdom, particularly Daya Mata, Swami Sri Yukteswar, and Paramahansa Yogananda.

My extraordinary writing coach, Bill Johnson, and deft line editor, Charity Hogge. My friend and advisor Salli Slaughter.

My friend Adrianne Brockman, for use of her prize winning photo, *What Joy!*, which she graciously provided for the cover of this book.

The members of my spirituality and healing groups for their invaluable commentary on how the ten-step healing model works in their lives.

My friends Jane Ahearn, Steve Ahearn, Allie Aller, Madelyn Antinucci, Steve Bearden, Phil Bolton, Barbara Colleran, Monica Desmond, Mary Faulkner, Royal Harris, Kent Hathaway, Sue Hathaway, Janice Hays, Jeff Hays, Meg Kaveny, Terra Kelsey, Corbett Monica, Stacey Moret, Rhandi Summers, Anthea Summers, Teddy

Taegder, and Jeanne Thorpe for their kindness and counsel on spiritual matters.

My sons, Jon and David, and daughter-in-law, Siobhan, for their loving patience while I have been immersed in this project

My phenomenal wife, Sharon Whitney. She knows things. She is the Goddess of Culture. She is my muse. She protected the space needed to create this book. She makes me laugh.

I bow to you all. May God bless you.

PART ONE
TEN STEPS

CHAPTER 1

INTRODUCTION

The great metaphysician Siddhartha Gautama, the Buddha, began his campaign 2600 years ago for the relief of human suffering with a simple diagnosis and treatment plan, known famously as the Four Noble Truths. The first of these truths is: life is painful. The Buddha outlines the root cause of human suffering and prescribes a set of healing practices designed to cure the pains of life. Compassionate service is the medication; peace of mind, the result. The Buddha shows us how to heal our pain with such practices as mindfulness, meditation, and service. The result is serenity and joy. In essence, the Buddha is a masterful pain manager. He teaches us how to transform our suffering into spiritual power.

What is the relationship between the enduring pain management program revealed by the Buddha and healing in today's medical system? Ample scientific evidence indicates that an active spiritual belief system such as Buddhism or any of the great faith traditions has a positive healing effect in all medical fields. Those who have a spiritual practice have better outcomes in medicine, surgery, mental health, and addiction. It is now a scientifically proven "Noble Truth" that spiritual belief systems have a role in healing the body, mind, and soul.

In my work as a psychiatrist during the last 30 years, I have been impressed with the power belief systems have in helping people manage harsh realities. Religion and spirituality give meaning and purpose to the mystery of life. Without this incentive, the painful problems of life tend to linger and grow. Those with an active spiritual belief system experience pain relief and healing. Although problems may not magically disappear, they become more manageable.

Life is difficult. Our problems are deep, complex, and severe. Often we find ourselves caught in a web of pain. We don't know how we got there and we don't know how to get out. Because we manage our pain poorly, we find ourselves in more trouble. Poorly handled problems are a source of untold difficulty. We need help. We need to learn more about the origin of our suffering so we can manage it more skillfully. Then, instead of dragging us down, our problems become a source of strength and peace.

We need solutions that directly address the root causes of our suffering. To this end, I have extracted and organized universal spiritual principles, methods, and qualities from the world's great religious traditions into a ten-step, self-help model designed to aid the reader in transforming any troubling problem into spiritual power.

Like the Buddha, by tracing the course of our pain, we can arrive at some very important truths. When confronted with any difficulty, we shift out of our psychological comfort zone and experience insecurity, worry, and doubt. A new lump, unfamiliar pain, or any lingering discomfort disturbs the routine defenses that give us a feeling of safety. The flicker of a single thought, such as, "This could be serious!" creates anxiety.

An alarm goes off. "Am I OK? Safe? Or am I going towards what I fear the most--intense suffering, disability, or even death, with its associated fear of the unknown?"

Such feelings of insecurity are linked, often unconsciously, to the big questions of life, questions that form the core of spiritual belief systems:

- Why was I born?
- Who am I?
- What is the purpose of my life?
- Is there a God, and if so, what is God's nature?
- Why is there so much suffering and evil in the world?
- How can I find peace, love, and joy in the face of suffering and evil?
- What is death?
- Where do I go after death?

These profound questions address the mystery and meaning of life. Usually such profound questions remain hidden in the unconscious mind while they manifest as anxiety on the surface of consciousness. Nevertheless, they are more likely to become conscious and active at times of crisis such as illness, disability, trauma, or loss. This affords patients, healthcare professionals, and the public a supreme opportunity to work in the territory of belief systems and healing.

Spiritual belief helps us deal with mystery, meaning, trauma, and loss, subjects that are relevant at the time of illness or crisis. When we suffer, we can take advantage of the healing power that is linked to spirituality. By intensifying our belief systems, we can kindle the infinitely intelligent, miraculous, healing power of our bodies, minds, and souls.

Mind-body medicine teaches us how to apply the power of belief to healing. It is emerging as a major force in health care. The burgeoning appeal of mind-body medicine is due to its scientific validity as well as its cost effectiveness: it is ultimately a self-help program. In *Timeless Healing, the Power and Biology of Belief,* Dr. Herbert Benson estimates that mind-body techniques are the treatments of choice in 60 to 90 percent of all doctor visits, and have positive effects no matter the illness.

The time has come for medicine to embrace four important areas in the study of disease and healing: the biological, psychological, social, and spiritual. We can find the cause and cure of disease in these four areas. Until recently in the West, our focus has been on the biological, with some emphasis on the psychological and social realms. Now, however, the scientific connection between spirituality and healing has been made, giving health care professionals, patients, and indeed everyone access to an expanded reservoir of healing power by activating their spiritual belief systems.

I write this book for my patients, colleagues, and the public. The purpose of this book is to help the reader in three ways:

1. Pain management: managing any physical, mental, or spiritual pain or problem;

2. Expansion of healing power: healing body, mind, and soul;
3. Spiritual evolution: the cultivation of spiritual qualities such as love, compassion, forgiveness, courage, strength, peace, wisdom, and joy.

This task may seem daunting. The variety of approaches to meaning and purpose in life is great. There are many religious, spiritual, cultural, and secular belief systems, variations within each, and differences between individuals. Although some people will want to learn, study, and gain expertise in mind-body practices, others with histories of religious disappointment or even serious trauma may not want to engage in this type of work. Some think they have all of life's dilemmas figured out and need no more help.

Despite these barriers, we can work with people from diverse backgrounds in an individualized, non-threatening manner. The connecting link between one's beliefs and the healing power they stimulate is always accessible, waiting to be tapped, free of cost. We can extract and translate universal truths from the great religious traditions into mind-body medicine practices. This book describes a variety of such healing methods.

The ideas in this book originate from a wide variety of teachings. There is no quarrel in the fundamentals of all the great faith systems; rather, they compliment each other. There is an abundance of inspiration to be found in their myriad expressions. Here you will find the wisdom pearls of the ages aimed at healing body, mind, and soul. If you choose to work toward these ends, you will see how your pain is the route to healing through the cultivation of spiritual qualities. In the midst of painful confusion and change, you will learn how to reach the changeless peace that resides within you. You will be able to take refuge in the inner palace of harmony and beauty, regardless of the harsh realities of life. Then you can assist others in their journey toward contentment and freedom. The next chapter describes how to use this book to build an individualized spiritual healing program.

CHAPTER 2

HOW TO USE THIS BOOK

My work as a psychiatrist has taken me to neighborhoods where I met people from vastly different cultures than my own. I have been the doctor for African-American and Hispanic people in Harlem and Bedford-Stuyvesant; Tlingit, Haida, Atthabascan, and Eskimos from the villages of the Alaskan bush; retired military, U.S. Coastguard, and postal workers in Portland, Maine; and many from a variety of other communities. While I have studied the nature of disease and suffering in textbooks and models, the greatest teachers have been these patients, bearers of the devastating aspects of life: war, racism, poverty, mental and physical illness, child sex abuse, rape, domestic violence, and addiction. These courageous people and the mean streets they walk continue to be my teachers of the harsh realities of life.

Because life can become brutal for any of us at any time, we all need ways to manage troubled and painful times. I have a passion for learning how healing power acts as an antidote to pain and devastation. I have studied with the teachers, masters, and gurus of psychology, psychiatry, and spirituality, searching their models with a fine toothcomb, looking for elements that strengthen our ability to heal.

Understanding the torment life brings while experiencing its beauty, grace, and healing power, I have developed a ten-step self-help model that I use myself and teach to my students and patients. The model has three parts:

1. The Ten Steps: The root causes of our suffering are addressed in steps 1-5. The corresponding solutions to these problems comprise steps 6-10. Here we learn how our pain is the route

7

to healing through the cultivation of Love. In this work, Love represents a composite of 100 spiritual qualities. I capitalize the word "Love" to emphasize its Divine Nature.

2. Spiritual Practice: Here you will find a description of twelve spiritual methods proven over the ages to be effective tools for cultivating spiritual qualities. Detailed instructions explain how these methods help us cultivate Love, peace, strength, and courage in response to any pain of the body, mind, or soul. With continued practice of the recommended spiritual methods, we can prepare for any difficulty life brings.

3. Spiritual Qualities: We certainly need to work with our issues, problems, illness, and flaws, but these are not who we are. Labels obscure our true selves. Rather than brand ourselves with labels or identify with our problems, we are encouraged to see our true self as the soul, a composite of spiritual qualities adding up to Love. The center of our being is Love. From a list of 100 spiritual qualities, ten are chosen for detailed study. Here we learn how to use our current problems as a springboard for discovering our spiritual identity of Love, compassion, warmth, and kindness. Love is more powerful than any pain or problem. It is the Great Healer. It is the fundamental solution to all of our problems. It is who we really are.

The purpose of this book is to share this model with a wider audience, those interested in doing spiritual work to stimulate healing power. The model can be used by:

1. Health care professionals interested in helping their patients increase their pain management skills and heal. The model supplements the healing practices of all medical specialties including mental health, substance abuse, and alternative health care.

2. Healthcare consumers looking for help in managing any symptom, disease, or disability;
3. Seekers in crisis struggling with severe problems;
4. Beginning or advanced seekers of spiritual knowledge;
5. People who want help with any pain or problem.

The model is for group or personal use. Healthcare professionals and physicians can teach the ten steps to their patients in hospitals and clinics. The model is also suited for self-help groups in the community.

I teach the steps in a group format that is primarily educational. We read a short passage followed by discussion and contemplation of its significance. This teaching method is appropriate for discussion groups run in clinics or hospitals, as well as in self-help groups independent of health care institutions.

My group does not focus on personal problems that require individual counseling. I do not try to fix other people's problems, nor do I ordinarily give advice or counsel. While all of us need advice or personal counsel from time to time, we always need the universal knowledge of how to expand our healing power, manage our pain more skillfully, and cultivate spiritual qualities. Groups should focus on spiritual practices that transform pain into spiritual power. However, we do not need a group or teacher. We can do this work at home, alone.

This book is an instruction manual. It gives step-by-step processes and examples of bringing spiritual concepts from the lofty penthouse to the ground floor of the daily routines of life. The aim of this book is not conversion, but rather inciting the reader to spiritual action and healing within their preferred system. For those building a personal spiritual program, this work offers a variety of ideas and methods to explore and practice. Other readers brought up in one of the world's great traditions such as Judaism, Christianity, Islam, Hinduism, or Buddhism, may be interested in adding universal spiritual principles and methods that will enhance their established belief system. In either case, whether you are building a program of your own or working from within a particular religion, spiritual practice will augment and intensify your healing power for its work on body, mind, and soul.

While this book is packed with powerful spiritual ideas begging for contemplation, it is no less rich in its practical, down-to-earth, how-to approach. For some, it will be a lifelong resource, as the sacred wisdom of the ages requires ongoing study, contemplation, and practice.

Spiritual work is like climbing a shining mountain. The mountain sparkles with higher states of consciousness and spiritual qualities. Though inviting and attractive, it is not an easy climb. You will need some equipment--some spiritual tools--to help you get a grip and keep your balance. This equipment must fit comfortably. It will vary according to your individual desires and needs.

All too often people argue about the equipment and the pathway. When the argument starts, climbing stops. The trails of history are populated with tragic stories about confrontations concerning the "one true way." When spiritual seekers become belligerent or even violent, not only does progress stop, but the combatants slip, slide, and ultimately fall off the mountain.

In this work, you are encouraged to build your own program in the spirit of "take what you need and leave the rest." This stance avoids controversy and debate while honoring individual preference and need. The book offers principles, methods, processes, affirmations, quotes, and homework assignments. If an idea or method is useful, pick it up and work with it. If it is not, modify it or skip it, and move on until you find something that works for you.

POINTS TO REMEMBER

- This self-help model describes 10 steps, 12 spiritual methods, and 10 spiritual qualities. Its purpose is to help readers expand their healing power, improve their pain management skills, and cultivate spiritual qualities.
- The centerpiece of the model is Love. Love is the greatest healer. It is the universal solution to all of our problems. I encourage

you to prove this to yourself through direct personal experience, by developing a spiritual practice.

The next section of the book describes the ten-step model. You will learn how to use the inevitable suffering of life to cultivate peace, Love, and joy. The result is a shift in the locus of control from the outer world of people, places, and things, to the inner world of peace, power, and strength: a world of our own definition.

CHAPTER 3

TEN STEPS TO PAIN MANAGEMENT AND SPIRITUAL EVOLUTION

Suffering is the Route to Spiritual Power

We seek unlimited peace, Love, and joy in an uncertain world where suffering is inevitable. Because we manage our pain poorly, we get into trouble. The wisdom of the ages, taught by the world's diverse religious traditions, offers a solution to this dilemma by pointing out the connection between pain management and the cultivation of spiritual qualities. When we develop a spiritual practice, we learn how to transform our suffering into spiritual power.

This chapter describes a self-help method of ten principles that propel spiritual evolution. The central premise is that life, through a series of painful lessons, teaches us that the peace, Love, and joy we seek in the outer world can and must ultimately be found within. The ten steps are:

1. The Core Drive
2. Duality and Brutal Reality
3. The Compromise
4. Bad Habits
5. Tools Become Barriers
6. The Seeker
7. Soul and Spirit
8. The School of Life
9. Spiritual Practice
10. Spiritual Experience

Steps 1-5 describe the evolution of our suffering; most of us mismanage our pain, ultimately making it worse. Reality can be fierce and cruel. The very thought causes us to feel threatened. We resist looking at the dark side. However, knowledge of what we are up against is our best defense.

If we understand the root causes of our suffering, we can build a powerful spiritual program in response and be more likely to succeed. We must not shrink, even in the face of the most frightening problems. If we face the brutal realities of violence, tyranny, war, crime, poverty, disease, fear of the unknown, and death, we can build corresponding spiritual responses. It may be difficult for some to read this analysis. Nevertheless, I encourage you to read on. See if you can recognize the root causes of your own suffering in these first five steps.

Steps 6-10 address the problem of suffering. Here we learn how our pain can be used as a stimulus to cultivate peace, Love, and joy. Step 6 describes a period of insight and searching. Step 7 explores the nature of our soul and Spirit.

Step 8 describes pain management in the school of life. Pain is the teacher. *Lessons have to do with learning how to Love when we do not.* Homework assignments and tests are designed to expose and eliminate the problems and flaws that restrict our ability to experience peace and joy. Pain is an intelligent guide, directing us to the work we need to do. When we learn how to extract the necessary lessons from our pain, we expand our Love and move forward.

Step 9 describes twelve spiritual methods derived from the world's great religions. These methods help us unlock healing and spiritual powers inherent in the body. Step 10 describes the revelations that occur when we develop a spiritual practice. Spiritual practice cultivates qualities such as Love, compassion, understanding, courage, perseverance, and humility. These qualities are the jewels of this life. They are healers. They help us eliminate or endure any painful condition of body, mind, or soul. They are more powerful than any barrier or challenge we may face. When we develop a spiritual practice, we slowly replace our limitations and flaws with spiritual qualities. We can then use these qualities to manage the turbulence of life.

While there is no easy way out of the dilemmas posed by life, there is much relief in the discovery that even in the throes of greatest turmoil, we exist somewhere on a 10-step map where suffering has a divine purpose: the development of spiritual power. We regain our bearings when we understand our pain is the stimulant for the growth of spiritual qualities.

By seeing the map, by finding our place on it, and knowing there are always steps to take in the right direction, we get tremendous relief. We see that there is a sense of meaning, purpose, and direction to all that happens, and that we can take back control of our destiny. We make progress and feel better. We see that results are actually quite spectacular although slowly produced, which we do not like. But we can put up with this as long as we define the problem and take steps toward a tangible goal.

We encounter trouble no matter which route we take, but the way offered here is the path of least resistance, the way through our pain to peace, power, and strength. As we move forward through the steps, we find ourselves living the richest possible life, a journey where our spirit is in charge and we are ready for anything!

CHAPTER 4

THE EVOLUTION OF SUFFERING: STEPS 1-5

The Inevitability of Suffering and How We Make It Worse

STEP 1: THE CORE DRIVE

We want to live in a house filled with unlimited peace, Love, and joy; a home where no pain or death can enter. This is our core drive. We crave a perfect world consisting of three parts:

1. The complete elimination of physical, mental, and spiritual anguish;
2. Unlimited peace, Love, and joy;
3. Immortality, the feeling that there is more time.

These elements drive all of our good and bad actions alike. Whether we rob a bank or serve the poor, the motivation is the same: we try to avoid suffering, seek Love, and want more time, afraid as we are of the unknown and death. Our quest to fulfill the core drive solely on the physical plane is doomed to fail, however, as material life is painful, the permanent solace we seek is transient, and death ultimately wins.

STEP 2: DUALITY AND BRUTAL REALITY

We do experience peace, Love, and joy on the physical plane, but it is limited and change is inevitable. It is only a matter of time before reality shifts gears and brings forth new suffering, sometimes difficult or devastating, often brutal. This is the law of duality, which rules the story on the physical plane. Duality is the law of polar opposites, the ups and downs of life: pleasure and pain, good and evil, joy and sadness, love and hate, gain and loss, health and disease, prosperity and poverty, wisdom and ignorance, strength and weakness, life and death, and so on. These opposites oscillate throughout our lives.

However we seek to avoid it, suffering is inevitable, time is limited, and the mysterious, infinite unknown, death, takes over in the end. It can be overwhelming. This is the harsh side of reality, here referred to as "brutal reality." Brutal reality includes three elements:

1. Death
2. Pain and suffering
3. The unknown

In effect, brutal reality is the dark side of duality: pain, limitation, and impermanence. It has great power and ultimately cannot be controlled. It asserts itself unpredictably in anyone's life at anytime, and in a seemingly endless variety of ways.

Brutal reality impacted my life before I was born. In 1943, I was a 7-month-old fetus in my mother's womb. A neighbor accidentally dropped my sister, Suzanne, who was 20 months old. That night she developed a fever and had a seizure. My parents took her to the hospital where a spinal tap revealed blood in her spinal fluid. She had a type of brain damage that caused muscle spasms, a condition known as cerebral palsy. Her life was one of severe and chronic disability. She had difficulty walking and often fell: loud crashes sounded in the house at any time. My parents and I would run to her in fear of what we might find. Would there be a broken leg, a cracked skull, blood? She would often choke or gag on her food due to muscle spasms that inhibited her ability to swallow, taking away in a flash the camaraderie of our family supper.

She was a beautiful person, physically and spiritually. I never saw her angry. She was pure Love. Despite her beauty, she remained homebound, isolated, and lonely, her disability preventing her from keeping up with her peers.

At age 24, a sudden loss of eyesight compounded her problems. She became blind over a few short weeks from a mysterious process no physician could diagnose. She went to a school for the blind and learned Braille, where she met the love of her life, a wonderful man who was also blind. It was her lifelong dream to get married, and she did at age 27. On the weekend of her honeymoon, she got sick. Six weeks later she was dead. The same mysterious neurological disease that caused her blindness destroyed her nervous system.

On that same day in 1943 when I was a 7-month-old fetus, thousands of people were executed in the gas chambers of the concentration camps in Europe because they were Jewish, homosexual, gypsies, or other such ill-fated, trumped-up categories. Millions of innocents were lost in the camps of the Holocaust.

We suffer brutal reality individually from disease, violence, racism, poverty, and injustice, and collectively from cataclysmic events such as political upheaval, earthquakes, and war. Since life eventually leads to death, brutal reality ultimately reigns on the physical plane. While the ordinary changes of life are a source of adventure and excitement, death is terrifying, as it forces us to leave behind everything we know.

In the card game of life, we must play the hand we are dealt. But death, that invisible, mysterious opponent, holds the ace. We do not like this power arrangement. In our attempts to get control and feel safe, we accumulate as many cards in the deck as possible, but brutal reality wins in the end. At death, when brutal reality finally plays its ace, we are thrust forward into the unknown at an accelerated pace. We are propelled into a personal form of future shock. There is a radical rapid shift into the heart of the mysterious infinite unknown.

We want to live painlessly and forever in perfect harmony. We try to achieve this core drive through the big show: the story of life on the physical plane. The action is attractive, fascinating, and seductive. It lures us into thinking we can achieve comfort and safety through our relationships, work, and recreation. We love the show. But the laws of duality and brutal reality rule the drama. Everything on the physical plane is temporary and limited, and suffering is inevitable. We try in vain to control our stories, but this is impossible. We cannot trust the external world to give us the absolute safety and perfect Love we crave. In the collision between the core drive and duality, we discover the need to compromise.

STEP 3: THE COMPROMISE

We compromise by creating an illusion of safety through our relationships and activities. Family, friends, work, recreation, culture, and hobbies provide us with a measure of Love and security. We are often comfortable and feel safe. However, no matter how we struggle to keep what we have, it is only a matter of time before instability is upon us again. Suffering is unavoidable and eventually everything succumbs, including the body. We do not like this set-up. We resist the pain of reality; we do not accept the compromise. Instead, we make a desperate attempt to eliminate *all of our suffering* through faulty mechanisms such as the cultivation of bad habits that create pseudo-relief from our pain.

STEP 4: BAD HABITS

Our relentless craving for perfect peace forces us all too often to act in desperate, destructive ways. We develop bad habits, power trips, materialism, hyperactivity, and codependency. In a mighty but misguided effort to ward off pain, we stuff ourselves with food, drugs, alcohol, and sex, and develop addictions. In our restless search for permanent joy, we strive for wealth, possessions, and power over others. We become activity junkies, hooked on work, watching and playing sports, glued to television, the Internet, movies, music and so on ... all the while actually seeking eternal Love and safety in a world where transience and limitation are the rule.

Our troubles deepen as these bad habits have a negative influence on us and others. Not only do we lose sight of the Love we seek, but we infiltrate our relationships and work with negativity. We dig ourselves into a deeper hole as we make the original, inevitable suffering on the physical plane worse through our misguided attempts to eliminate it.

EXERCISES

1. What is your core drive?
2. What dualities are present in your life?
3. What is your brutal reality?
4. Describe how duality and brutal reality affect your life.
5. Describe the relationship between the core drive, duality, and brutal reality in your life.
6. What is "the compromise" described in step 3?
7. How does this compromise play itself out in your life?

STEP 5: TOOLS BECOME BARRIERS

We use six tools to achieve the core drive of unlimited peace, that house where death and pain cannot enter.

1. Mind
2. Emotion
3. Desire
4. Body
5. Activities
6. Ego

While these tools are useful in helping us find some measure of peace, Love, joy, safety, and pain relief, they become problems themselves. We add to our suffering with our restless minds, high emotional reactivity, excessive material desire, improperly cared for bodies, hyperactivity, and egotism. Following is a discussion of how each of these tools helps us achieve our goals and how they too often spin out of control, add to our suffering, and become barriers to spiritual growth.

STEP 5.1: THE MIND

The mind is a very powerful and effective tool designed to help us in our pursuit of happiness. It shapes the meaning of our personal story and it is a brilliant problem solver. When difficulties arise, the reasoning mind activates its "fixing mode." With its powers of understanding, reason, creativity, imagination, and positive thought, we analyze our problems and develop plans of action. The mind does this work best when it is peaceful, positive, receptive, and resilient. From this position, it can meet the challenge of any problems, tests, and lessons that life presents.

Unfortunately, the mind does not always work this well. It has a complex bag of tricks that keeps us from our core mission. It seems to have a life all its own. It won't quit thinking often good, but sometimes useless, foolish, or destructive thoughts. It ruminates and obsesses, long after it has completed its work of shaping meaning and solving problems. Even when we try to control it, the mind demonstrates its relentless independence, becoming at times a formidable opponent in our quest for happiness and the elimination of suffering.

When stressful problems arise, the mind often reacts like an electrical wire carrying too much charge. Overheated, it inadvertently attacks us with highly charged negative, and often false thoughts. Negative thinking creates anger, depression, fear, and insecurity. We lose logic and flexibility. Distortion replaces truth. There is no problem solving. On the contrary, the mind in overdrive is a liability, contributing an additional layer of inner turmoil to our original painful problems.

Ideally, when we have done all that we can to work on the reversible component of a problem, the mind would return to its natural state of peace and poise. Instead, even after it performs well in "fixing mode," the mind remains hyperactive and restless, in perpetual motion like a rabbit living in the attic. If we try to grab it, it hops out of our grasp. Fast and slippery, it darts from one topic to another, compromising our ability to focus, concentrate, and relax.

While at times the mind bolts like a bunny from one topic to another, it can also get stuck in a rut. When a car is stuck in the mud, it is natural to respond by pressing harder on the accelerator ... but this makes the problem worse. The motor overheats, the rut deepens, and mud spreads around. Similarly, the mind gets hung up on a problem and goes over the same thoughts again and again, even after a solution and plans have already been determined. We keep thinking about the problem, which only serves to deepen the mental groove that carries the overworked pattern of thought. This common occurrence is called rumination. We think too much. Perpetual replays of our personal story are a form of addiction. Hooked to the soap opera of our own lives, we lose contentment and satisfaction.

An easily distracted, restless mind is a source of untold grief. It adds layer upon layer of unreality, distortion, and negativity over our true selves. It creates twists and turns that make life unnecessarily complex and stressful. It obsessively analyzes and fantasizes, creates unrealistic assumptions and expectations, and subjects itself to attractions and repulsions. It exaggerates the importance of events and infuses insecurity into our personal story.

Despite all of this, we seem to be in an unconditional love affair with the mind. We profoundly over-identify with it, no matter how much trouble it gives us. We consider our own thoughts, likes, and dislikes to be the final arbiter of truth. A bridge of arrogance spans events and the mind's interpretations of them. We let it dominate our consciousness even when it is wrong or hysterical.

The mind has a subtle, relentless grip on us. In the beginning we don't even know that this clever dictator has taken over, as it uses tactics that are elusive and beyond our grasp. Unaware of its wily ways, the mind keeps us under its hypnotic control. This state of consciousness is so habitual, we do not see the enemy within.

We need to understand how much trouble the shrewd and cunning mind causes. Then we can take steps to reduce its negative power and return it to the instrument it should be of creativity, imagination, problem solving, and story shaping. In step 9, spiritual practice, we learn how to do this. There is a description of several spiritual techniques including affirmation, meditation, mindfulness, and yoga. These techniques help us realign the mind with its natural state of peace, poise, positive resilience, openness, and flexibility.

STEP 5.2: EMOTION

Emotions are natural, healthy, and intelligent. They carry important information about our issues, problems, solutions, strategies, and lessons. When we learn how to extract this information from our feelings, we gain self-knowledge: knowledge of our personal story. There are times when we have to go through emotional pain and learn from it in order to move forward. Translating emotion into self-knowledge is a valuable skill. When we know how to do this, we can transform our suffering into peace, joy, and strength.

Too often, however, we suffer from highly reactive and volatile emotions that we do not understand. Most of us have had no training in emotional pain management. Because we don't know what to do with these feelings, we instinctively try to keep them from conscious awareness by denying their existence, avoiding them with bad habits, or pushing them into the subconscious and body where they are stored in latent form. The unprocessed emotion remains in the body and subconscious mind, however--waiting, if not begging, for recognition.

While in storage, painful, unprocessed emotions have a negative impact on our physical, mental, and spiritual health. We develop negative attitudes, distorted thinking, and behave in destructive ways. In the worst-case scenario, suppressed emotions overwhelm our defenses and we lose control, subsequently endangering ourselves and others. Unprocessed emotions reap untold havoc on our lives.

There is a powerful narrative embedded in our feelings about our personal story. We need to learn how to process our emotions by letting our story unfold naturally. Then we need to learn to spiritualize our story. The spiritual practices described in step 9 teach us how to do this. When we develop a spiritual practice, we learn how to transform painful emotions into self-knowledge.

STEP 5.3: DESIRE

We love the show, the play of life on the physical plane. Its fascinating stories and alluring material objects capture our attention and desire. We want loving relationships, prosperity, and health. These desires are good. They help us achieve peace, safety and joy. Problems occur when we hold on to our possessions with fierce tenacity and when we ceaselessly desire more.

If not careful, our attachment to what we own and our thirst for more can slip into addiction. It is all too easy to become obsessed with power, sex, relationships, money, success, status, material objects, food, drugs, or alcohol. These addictions weaken and eventually paralyze our will, destroy our character, and bury our souls. Their root cause is excessive, uncontrolled desire.

Desire itself is the problem. Even though some desires are positive, leading to success, health, and prosperity, they do not stop here. Desire begets desire. We want more *things*, even when we have enough. When desires are not met, we become angry, frustrated, and tense. When desires are satisfied, we are still not happy because another desire inevitably crops up and steals our peace. In our dissatisfaction and restlessness, we seek relief by quenching the next wave of desire. We cannot seem to get enough of what we think we want, because once we get it, we are stimulated to get more. If we keep pursuing happiness in this seemingly endless procession of want, we become caught up in a cycle of bad habits and addiction, greed and anxiety, attachment and exhaustion.

Excessive material desire is a root cause of dissatisfaction. Our attachments and bad habits separate us from others. We feel alone, insecure, and frightened. We act against our own will and the best interests of others. We are out of control, in a vicious cycle that is difficult to break. If we do not disrupt this cycle, we can experience panic, terror, depression, anger, and even rage. These painful emotions dominate our consciousness and impede our ability to live a spiritual life. There can be no peace when our minds are restless and our emotions easily triggered. It is hard to love if we are on a power trip or greedy for more money. The spiritual practices described in this work help us transform excessive material desire into inner peace and contentment. Then we can appreciate what we already have.

STEP 5.4: THE BODY

The body is our vehicle for engaging life, the doer of all activities as we seek the many joys life has to offer. However, the body throws us many challenges. It annoys us when it pulls and tugs, gets tired and heavy, or is too hot or cold. It longs for relief from desire, hunger, and discomfort. It tosses us between pleasure and pain, illness and health, life and death. It subjects us to its demands which sometimes lead us astray, into bad decisions and bad habits.

Some abuse the body by eating, drinking, and smoking too much. Many are in poor shape, not getting enough physical exercise. We all suffer from a variety of physical pains and progressive disability as the years pass, and ultimately of course the body ends in death.

We strongly identify with the body. It is our greatest attachment. We cling to the body in life and even at death. We hold on to it as though it were the only boat in the ocean. We think that letting go means drowning.

Fear of death causes many to become over-involved, even obsessed with their physical appearance, refusing to accept the body's progression into old age. Some of us choose cosmetic surgery, a stitch here, a tuck there, attempting to ward off what we fear the most: annihilation of the body and extinction of consciousness.

Despite all of the trouble, the body is of magnificent design. It has inherent miraculous healing powers, spiritual qualities embedded in our genetic code, and it is the carrier of our potential spiritual enlightenment and liberation. The body is a temple, harboring higher states of consciousness. We can experience deep peace, Love, and joy of the soul when we develop a spiritual practice. Therefore, taking control of and being responsible for the maintenance of our bodies is imperative for healing and spiritual evolution.

STEP 5.5: ACTIVITY

During the day, we walk, talk, work, shop, cook, clean, care for children and parents, exercise, study, read, play, go to church, mosque, or synagogue, play sports .... Most of us are in a state of perpetual motion from the time we get up in the morning until we go to bed at night. Being active is good, a natural part of life. But popular culture would have us believe that work, recreation, and leisure will give us the peace of mind we seek. Experience dictates otherwise.

In the course of living, we find the joys and pleasures of the outer world are limited and ephemeral. The world of events, objects, and people is always changing. Everything has a beginning, middle, and end. Joy alternates with sadness, peace with anger, health with sickness, success with failure, and pleasure with pain. We cannot avoid the ups and downs of life. Worldly pleasures do not last and suffering is inevitable.

Although we cannot be completely satisfied with our lives on the physical plane, the wisdom traditions point to our inner being as a source of lasting peace. Discovering the inner path to contentment is difficult, however, as the external world is powerful and attractive, continuously seducing us into the illusion that happiness is within our grasp and the price is right.

Activity becomes a barrier to spiritual growth when it is compulsive, addictive, or used as a substitute for searching within for the transcendent peace, Love, and joy bred of stillness. We can bring stillness into our lives when we learn such practices as contemplation, introspection, and meditation, as described in step 9.

STEP 5.6: THE EGO

The ego is the chief executive officer of our physical plane consciousness. Its job is to satisfy the core drive. It does this by establishing our place in the world of relationships, work, and recreation. This is good. However, the ego has become a problem, as it has seceded from the union with our higher self, Higher Power, and creation. Like a rebel monarch, it declares itself the sole owner and operator of consciousness. It tricks us into thinking that material consciousness is the only reality. Forcing out all experiences of higher consciousness, it would have us believe that we are alone and limited.

The ego has surreptitiously taken over the control rooms of the mind, emotion, desire, body, and action. It uses these tools in its desperate search for immortality and permanent peace. The search is in vain, however, as the ego runs into the brick wall of limitation and inevitable suffering on the physical plane. Nevertheless, the ego does not give up its battle. It counters with an insatiable desire for recognition, success, and power. This results in excessive attention-seeking, inflated self-importance, accumulation, and empire building.

The ego behaves like a dictator, using a variety of tactics to gain power over others, including subtle manipulation and overt aggression. Concerned primarily with itself, the ego behaves as a greedy narcissist. "I! Me! Mine!" Territorial and self-important, it tries to manipulate others to its own ends and purposes. With a voracious appetite for control, it stifles dissent and ignores criticism.

Even if the ego's works give us success, power, and wealth, we are still in trouble. No matter how important we become, under the control of the ego we remain separate from the vast kingdom of peace within ourselves. Since it has no foundation, at its core the ego is insecure and fears extinction. Thus it is paranoid and defensive when it does not need to be and tries to be right all of the time, even when it is wrong.

Because the ego lacks introspection on its own problems, it remains self-righteous while it scapegoats others. The ego resists change and continues to hold on to outmoded ideas. It leads us into the dead end streets and dark alleys of our consciousness. With the ego in charge, we remain troubled, insecure, alone, and frightened.

Clearly, we must address the problem of the ego on the spiritual path. In the section on spiritual practices, we learn how to reduce and ultimately replace the ego with the power and wisdom of the soul.

POINTS TO REMEMBER

The first five steps describe the evolution of suffering on the physical plane. In summary:

- We want (1) complete elimination of suffering, (2) unlimited peace, Love and joy, and (3) immortality. This is the core drive.
- We attempt to achieve the core drive through our relationships, work, and recreation but these prove inadequate since life on the physical plane is dual. There is limitation, impermanence, and some suffering is inevitable.
- We cultivate bad habits in an attempt to eliminate our pain.

- There are six tools that we use to achieve the core drive: Mind, emotion, desire, body, activity, and ego. While these tools help us, they can also spin out of control and add to our suffering.

EXERCISES

1. Step 5 describes how the mind, emotions, desires, body, activities, and ego are assets that become liabilities. Review how each of these tools presents both opportunities and challenges in your life.
2. Does your mind both solve and create problems for you?
3. What kinds of problems does your mind create?
4. Would you like to be able to control your mind but don't know how?
5. Do you struggle with painful emotions that seem excessive and get you into trouble?
6. What are some examples in your life of how desire led to attachment and a bad habit or two?
7. Have your bad habits lead to excessive emotional reactivity?
8. Do you fill your waking life with continuous activity?
9. Do you have built-in periods of retreat and solitude for rest and regeneration?
10. Describe how your ego gets you into trouble.

In this chapter, we studied steps 1-5. These steps describe three levels to our suffering:

1. Suffering is inevitable;
2. Pain is often self-inflicted from our bad habits;
3. The six helpful tools often spin out of control.

Steps 6-10 address each of these levels. In the following chapters, we will learn how *pain management and spiritual practice lead to the recovery of the soul and Higher Power as the peace, Love, and joy we crave.*

CHAPTER 5

SEEK AND YOU SHALL FIND: STEPS 6-7

Spiritual Qualities, Soul, and Spirit

STEP 6: THE SEEKER

We want permanent peace, Love, and joy, no suffering, and unlimited time. We cannot satisfy this core drive on the physical plane where limitations abound and suffering is inevitable. We compromise by creating an illusion of safety through our relationships, work, and recreation. However, since we do not accept the inevitable suffering of life, we often try to escape our pain by developing bad habits. While mind, emotion, desire, activity, body, and ego help us achieve our goals, they spin out of control and add yet another layer to our suffering. Our pain deepens. We may develop symptoms and become less able to function productively. Moreover, there may be an impending or actual loss of control with danger to ourselves or others. Our suffering leads us to a period of questioning. We recognize the need for help. We become seekers.

This is a difficult stage to achieve, because of the ego. The ego, considering itself the king/queen of truth, denies any problems under its leadership. It sees no need for consultation. This sets up a fierce battle between our pain and our egos. Our pain demands that the ego get out of the way so new knowledge can flow in to save the day. Sensing a threat and a potential humiliating defeat, the ego clings to the status quo as it fights off new ways of understanding and perception.

If insight is to prevail, however, we must seek help. We must reduce the ego to learn new and better ways of managing our pain. When our suffering becomes unbearable and the ego has finally had enough, it gives up a little territory and surrenders into the pain. At this point, humiliation becomes humility. The soft inner core of our being opens. Now we can learn. Now we can go deeper, ask the big questions, and seek new ways of understanding.

Our search for meaning takes us to the dark side of duality: failure, defeat, loss, separation, abandonment, rejection, sickness, violence, poverty, war, death, and evil. What possible spiritual explanation can there be for slavery, the Holocaust, famine, or a terror attack perpetuated by criminal extremists? Why do murder, sex abuse, and rape exist? Why is reality so brutal? While our minds crave an explanation, our souls yearn for relief. But the spiritual mathematics in these shadows present a big challenge, and knowledge of the absolute is elusive. We persist. Is there anything to hold on to? Is our search for permanent Love and safety futile on this earth where limitation and insecurity seem to have the upper hand? If the physical plane cannot satisfy our deepest yearning, is there another dimension to life, perhaps higher or more subtle, that can help? Can the terror associated with the unknown be transformed into awe, curiosity for adventure, and creativity? Is there anything that doesn't change, which gives stillness and peace? Is there something in this life and after death in which we can trust?

Our search takes us to spiritual belief systems. World religions delve into the heart of the mystery and suffering of life and emerge with a prescription for our difficulties. We can heal ourselves, religion teaches, if we learn how to manage our pain by developing a spiritual practice. When we practice spiritual disciplines such as meditation, mindfulness, service, and yoga, we cultivate ever-expanding Love; moreover, we discover this and other wonderful spiritual qualities are of the same nature as the soul and Higher Power.

Pain management and spiritual practice lead to the discovery that the soul and Spirit are indistinguishable from the unlimited Love we so crave. This is the core drive resurrected! But now, armed with the wisdom of the great world religions, we understand that the Love we have been seeking in the outside world can and must ultimately be found inside. Step seven elaborates on the nature of the soul and Spirit.

STEP 7: SOUL AND SPIRIT

SOUL

Religious traditions point to spiritual qualities as the nature of the soul and Spirit and recognize these qualities as the goal of all spiritual work. If we extract the quintessence from the texts and stories of the sacred traditions and summarize them in one-word qualities to sell as a tincture of religion, these qualities would be found:

SPIRITUAL ALPHABET

1. acceptance	35. honesty	69. pure awareness
2. appreciation	36. hope	70. pure consciousness
3. balance	37. humility	71. purity
4. beauty	38. humor	72. receptivity
5. belief	39. immortality	73. reverence
6. changelessness	40. infinity	74. rhythm
7. cheerfulness	41. integrity	75. safety
8. clarity	42. interconnectedness	76. security
9. community	43. introspection	77. self-control
10. compassion	44. intuition	78. service
11. confidence	45. joy	79. silence
12. contentment	46. justice	80. simplicity
13. courage	47. kindness	81. sincerity
14. creativity	48. knowledge	82. spaciousness
15. desirelessness	49. laughter	83. stillness
16. devotion	50. light	84. strength
17. endurance	51. listening	85. success
18. energy	52. loyalty	86. surrender
19. enthusiasm	53. mercy	87. sweetness
20. equality	54. mindfulness	88. tenderness
21. eternity	55. mystery	89. thoughtfulness
22. even-mindedness	56. non-attachment	90. tolerance
23. faith	57. non-injury	91. trust
24. fearlessness	58. oneness	92. truthfulness
25. forbearance	59. openness	93. unconditional love
26. forgiveness	60. order	94. understanding
27. freedom	61. patience	95. unity
28. friendship	62. peace	96. usefulness
29. fun	63. perfection	97. warmth
30. generosity	64. perseverance	98. will
31. gentleness	65. play	99. wisdom
32. gratitude	66. positive thinking	100. witness
33. harmony	67. power	101. other
34. healing	68. practicality	

The *Bible, Koran, Bhagavad Gita,* and all sacred texts speak to these qualities. Christ, Buddha, Krishna, Mohammed, the Bal Shem Tov, gurus, Zen masters, and yogis teach these qualities. They are at the core of every spiritual story. They represent the basics, the alphabet: the periodic table of spiritual elements.

Spiritual qualities describe who we really are. We are born with them. They are standard equipment, built into the human genetic code. As Dr. Herbert Benson argues in *Timeless Healing,* we are "wired for God." The higher self is pure and perfect, loving and calm, wise and compassionate. This is our genetic birthright.

The roles we play in life, our educational level, economic status, race, ethnicity, and age obscure our true nature. We are not ultimately described by our bodies, personalities, or roles. Similarly, we are not our problems, flaws, or illnesses. These superficial identifications veil our inner identity or true self, the soul where we find all of the spiritual qualities.

The list of spiritual qualities is long and may appear formidable. It need not be. All of the qualities are connected, and Love is the root. If we improve our ability to Love, the rest of the qualities simultaneously grow. Similarly, if we cultivate any one of the qualities, our Love grows. We can pick one or a few qualities to work on at any given time. It does not matter which ones we choose.

Nor does it matter what religion we practice. It does not matter if we practice a religion at all. What *does* matter is the level of our development of our souls' qualities, or Love. If the fruit of a religion is Love, it is good; if not, there is a problem.

Love is the soul, composed of the 100 qualities listed in the spiritual alphabet. For our purposes, each time you read the word "Love," you can consider that as one or a combination of the spiritual qualities listed in the spiritual alphabet.

The soul is the deepest aspect of our being, a calm center which is *always there,* no matter how turbulent or chaotic our life. We can always turn to the soul for refuge, comfort, and rejuvenation. No matter what external problem we face, the soul offers harmony.

"Love" is not merely a word but an actual healing power, a concrete, tangible force with an identity and life all its own. We can cultivate Love through the practice of a variety of spiritual methods. We know how to make it grow. And as it grows, our healing power grows.

Love and its associated spiritual qualities are the healers. They broker and buffer the pain of life. Such healing powers as compassion, understanding, forgiveness, and humility will contain, reduce, or eliminate any barrier we encounter.

We can trace the root of all of our problems to a lack of Love. Similarly, Love is the solution to all of our problems. Knowing this kindles hope, which is necessary to start the healing process. Hope is the match that lights the fire necessary for spiritual growth and evolution. The cultivation of Love & Co., the goal and the reward of the spiritual path, is the true revolution.

We can contact the soul through meditation, prayer, and contemplation. These methods bring us to a quiet state needed to hear the still, small voice within. This voice, an inner guide, can show us the way to compassion, kindness, and courage. Deep inside the soul, we are all a composite of spiritual qualities: warm, loving, human beings filled with strength, wisdom, and joy. This is our spiritual identity, our Buddha nature, the image of God within. It is who we really are. Part of the spiritual journey is spent searching for and finding this inner reality, a search that also involves defining for ourselves the nature of our Higher Power.

SPIRIT

In this work, "Spirit" or "Higher Power" refers to:
- Higher meaning and purpose
- The higher or true self
- Higher states of consciousness
- The God of your understanding

It is very helpful, on the spiritual path, to define the nature of our Higher Power for ourselves. Once we have a working image of a Higher Power, we can tap into it as a source of the Love we seek. Following is a breakdown of some of the ways that spiritual belief systems describe the nature of Higher Power:

- OMNISCIENT, OMNIPOTENT, OMNIPRESENT: In Christianity, Judaism, Islam, Hinduism, and certain aspects of Buddhism, God is present everywhere as an all-knowing, all-powerful, conscious Universal Being to whom we may appeal and receive a response through grace.

- GOD IS LOVE: There is a personal relationship with God as Father or Mother, Friend, Confidante, Beloved, Teacher, Protector, Guide, Healer, Counselor, or Physician through communion, prayer, affirmation, meditation, service, and/or yoga.

- CONSCIOUSNESS: Many people do not feel comfortable relating to their Higher Power in a personal way. They feel that any attempt to think of God in human terms is limiting, if not confusing. These individuals may pursue an elevation in consciousness but do not believe in a God to whom they can appeal. For example, some who practice Buddhism may focus on purification or elevation of their awareness, energy, and consciousness.

- THE MASTERS SUCH AS CHRIST, BUDDHA, KRISHNA, MUHAMMAD, THE BAL SHEM TOV: God-realized masters embody the great spiritual qualities as a model for humanity to follow.

- THE CHANGELESS ONE: This is God as the One Life that flows through, pervades, and unites everything, a oneness of life that is changeless and eternal, the source of all that is, and the place to which we all return. This pure consciousness and awareness cannot be cut, burned, or hurt in any way.

- NATURE: Some commune with nature, energy, or Mother Earth.

- HIGHER PURPOSE AND MEANING: Others believe in a higher purpose and meaning. They seek spiritual qualities as part of their higher self. The tools for growth are reason, feeling, dreams, and the subconscious mind.

- AN INFINITE OCEAN FILLED WITH OMNISCIENT LOVE: This is God as the Great Physician with infinite healing power. We can enter this field via meditation and prayer.

- THE INFINITE MYSTERIOUS UNKNOWN: No words can describe this state. It is beyond the meager adjectives of human conception.

- Many other concepts, images, and ideas.

We can specifically define those aspects and images of a Higher Power that are comfortable, approachable, and accessible. Then we can use our concept as a source of continuous guidance in our response to any problem or pain.

In this work, I will employ all of the aspects described above in discussion, affirmations, and processes. If you have difficulty connecting to an image I am using, I encourage you to replace it with one that can work for you. For example, if I refer to God, you might choose consciousness. If I choose Father, you might prefer Mother. God may be seen as male, female, both, or neither. I alternate between male and female pronouns and other aspects such as Teacher, Physician, Ocean, Changeless One, or Counselor to emphasize the multi-faceted nature of the Higher Power.

POINTS TO REMEMBER: STEPS 6-7

- Painful crises lead to a search for meaning and purpose.
- A study of spiritual belief systems reveals a connection between spiritual qualities, the soul, and our Higher Power.

- The qualities listed in the spiritual alphabet tell a story about Love.
- Our true nature is Love.
- "Love" in this work is shorthand for the 100 qualities comprising the spiritual alphabet.
- The development of spiritual qualities is the central purpose of spiritual practice.
- When we activate Love, our healing power expands.
- Spiritual qualities impact healing operations in some yet-to-be-determined way at the molecular, cellular, and electrical-magnetic levels of the brain and body.
- Developing a comfortable, approachable, and accessible concept of a Higher Power is useful for managing problems.

EXERCISES

1. Has your suffering led you to search for meaning and purpose?
2. What is the meaning and purpose of your life?
3. What role does your belief system play in giving meaning and purpose to your life?
4. What is your concept of soul, or true self?
5. Do you have a Higher Power?
6. What is your concept of a Higher Power?
7. Is your Higher Power loving and forgiving or judgmental and punitive?
8. To develop your concept of a Higher Power, think of some of the brutal realities that have or might occur. Is your connection to your Higher Power stronger than the worst experience that has happened or that you can imagine? What would it take to get you through that?

CHAPTER 6

SHIFTING THE LOCUS OF CONTROL: STEPS 8-10

Pain Management and Spiritual Practice Give Us the Peace, Love, and Joy We Crave

Step 7 defines the nature of the soul and Higher Power as Love. Knowing this, however, does not give us the pain relief we seek. The next step is to learn how to manage our pain more skillfully: Step 8 describes pain management in the school of life.

Step 9 describes spiritual practices. Step 10 describes the spiritual experience of ever-expanding Love.

STEP 8: PAIN MANAGEMENT IN THE SCHOOL OF LIFE

The sacred traditions describe the experience of higher consciousness as a vast stillness, changeless peace, and infinite Love. Yet daily we experience turbulence from life on the physical plane. We have little or no control over the evolution and spin of the show. We love the positive side of the story, but the intrusion of brutal reality throws us into high mental and emotional reactivity. The harmony we seek disappears and we no longer enjoy the show.

We cannot change duality, but we can change our response to it. We can learn new ways to manage pain by viewing life as school. The purpose of the school of life is to learn who we really are: soul connected to Spirit. This involves accepting pain as a stimulant for the growth of spiritual qualities. Then we discover our true identity of unconditional Love and changeless peace.

Every experience, event, and person is a teacher in the school of life. *Lessons have to do with learning how to Love when we do not.* There are homework assignments and tests designed to bring out our painful physical, mental, and spiritual problems. The blocks to our spiritual growth must be exposed before they can be eliminated. Pain tells us where to work. It is intelligent. It bears messages. By enduring and working with our pain, we learn our lessons, expand our Love, and grow.

Life expects us to do the homework every day. Daily assignments in the outer world often involve our jobs, school, relationships, and service. Daily assignments in the inner world include practicing affirmations, meditation, mindfulness, and other spiritual methods.

When we attend classes and do the necessary homework, we learn lessons and pass the tests. To pass a test requires using our suffering as a stimulant for the cultivation of spiritual qualities. We are to respond to all of our painful problems with ever-increasing Love, compassion, understanding, strength, courage, and other qualities as listed in the spiritual alphabet. When we pass our tests and achieve mastery, we move on to the next grade, where a new set of problems and higher standards emerge. However, when we play hooky from class and neglect our homework, assignments pile up and problems remain unresolved. We fail the test and repeat the class.

For example, some of us have a lifelong problem with high emotional reactivity. Our daily routine often includes setups: events that cause us to over-react. When we begin our spiritual practice, we must make a conscious decision to remain calm and patient, no matter the provocation. With spiritual practices such as meditation and mindfulness, we slowly transform excessive emotion to even-minded patience. We know that we have advanced when the circumstance that aroused excessive emotion in the past brings forth a peaceful response instead. When we master a certain level of grace, new, unexpected, and usually more difficult setups arise to test our ability to remain calm. In this way, the bar is raised so that we can continue to expand our peaceful response.

Sometimes life assigns very painful problems that need much study and work. In these more difficult classes, there is great potential for learning and growth as long as we use our pain to cultivate Love. On the other hand, if we resort to destructive, pain-killing devices such as substance abuse or other such bad habits, these difficult assignments will be lost as opportunities for spiritual growth, and their lessons will ultimately need to be repeated.

Many do well in the school of life when times are good, but poorly when tragedies or crises occur. A strong spiritual program must include all of life's events, including the most painful. When pain is accepted as the teacher, no barrier can stop us; even those that are apparently or obviously evil can be used to propel us forward to courage, strength, and wisdom.

The school of life never closes. There is always room for improvement when developing spiritual qualities. It is wise to do the homework daily. We cannot cram for the final exam the night before ... the final exam being entry into the vast unknown mystery at the time of death. Don't you want to be prepared?

STEP 9: SPIRITUAL PRACTICE

Many people go to synagogue, church, or mosque, perform rituals, sing and chant, listen to sermons, and study scripture. These good acts are a part of external worship. We get inspired, behave ethically, and may have some direct spiritual experiences.

The methods described in this work have to do with internal spiritual practice. These methods require an additional level of commitment, discipline, and time. The body is the temple. The pursuit is internal. The goal is translation of concept and belief into tangible experience and perception, going deeper into the realm of Spirit.

The spiritual practices described in this work are:

1   Affirmations
2. Habits
3. Progressive Muscle Relaxation
4. Breathwork

5. Contemplation
6. Meditation
7. Prayer
8. Mindfulness
9. Practicing the Presence of God
10. Service
11. Yoga
12. Transformation of Emotion

These methods help calm the restless mind, transform turbulent emotions into self-knowledge, excessive material desires into inner contentment, and the selfishness of the ego into gentle acts of humble service. We can practice these methods in response to any pain or problem. The result is a variety of positive spiritual experiences.

STEP 10: SPIRITUAL EXPERIENCE

Pain management and spiritual practice lead to the discovery of the soul and Higher Power. We can prove that we have a soul made in the image of Love if we practice spiritual disciplines in response to life's problems. When we do the work, we experience ego reduction, pain relief, problem resolution, healing, guidance, and protection. Spiritual qualities such as courage, strength, gratitude, humility, and forgiveness slowly grow.

As we advance, there may be an unmistakable change in consciousness. We experience the peace that surpasses understanding, unfathomable stillness, pure Love, ecstatic joy, cosmic sound and light, intuitive knowledge, visions, and pure disembodied consciousness.

With continued practice, our spiritual qualities become strong enough that no external drama or condition of our bodies can shake them. We remain peaceful, positive, and poised no matter what life throws. We are awake, aware, and ready for anything. Serene and compassionate service to humanity is the natural outcome of this state of consciousness.

At mastery, we experience the soul and Higher Power as a durable Love born of ever-expanding compassion, understanding, wisdom, and joy. We know we are the immutable peace of the soul, connected to Spirit, eternally safe and protected. We know our Love is greater than any pain or problem. We can get through any barrier, no matter how insurmountable it appears. Nothing can stop us. Nothing can touch us. This is the core drive, resurrected!

POINTS TO REMEMBER: STEPS 8-10

- To grow spiritually, we have to effectively manage our pain and develop a spiritual practice.
- In the school of life, pain is the teacher and a stimulant for the growth of spiritual qualities. Through a series of painful lessons, we learn that what we were looking for on the outside, we can and must eventually find inside.
- There are proven spiritual methods to help cultivate spiritual qualities.
- Pain management and spiritual practice lead to a variety of wonderful spiritual experiences!
- As we get better at managing pain and problems through the cultivation of spiritual qualities, our locus of control shifts from outside to inside ourselves. Eventually we come to understand that *everything we are looking for is inside.*

EXERCISES

1. Using the metaphor of life as a school, how would you describe some of the classes that you are in at this time?
2. What lessons are you learning?
3. Discuss pain as a stimulant for the growth of your spiritual power.
4. Do you have a spiritual practice?
5. What spiritual methods do you use?
6. Do you need to expand your spiritual practice?

7. Review the list of spiritual qualities. Which of these would you like to grow?

In the next section of the book, you will learn how to practice several proven spiritual methods. Regular, consistent practice of these disciplines will change your life. If you do the work, the virtues of the great saints and sages will slowly add on to you: peace and strength, compassion and courage, service and wisdom.

PART TWO
SPIRITUAL
PRACTICE

CHAPTER 7

GETTING STARTED

In spiritual books and sacred texts, we read stories about the heroism, courage, power, and selfless service of the saints and masters. There are anecdotes about miraculous healings, descriptions of eternal life, and discourse on the nature of truth. Prayers, poems, affirmations, and pearls of wisdom allude to unlimited peace, unconditional Love, ecstatic joy, and wisdom. The world's religions claim that the body is the temple which secretly harbors the actual God of the universe, or, similarly, that the body is the bearer of higher states of consciousness.

We can test the truth of these and other wonderful spiritual ideas through direct experience, but only if we develop a spiritual practice. While there may be no absolute scientific proof, we can use our intellect, feeling, intuition, and personal experience as tools for interpretation. The experiment is life itself. The test tube is the body. The material worked with is consciousness, energy, thought, feeling, desire, and behavior. This is the scientific method in metaphysics.

Spiritual practice leads to concrete, tangible results reproduced across cultures and historical periods. The methods described in this work have withstood the test of history. Millions have found their value as tools for the cultivation of spiritual qualities and experiences. These methods are:

- Affirmations
- Habits
- Progressive muscle relaxation
- Breath work
- Contemplation
- Meditation

- Prayer
- Mindfulness
- Practicing the Presence of God
- Service
- Yoga
- Transformation of emotion

The purpose of practicing these spiritual disciplines is to cultivate spiritual qualities in response to the inevitable suffering of life. We can transform our suffering into peace, Love, joy, and wisdom when we practice yoga, meditation, mindfulness, and the other methods listed above.

Before we begin the detailed study of these spiritual techniques, we will review eight suggestions for starting a successful spiritual practice, the Serenity Prayer, and a universal spiritual method.

SUGGESTIONS FOR STARTING A SUCCESSFUL SPIRITUAL PRACTICE

Following are eight essential principles of spiritual work, healing, and transformation:

1. Support: Get a support network of like-minded people.
2. Solitude: Learn how to be alone.
3. Self-reform: Change the world by changing yourself.
4. Ego reduction: Reduce your ego to expand your soul qualities.
5. Spiritual healing: Recognize the difference between physical and spiritual healing.
6. Self-acceptance: Accept where you are while striving to improve.
7. Discipline: Realize that suffering is a stimulant for the cultivation of spiritual power.
8. Expectations: Spiritual rewards occur on their own timetable.

SUPPORT

GET A SUPPORT NETWORK OF LIKE-MINDED PEOPLE

We need support from others to achieve any material or spiritual goal. In the spiritual life, it is important to find people who have similar ideas, aspirations, and practices. The spiritual path is difficult. There are barriers, tests, trials, and temptations that lead us off the path.

For support and encouragement, we need a network of people who love, care, understand, and forgive. When we see spiritual qualities such as strength, courage, and humor manifested in others, we gain the necessary guidance and inspiration to keep going, no matter what form resistance may take. While a supportive network of like-minded people is essential for spiritual growth, it is no less important that we build in ample time for solitude.

SOLITUDE

LEARN HOW TO BE ALONE

Popular culture would have us believe that success, money, power, and status bring security and happiness. Experience suggests otherwise. In the course of living, we find the joys and pleasures of the outer world are limited and ephemeral.

The wisdom traditions point to our inner being as the source of lasting happiness, peace, and safety. Discovering the path of wisdom is difficult, however, as the external world is powerful and attractive, continuously seducing us into the illusion that we can find in it the joy and security we crave.

The secret to discovering what is sacred and making it a part of our life is to develop a habit of solitude for study, contemplation, and meditation. But our addiction to the outer life makes it difficult to retreat for purposes of quiet reflection and stillness. Cultivating the new ground of solitude is akin to withdrawing from a substance of abuse like alcohol, drugs, or tobacco. When we retreat, we may feel anxious and crave our habitual pattern of activity. If we answer the call of this craving too quickly and fail to go through the rigors of the withdrawal, we do not bring the critical ingredient of solitude into our program.

When we suffer, we turn to other people, work, recreation, and entertainment for support and relief. While it is obviously helpful to have the support of loving people and constructive meaningful activities, an important part of spiritual growth is shifting the locus of control from outside to inside. At times of crisis, the ultimate defense is inner strength and courage. Spiritual qualities are best cultivated in solitude, slowly, and over time through such practices as meditation and the contemplation of sacred texts. Without stillness and solitude, the growth of spiritual qualities is stunted.

SELF-REFORM

CHANGE THE WORLD BY CHANGING YOURSELF

If we want to change the world, we need to start by changing ourselves. We will soon see how difficult a job that is! Gandhi once said he had three major opponents: the British people, the Indian people, and himself, and that by far, the most formidable was himself. Changing ourselves is more than a full time job. When we focus on self-reform, we won't have the time or energy to dwell on the problems or flaws of others.

Most of us have made the mistake of thinking that we can change other people. This is generally not possible. When we try to remodel the character of others, we can expect stiff resistance.

The way to influence others is to develop a spiritual practice which enriches the spiritual qualities in the soil of our own consciousness. When we are more compassionate, understanding, forgiving, peaceful, and wise, those around us who can will profit from our development. They will be inspired to bring out these qualities in themselves. We will gain more ground in this way than by pushing them.

EGO REDUCTION

REDUCE YOUR EGO TO EXPAND YOUR SOUL QUALITIES

The goal of spiritual practice is the cultivation of the soul qualities of the spiritual alphabet. But these qualities cannot grow unless the ego is reduced and ultimately replaced as it occupies the space rightfully owned and operated by the soul. However, the ego does not give up its space so easily. It sets up camp in spiritual territory and will not budge, believing that any surrender of turf may lead to its own demise. On the spiritual path, then, a battle ensues between the fiercely territorial ego and the soul qualities, yearning to blossom with full expression.

Our daily routines abound with opportunities to reduce the ego. By practicing the spiritual methods described in this book, we can replace the ego with spiritual qualities in a process of purification-- sometimes purification by fire. Introspection is necessary, and pain is often involved. Those who are not willing or able to go through such rigors get stuck. However, when we submit our ego for reduction in a spiritual process, the rewards are great; as the ego is dissolved, humiliation is replaced by humility, insecurity by peace, resentment by compassion, anger by Love, ignorance by wisdom, and sadness by joy.

The ego fights a bitter, resourceful war to the end. It resists every attempt of the soul to take over, and it does this is in subtle and devious ways. Often we don't even know that it is present and in control. When we discover and work to dissolve a layer of ego, another layer quietly takes over, silently waiting for an opportunity to cause trouble.

Ego reduction is slow and difficult. However, victory is inevitable to those who persist. The ego cannot survive the expansion of soul qualities that result from spiritual practice. The soul is more powerful than the trickster ego.

SPIRITUAL HEALING

RECOGNIZE THE DIFFERENCE BETWEEN PHYSICAL AND SPIRITUAL HEALING

Spiritual practice results in the healing of the body, mind, and/or soul. However, healing of the body may not always be possible since some conditions are chronic, progressive, and irreversible. In such cases, spiritual healing can still be relied upon.

Spiritual healing is independent of the healing of the body. Spiritual healing is a process of purification which involves reducing and ultimately replacing the ego with spiritual qualities. Our physical illness may improve, stay the same, or worsen, but we can always work on ego reduction and expansion of spiritual qualities. No matter the outcome of our physical pain and problems, with the practice of spiritual methods, we reduce the ego and grow spiritual qualities. We may get a chronic, progressive, or fatal illness but our spiritual healing process continues as we cultivate unconditional Love, patience, courage, endurance, surrender, and self-control.

Some people give up their work if they don't see their physical problems going away. This is a mistake; the point of spiritual work is the purification of consciousness, whether or not the body heals. In this sense, effort is progress, since spiritual work will always bring the expansion of spiritual qualities, even while physical pain persists.

SELF-ACCEPTANCE

ACCEPT WHERE YOU ARE WHILE STRIVING TO IMPROVE

The list of qualities in the spiritual alphabet is long and may seem daunting. Just thinking about unconditional Love is enough to stop some people from trying. If we think Love or any spiritual quality is unobtainable, we may not be able to look within, discover our current limitations, and begin the necessary work to improve.

We can avoid this dilemma if we accept our current state while at the same time make an effort to improve. We can remain relaxed, compassionate, and gentle with ourselves even as we see the distance between where we are and the top of the high spiritual mountain we are climbing.

Most of the time, there should be little or no guilt. When we are wrong guilt may occur, but only to show us where to work; its purpose is not to create lingering feelings of low self-esteem. We should look at our past mistakes with compassion and forgiveness. We can use the past as a reference point and not dwell there. We should extract what lessons we can from the past and then let the experience go.

To avoid neurotic perfectionism we give our best each day, knowing this is all that is expected. We must accept mistakes, failure, and awkwardness as part of the natural process of growth. We should see setbacks as opportunities to discover what we need for future successes. While engaged in the struggle to improve, we can cultivate humor, fun, laughter, and joy. This helps us not take ourselves too seriously.

DISCIPLINE

SUFFERING IS A STIMULANT FOR THE CULTIVATION OF SPIRITUAL POWER

You may not have found a spiritual path that suits you. You may have only recently found your way, and are just beginning. Or perhaps you are well along on a path with a teacher, teachings, and techniques that fit your needs. In any case, a good understanding of the nature of the struggle is important.

The spiritual path is slippery. It is easy to slide off and fall. We might be tempted to throw in the towel early on, not foreseeing how difficult it would be, nor how uncomfortable. It is a mistake to underestimate the work, effort, and discipline required. The transformation of ordinary to spiritual consciousness is no easy task. Life is painful. Change is difficult and slow.

Hard times are especially risky if we do not understand the connection between suffering and the development of spiritual power. If suffering appears meaningless, we may become frightened and turn to unhealthy pain-killing habits such as substance or sex abuse, excessive dependency on others, addiction to the Internet, television, and so on. On the other hand, if we understand that pain is a teacher and stimulant for the cultivation of spiritual qualities, we are much less likely to become frightened and abandon the path.

A comprehensive spiritual program helps us expect, rise to, and work through any challenge. When difficulties arise, we respond with spiritual practices that help us cultivate Love, strength, courage, and endurance. The expansion of these and other spiritual qualities will help us transcend any challenge.

When we have finished a set of problems or have passed some of life's tests, we experience the reward of happiness and tranquility. We love that part of the show when we celebrate life as pure entertainment and joy. It is only a question of time, however, before a new set of difficulties arise. As we move forward on our path, the bar is raised. More advanced problems and challenges arrive. How else would we develop our spiritual muscles? It is a marathon, not a sprint!

Finding and following a spiritual path requires self-control, stamina, and balance. We need to follow the path with devotion and loyalty. This involves making choices that build strength, courage, and endurance. The struggle is daily and continues until our last breath is taken. We need discipline to maintain our direction when in crisis. We need patience and perseverance for the long course of life. We must face the pain of reality in order to achieve higher states of consciousness. Running away from troubles and difficulties does not work. There can be no denial or avoidance on the path. We may rest, take time out, pace ourselves, and even backtrack when necessary, but ultimately we must do all of the work. Reality can be harsh and brutal. However, with spiritual practice, we can face whatever comes our way, understand it, learn from it, and move on to higher spiritual realms where the rewards are great.

EXPECTATIONS

SPIRITUAL REWARDS OCCUR ON THEIR OWN TIMETABLE

In any endeavor, it is good to have realistic expectations. Spiritual belief systems make many grandiose, idealistic promises, such as eternal peace, unconditional Love, and abundant joy. In the beginning, it is the hope for such experiences that gets many people involved in the rigorous discipline of the spiritual path. And after doing the work, it is a natural human tendency to expect the rewards promised. However, there will be times when there seems to be nothing but work, struggle, effort, and pain without compensation. Progress towards higher states of consciousness can be very slow or seem non-existent.

It is best to have no expectations; if our demands are not met, we might stop doing the work. If we are patient and try not to imagine how fast our growth should be, we can persevere and stay on our chosen path. Though results are often slower than we would like them to be, spiritual growth always occurs if we make the effort. If we give our best effort without the expectation of reward on a particular schedule, we will eventually enjoy the fruits of our spiritual work. Peace, Love, joy, power, and wisdom lie on the other side of every painful problem, but they arrive on their own timetable.

POINTS TO REMEMBER

- We can test the reality of any spiritual idea through direct personal experience when we develop a spiritual practice. This is the scientific method in metaphysics.
- Spiritual healing is the reduction of the ego and the expansion of soul qualities, independent of whether or not the body heals.
- We can use our suffering to expand our spiritual power if we have a spiritual practice.

AFFIRMATIONS

If you do not know how to do affirmations, please refer to Chapter 10.

- I balance support and solitude for maximum spiritual growth.
- To change the world, I reform myself.
- I embrace ego reduction through expansion of soul qualities.
- My body may not heal but I can always expand Love, peace, courage, and strength.
- I accept my present state as I make the spiritual climb.
- Peace, joy, Love, power, and wisdom are on the other side of every painful problem.
- Spiritual power comes on its own schedule. I wait patiently.

EXERCISES

1. How does the scientific method apply in metaphysics?
2. Why is it important to have a spiritual support network?
3. What is the purpose of solitude on the spiritual path?
4. How does a reduced ego assist in spiritual growth?
5. What is the relationship between ego reduction and spiritual healing?

In the next chapter, you will learn how to apply the Serenity Prayer to your spiritual practice.

CHAPTER 8

THE SERENITY PRAYER

Will and Surrender

The Serenity Prayer addresses two spiritual powers: will and surrender, both of which are monumentally important every step of the way on the spiritual path.

The Serenity Prayer is: "God grant me the serenity to accept the things I cannot change, courage to change the things I can, and the wisdom to know the difference."

In the pursuit of any spiritual goal, we need a strong will, the humility to surrender, and the wisdom to know the difference. We need will to change what is changeable. We must surrender or accept what we cannot change, and often, we need the ability to do both. Many problems require both will and surrender. We can work on a problem with our will, while accepting it as long as it remains. Wisdom is making the distinction between problems that require our will, surrender, or both.

Wisdom does not come easily. Often we apply our will to problems that need acceptance. This leads to frustration, anger, and demoralization. Similarly, we often make the mistake of accepting problems that could be solved by will and action, thus cutting ourselves off from growth, healing, and accomplishment. This leads to guilt and low self-esteem. With experience, we can gain the wisdom to know when to use our will, surrender to the inevitable, or both.

The Serenity Prayer helps us maintain peace of mind during all phases of our spiritual work, including those times when we feel we are not making any progress. This chapter describes how our will and surrender work separately and together for maximum spiritual growth.

WILL

HOW TO DEVELOP WILL POWER

Will has two elements, free will and will power. Free will is our ability to choose. It determines our direction. Will power is the degree of intensity and passion given to our choices. Our will shapes every moment of our lives, as we are always making choices in our thoughts, values, attitudes, desires, emotions, and actions.

Will is enormously important on every step of the spiritual path. It is involved in determining if we choose a spiritual life, which path we choose, and how much time, energy, and devotion we invest on that path. Each of the spiritual methods described in this work requires the use of our will power. In step 6 of the universal spiritual method described in the next chapter, we will review the importance of will in developing one-pointed, calm concentration in the performance of every spiritual method. In the lesson on the science of affirmations, we will learn how will is intimately involved in our choice of thoughts, which in turn have a profound effect on how we see, feel, and act in the world. Will determines how much spiritual work we do. The more work we do, the better our results. Will and thought help us eliminate bad habits, get through barriers, change, heal, grow, cultivate spiritual qualities, and never give up. Following is a discussion on how to expand our will power.

CULTIVATING WILL POWER: FROM SPARK TO BONFIRE

The universe simply will not leave us alone!

Tests, trials, and temptations inevitably interrupt our peace and stability. In response to life's difficulties, we have the choice to react in a positive or negative fashion. However, no matter how hard we try to choose rightly, at times we get lost in negativity.

The restless mind, unbridled emotions, excessive material desires, physical pain, bad habits, and egotism present an imposing array of problems for us to manage. Sometimes our problems take over. We get stuck in old, negative thought patterns and habits that automatically choose our path for us. We cannot seem to get out.

When locked in any painful struggle, our salvation lies in our free will and will power. In response to life's challenges, we can always choose to cultivate spiritual qualities by practicing a spiritual method. For the method to be effective, however, we need our will to be strong and determined, or we may not be able to work our way through the problem. When we apply all of our will power to the chosen spiritual method, spiritual qualities will grow. The remaining question is: How do we maximize our will to fully empower our spiritual practice?

Our day may be progressing pleasantly, until one of the setups of life disrupts our harmony. Perhaps a rude bus driver does not accept your bus pass; a nurse calls you from the doctor's office with the news that you need further testing because of a dark shadow in your chest x-ray. She does not give you any other information, and her attitude was cold and detached.

On the spiritual path, we try to respond to such difficulties with one or a combination of spiritual qualities. Though the bus driver might have been wrong and the nurse behaved unprofessionally, we try to remain calm, compassionate, and patient. Often, however, we lose control and contribute to the negativity with our own frustration and anger.

To regain a positive response as soon as possible when we lose control, we need spiritual methods such as affirmations, breathing, mindfulness, and prayer, and we need ever-expanding will power. Step 6 of the universal spiritual method outlines the necessity of bringing all of our heart, mind, might, and soul to the chosen method. To handle problems in life we need one-pointed, calm, concentration involving the totality of our being. A spark of will power will not do. We need a bonfire!

If our will is weak and we run into a large barrier, we will not have the power to get through. However, when our will is strong, we can burst through the barrier that stands in our way. The stronger our will, the easier barriers are to breach. With continued practice, we can get through anything. To understand the expansion of will power, imagine increasing physical strength.

Let's say you're able to do 12 pushups. You set a goal of 25. To achieve 25 pushups, you need to reach the current boundary of 12, and push past it with several repetitions of 13. With the sustained effort of pushing past your current limit, you will get to your goal of 25 push-ups. As you push through and expand your boundaries, your will power gets stronger.

Will is the invisible muscle of our life, the power that gets us through an obstacle to our desired goal. As with physical muscles, our will power expands or atrophies depending on how much exercise it gets. We can use this principle to understand how our willpower grows.

When life springs a challenge, such as the rude bus driver or the cold-hearted nurse, we can respond with frustration and anger, or we can do an inner spiritual workout. The inner workout utilizes our will with a spiritual method to cultivate a spiritual quality. For example, we could do some inner pushups such as deep breathing, and affirmations of loving-kindness. With repetition and practice, we expand our ability to give a compassionate response to irritable, rude, provocative people. When we do this, we cultivate inner strength and peace while others profit from our work, as we do not add fuel to their fire.

For maximum spiritual growth, we should identify realistic, attainable goals and pursue them no matter what obstacles arise. We set our desire and effort at 100%. We do not let up. We do the work in a calm and continuous manner, chipping away at each barrier with all of our determination until it dissolves.

Mistakes are part of the process. However, if we maintain our effort despite setbacks, eventually we progress. As we work our way through obstacles and resistance, we exercise our will and thereby increase its power. The more our will is exercised, the more will power we build. This cycle repeats itself with new barriers, forcing our will to higher levels. This is how we can increase our will power from a spark to a bonfire, a necessity on the spiritual path. We will need ever-increasing will power to help us through the trials and tests of life.

"TWO FROGS IN TROUBLE"

From the writings of the renowned yogi, Paramahansa Yogananda:

Once a big fat frog and a lively little frog were hopping along together when they had the misfortune to jump straight into a pail of fresh milk. They swam for hours and hours, hoping to get out somehow; but the sides of the pail were steep and slippery, and death seemed certain.

When the big frog was exhausted, he lost courage. There seemed no hope of rescue. "Why keep struggling against the inevitable? I can't swim any longer," he moaned.

"Keep on! Keep on!" urged the little frog, who was still circling the pail. So they went on for awhile. But the big frog decided it was no use. "Little friend, we may as well give up," he gasped. "I'm going to quit struggling."

Now only the little frog was left. He thought to himself, "well, to give up is to be dead, so I will keep on swimming." Two more hours passed and the tiny legs of the determined little frog were almost paralyzed with exhaustion. It seemed as if he could not keep moving for another minute. But then he thought of his dead friend, and repeated, "To give up is to be meat for someone's table, so I'll keep paddling until I die--if death is to come--but I will not cease trying. While there is life, there's hope!"

Intoxicated with determination, the little frog kept on, around and around and around the pail, chopping the milk into white waves. After awhile, just as he felt completely numb and thought he was about to drown, he suddenly felt something solid under him. To his astonishment, he saw that he was resting on a lump of butter, which he had churned by his incessant paddling! And so the successful little frog leaped out of the milk pail to freedom.

GOAL SETTING

Following is an exercise in goal setting. This exercise will demonstrate how to use will, thought, and action to accomplish any goal on the spiritual path.

1. Goal
2. Thought
3. Will
4. Action
5. Tests
6. Persistence
7. Success
8. Confidence
9. Goal

1. Goal: Pick a realistic, attainable goal. Choose a goal that is good for you, others, and the world.

2. Thought: Thoughts are very powerful, whether negative or positive. Keep your thoughts positive in the direction of your goal. Negative thoughts will only delay your progress. Remove all traces of negative thinking. You might try some of the affirmations related to will at the end of this chapter.

3. Will: Use the full force of your will to accomplish your goal. Gather all of your strength, might, and determination until your intent is unbending. Set your mind to absolute victory.

4. Action: With a positive mind aimed at your target and your will at full throttle, perform all of your actions in the direction of your goal.

5. Tests: Expect many tests. Tests come in the form of difficulties, barriers, and obstacles. Exercise your will and thought power against this resistance.

6. Persistence: Do not allow any negative influence to weaken the developing power of your will. Refuse to lose. Never give up. The only way to stop your spiritual growth is when you give up: then you lose. On the other hand, if you choose wisely and keep battling, you will move forward and ultimately succeed.

7. Success: When you follow the steps outlined above, your thought and will power increase and you accomplish your goals.

8. Confidence: Confidence grows when you succeed.

9. Goals: Set a new goal. Over time, you can pursue goals that are more complex and difficult to achieve. However, with too many goals, you can scatter your energy. Do not leave something half done to start a new goal. To avoid this problem, devote all your will power to mastering one goal at a time.

Remember to remain calm as you work your way through each of these steps.

An example of goal setting:

1. Goal: Joe wants to quit smoking.

2. Thought: He makes up his mind and begins using the following affirmations: "I can change. With will and thought, I cultivate strength and peace. With great determination, I create new good habits and spiritual qualities. I make up my mind strongly now. I am busy doing my part because God helps those who help themselves."

3. Will: Joe knows his cigarette habit is very powerful so he will need the full force of his will. He starts working with these affirmations: "I have the will to change. I will change. I use the full power of my will to transform negative to positive thoughts. Nothing can stop me. I am strong. I give 100 % of my effort."

4. Action: With his mind set at success, Joe conducts all of his activities in accord with his goal. His intent is unbending. He refuses to smoke.

5. Tests: There are many tests. Cigarettes are everywhere. When Joe sees other people smoking, he wants to retreat to his bad habit but resists the craving by using the following affirmations: "I use any obstacle to stimulate me towards greater effort and therefore greater achievement. The craving for cigarettes tries to throw me off balance but my inner strength keeps me steady. With great determination, I create new good habits. The more work I do, the more results I get. When I resist the craving, it disappears like a wave in the ocean, only to be replaced by strength and peace."

6. Persistence: Joe knows his battle against cigarettes is long-term. A friend offered him a cigarette at a wedding celebration. He relapsed and gave in, but quickly picked himself up, using the following affirmations: "No matter how many times I fall down, I pick myself up and struggle again towards my goal. When a host of difficulties and obstacles arise, I refuse to give up. I possess the power of will and the power of thought. I make the effort now to draw these powers out through practice in the daily routines and challenges of my life."

7. Success: Joe experienced difficulties and setbacks on his way to success but because of his persistence, he gave up smoking and no longer craves it. By exercising his will and affirmations, he replaced his smoking habit with peace of mind and strength. He affirms: "I am victorious. I am successful. I am calm and strong."

8. Confidence: Because of his success, Joe is more confident in himself. He is especially buoyant as he has discovered the scientific method of healing through affirmations and will.

He is amazed at how the wonderful gift of will power works. By simply learning how to think correctly, he knows how to expand his healing power, positive energy, and will. He beat the habit because he was thinking scientifically. He affirms, "I meet everybody and every circumstance with courage."

9. Goal: Joe sets new goals as he realizes that he can use his newfound positive energy to benefit himself, others, and the world. He affirms: "I am a strong willed person who can accomplish much good in this world. I exercise will and thought to help others and myself. I try to make this earth a better place to live by using my tools of will and thought. No matter what challenge comes my way, I remain positive and live constructively."

Clearly, will is important on the spiritual path as it helps us change, heal, grow, eliminate bad habits, move through barriers, accomplish goals, cultivate spiritual qualities, and serve the world. However, some conditions do not respond to will power. When we have applied all of our will, thought, and action to a painful problem and the problem remains, we can invoke will's partner, surrender.

SURRENDER

LEARNING TO LIVE WITH WHAT WE CANNOT CHANGE

Surrender is acceptance of the painful conditions of our current reality. Surrender is the opposite of resisting, running, or hiding. It means going through whatever comes our way in order to find our personal brand of knowledge, power, courage, humility, endurance, and wisdom. We must face our pain thoroughly and completely, for our most triumphant spiritual assets reside in the depths of our suffering. Pain is the teacher. It carries our personal story, meaning, and lessons. The lessons have to do with expanding our Love.

Athletes train their bodies for the exertion of their sport. Spiritual seekers must also train. They work out their inner body of thoughts, feelings, desires, and energy. The inner workout includes introspection and transformation. Introspection is looking within to uncover issues, problems, bad habits, and flaws. Transformation is making the necessary changes. Pain, once accepted, is the purifying agent that transforms negativity into spiritual power.

In the beginning, we may not understand pain's positive role of teaching, transformation, and purification. We can, however, demonstrate for our own satisfaction the important spiritual principle that suffering is packed with personal meaning. When we learn how to do the inner workout called surrender, we can discover for ourselves that when we inspect our pain, it reveals the lessons we need to learn.

The power of surrender is great. When fully developed, it can get us through anything. Through surrender, we discover personalized spiritual knowledge on the other side of our pain and problems. When we realize this principle, we will be inspired to drop our defenses and resistance, which do nothing but add tension and delay learning. Instead, we will enter the pain, eliminate negativity, and cultivate peace, joy, Love, wisdom, and strength.

Moving into the center of our pain requires much courage, as we may have some dark days when nothing seems to make sense. However, if we trust pain as our teacher, we will see the evolution of our personal story taking the high road of wisdom. Pain is intelligent. It takes us where we need to go. It reveals its hidden secrets and meaning as it leads us through the maze of our troubles and difficulties into the light of spiritual wisdom.

When we apply our will to a problem and it remains, we can accept the problem as a guest-teacher who has come to reveal a hidden secret. Following is a technique for unpacking the spiritual knowledge carried in our pain.

A TECHNIQUE TO SURRENDER

1. Introspection
2. Higher Power
3. Spiritual qualities and methods

1. INTROSPECTION

Take several slow deep breaths. If you know a meditation technique, use it now to invite as much stillness as you can. Assume an attitude of gentle, compassionate understanding toward yourself. Surrender to the pain. Feel it fully. Listen to it. Learn from it. Ask the pain, "Why are you here? What do you want? What do you have to teach me? What lessons do I need to learn? What problems remain hidden from my view? What spiritual qualities must I develop in response to you?" The pain will point you in the direction of your inner work, which always has to do with expanding Love.

2. HIGHER POWER

Ask for help from your Higher Power.

3. SPIRITUAL QUALITIES AND METHODS

Love is the greatest healer. When we align ourselves with Love, we purify, heal, and transform. Choose a spiritual method and begin the work of cultivating Love in response to your pain. Focus on Love as your true identity.

When we surrender, we drop our resistance and enter the pain that will not otherwise go away. Through introspection, pain informs us of the nature of our problems. Through transformation, we respond to all of our problems with Love and its escorts: peace, compassion, understanding, or any combination of spiritual qualities from the spiritual alphabet.

Surrender, introspection, and transformation activate the healing power that resides and operates within every cell of the body. We can deploy this process of purification with any type of problem. With practice, we will see how this miraculous, intelligent healing power works. It is incomparably brilliant! The transformation of pain and problems into spiritual qualities through surrender is one of the inherent miracles of the body. Do not miss the opportunity to demonstrate this marvelous power when presented with a problem or condition that does not respond to your will.

The purpose of suffering that does not respond to will is to help us work on our inner being. It purifies, purging everything that is not Love. In this sense, all pain is a blessing. It is for you to decide if your suffering is God's will, but no matter what your beliefs, you can always be in school, learning the lessons and cultivating the qualities having to do with Love. To set yourself up for healing, surrender to the pain and let your story unfold in the direction of Love. This is the secret of pain management through surrender. Make contact with and befriend the great power of surrender. It will get you through anything.

MANAGING PROBLEMS WITH WILL, SURRENDER, OR A COMBINATION OF BOTH

The Prayer of Relinquishment:

I am faced with this problem at the moment:
I won't run away from it.
I'll do my best to overcome it.
But the outcome is in the hands of my loving Father;
Whatever He wills, I accept.

The Prayer of Relinquishment describes the balanced use of will and surrender. The prayer reminds us to do our part of the work and accept life just as it is. While we use all of our initiative to work on a problem, we simultaneously surrender the results to our Higher Power. This is difficult. All of us miss the balance point between will and surrender a countless number of times. Mistakes are inevitable. We are either too active or too passive. When too passive, we feel poorly about ourselves and do not live up to our potential. When too active, we create new problems.

What is the right combination? How do we know whether a condition requires more or less will or surrender? Often, we do not; but we can improve. Stillness is the key. When we are alert, aware, and calm, we can hear the still, small voice within, guiding us to a balanced combination of will and surrender.

Pain may come subtly at first, trying to gently coax and persuade us to discover and work on our problems. If we are mentally restless, however, we may not recognize its purpose. When we do not sense and listen to it, we cannot extract the necessary lessons. The underlying problem remains and our pain grows. We feel tension and pressure. If we do not do the work at this stage, our pain may expand into symptoms, ultimately impairing our functioning and resulting in potential crisis and danger. At this point, there is neither a balance of will and surrender, nor wisdom to know the difference.

With sustained spiritual practice, our foundation of inner peace broadens and deepens. We can maintain inner harmony and balance even when challenged by painful difficulties. The mind remains calm and we hear the messages from that voice within. When we learn how to listen in stillness, we can find our problems through introspection, and transform ourselves through the cultivation of spiritual qualities. When we take responsibility for our problems by using pain as our guide, we make fewer mistakes in our attempts to balance will and surrender. As long as we remain calm and unruffled, pain, the great teacher in life, helps us know when to act and when to remain silent.

The goal of life is Love and service. To achieve this grand purpose, we must learn when to surrender and when to act with will. We need one pointed, calm, continuous use of our will to change what we can, and to surrender and expand our Love in response to what we cannot change. With time and practice, we can use will, surrender, or combinations of both in increasingly sophisticated ways, thus expanding our Love and our usefulness.

POINTS TO REMEMBER

- We can exercise will consciously and continuously by simply remembering to use it throughout the day.
- When we exercise our will, it grows.
- With continuous will, thought, and activity, we can accomplish any realistic goal.

- While we practice all spiritual methods with intensity, our effort should remain smooth and steady. Anxiety and tension reduce our effectiveness. The formula for success is calm, single-minded concentration.

- Anxiety reduces will power, as it uses up the energy that we could otherwise use to accomplish our goals. Overcome obstacles by practicing deep breathing with affirmations of peace, courage, and faith.

- When we cannot change an outer condition, we retain the freedom to choose our inner response. We use our will to choose positive thoughts, values, attitude, feelings, desires, and actions no matter what other people do.

- We are control artists. Pride keeps us from letting go. We fear humiliation. We worry about appearing weak. We think surrender implies passivity. We think if we give up control, we are going to get hurt. While it is true that when we surrender, we stop trying to solve external problems by changing others and controlling events, paradoxically, we gain control: surrender breeds an imperturbable state of inner strength and peace.

- Surrender is a powerful tool because it allows us to be at peace even though conditions and circumstances may be rough.

AFFIRMATIONS OF WILL

- I can change.
- I will change.
- I am successful.
- I make up my mind strongly now.
- My mind is set. My will is strong. I am ready to take on the challenge.
- I meet every circumstance with courage.
- No matter the challenge, I stay positive.
- God helps those who help themselves. I am busy doing my part.
- I possess the power of will and the power of thought.

- I use my will and thoughts to accomplish my goals, every step of the way.
- With will and thought, I work through any barrier.
- I act until my goal is accomplished.
- With great determination, I cultivate Love, peace, and strength.
- The more work I do, the more results I get.
- No matter how many times I fall down, I pick myself up and struggle again towards my goal.
- I use my will and thoughts to Love and serve.
- With will and thought, I make the earth a better place to live.
- When difficulties arise, I refuse to give up.
- Love is my reason for being. I use my will to carry it out.

AFFIRMATIONS OF SURRENDER

- I accept the things I cannot change.
- I remain unruffled no matter what comes.
- I have done all that I can. Now I surrender to the will of God.
- I have done all I can. Now I expand my Love.
- Love is the greatest healer.
- Love transforms my suffering into peace, compassion, and understanding.
- No matter what circumstances arise, I trust in a higher, invisible order.
- I used to try to control everything. Now I have trust and remain calm in any circumstance.
- I face my fear by surrendering it to God's hands, having complete faith in His will.
- I know when to resist my problems and when to resign myself to them.
- In response to any painful condition, I cultivate strength, courage, and endurance.
- I remain loving, compassionate, and gentle with myself while I try to change for the better.

EXERCISES

1. What is the Serenity Prayer?
2. What are the two components of will?
3. What is surrender?
4. What is the way to increase will power?
5. Describe the nine-step method for setting goals. Choose a goal and apply this method.
6. Describe the technique for surrender. Practice this method for any painful problem.
7. Can you think of a time when you were willful when you should have surrendered?
8. Can you think of a time when you surrendered when you should have been willful?
9. Can you think of a time when you have used will and surrender on the same problem?

In the next chapter, there is a description of a universal spiritual method that can be used to transform any type of suffering into spiritual power.

CHAPTER 9

A UNIVERSAL SPIRITUAL METHOD

A Ten-step Method for Working With any Pain or Problem

Life is a series of tests and trials, every step of the way. We all experience physical, mental, emotional, and spiritual problems throughout our lives. These problems range from minor irritations to major crises. Following is a list of some of our most common problems:

a. Physical pain
b. Disease
c. Disability
d. Trauma
e. Restless mind
f. Painful emotion
g. Excessive material desire and attachments
h. Bad habits or addictions
i. Hyperactivity: always have to be busy
j. Egotism or selfishness
k. Loneliness and fear of being alone
l. Too dependent on others
m. Any conflict
n. Denial of problems
o. Controlling and rigid
p. Perfectionism
q. Negative attitude
r. Loss of status, possessions, people, or self-esteem

s. Feeling unworthy, guilty, or ashamed; self-hatred
t. Feeling rejected, abandoned, or humiliated
u. Hatred
v. Prejudice: judging others by their role, body, personality, age, race, religion, nationality, sexual identity, economic class, or disability
w. Indifference or boredom
x. Fixed false religious beliefs
y. Fear of the unknown, the abyss, and death
z. Lack of meaning and purpose
aa. Any other painful problem or character flaw

When a painful problem arrives, it disturbs our peace and indicates an area where we could use some work. The school of life is in session. We have homework. Pain teaches us, directing us to cultivate certain spiritual qualities in response to our problem.

Following are ten steps we can use to work our way through any pain or problem, however mild, severe, or extreme:

1. Introspection: Discover your issues and problems.
2. Higher Power: Get help from your Higher Power.
3. External action: Take action in the external world.
4. Spiritual qualities: Choose one or a combination of spiritual qualities in response to your problem.
5. Spiritual methods: Practice one or a combination of spiritual methods to cultivate spiritual qualities.
6. Will: Apply all of your power to the chosen spiritual method.
7. Grace: Gain access to the vast intelligent healing power within and around you.
8. Expansion of spiritual qualities: Expand your spiritual powers in three stages.
9. Repeat steps 1-9: Develop a lifelong process.
10. Mastery: Attain superconsciousness in both meditation and activity.

1. INTROSPECTION

Introspection is self-analysis. It brings us to recesses of the mind that ordinarily remain hidden. It allows us to see our strengths and virtues as well as our flaws and limitations.

In practicing introspection, we are encouraged not to deny or suppress our problems, but to find them. All of us have issues and flaws. The advantage of finding out what they are is that once discovered, we can develop a plan for improvement.

An honest look at our problems can be threatening or even shattering to the ego, but the goal is not to tear the self to shreds. The purpose of introspection is to discover what needs to change without inflicting any unnecessary guilt, low self-esteem, or humiliation upon ourselves. Rather than feel bad about our problems, we can feel good that we have the courage to face them and the integrity to change for the better.

Retreat to a quiet place.

To help create a safe healing space within, take several slow deep breaths. If you know a meditation technique, use it now to bring in as much stillness as you can. To facilitate the healing power, assume an attitude of compassion, understanding, and gentleness toward yourself. Now do a deep, honest, and fearless search for any issues, problems, or flaws that may need some work. Make a problem list, and a list of your strengths and accomplishments.

2. HIGHER POWER

We can get help from a Higher Power. To get help, we need to develop a concept or image that is comfortable and reachable. There are a variety of ways to conceptualize a Higher Power. Some examples are:

- The Omniscient, Omnipotent, Omnipresent God to whom you may appeal and get a response through grace;
- A personal relationship with the God of Love manifesting as Father, Mother, Friend, Confidante, Beloved, Teacher, Protector, Guide, Healer, Counselor, or Physician;

- A personal relationship with a God-realized master as the embodiment of spiritual qualities, for example, Christ, Buddha, Krishna, Mohammed, or the Bal Shem Tov;
- God as the Great Physician, a vast field of intelligent Love filled with infinite spiritual qualities and healing powers;
- The Teacher: Every person, event, experience, and all of life is the Teacher;
- Higher meaning and purpose: for example, compassionate service to humanity;
- The higher self as an embodiment of spiritual qualities;
- Higher states of consciousness;
- Communion with nature or Mother Earth;
- Reason, morality, and the subconscious;
- The infinite mysterious unknown;
- Many other concepts, images, and aspects.

Define the aspects or images of a Higher Power that are comfortable, approachable, and accessible. Install that image in your consciousness and use it as a source of continuous guidance and inspiration. Your concept can help you in your relationships with people, in conducting the business of life, with minor irritations, or in major crisis. Sometimes we experience overwhelming pain. Sometimes we feel that we might shatter and never put the pieces back together again. Sometimes we do shatter. In any case, whether our problems are minor or extreme, our Higher Power can be a source of strength, courage, and wisdom.

3. EXTERNAL ACTION

We do everything we can to solve our problems with reason, will, and action in the external world. For example, when we have symptoms of an illness, we go to the doctor for medicine. If we are in conflict with someone, we work on interpersonal communication and problem solving. When we suffer, we turn to our loved ones, work, recreation, cultural events, and hobbies. However, when a problem remains after we have done externally what we can, we can use the problem as a stimulant for the cultivation of internal spiritual qualities.

4.   SPIRITUAL QUALITIES

Life is school. Pain is the teacher. The lessons have to do with expansion of spiritual qualities. We can respond to any problem with Love and its associated qualities. For example, we can cultivate patience when angry, peace when anxious, even-mindedness for excessive emotional reactivity, and strength for long-term illness.

Review the spiritual alphabet. Here you will find an army of 100 spiritual qualities. These healing powers are always available at no cost, in unlimited quantities, right inside of our bodies. Cultivate any one or combination of these powerful healers in response to your problem, test, or trial.

Do not focus on your problems or flaws. This makes them stronger. Instead, focus all of your attention on the spiritual quality. You are not your problems. You are a composite of the spiritual qualities listed in the spiritual alphabet. You are compassionate, loving, kind, understanding, courageous, and strong. This is your true identify.

5.   SPIRITUAL METHODS

We can choose any one or combination of the following methods to cultivate the desired qualities in response to any pain or problem. With regular and consistent practice of these powerful techniques, we can transform our suffering into spiritual strength.

- Affirmations
- Habits
- Progressive muscle relaxation
- Breathwork
- Contemplation
- Meditation
- Prayer
- Mindfulness
- Practicing the presence of God

- Service
- Yoga
- Transformation of emotion

For example, to help transform high emotional reactivity to even-mindedness, we can use any of the methods described in this work. We might choose meditation, mindfulness, and service. We might change the combination of methods another day to affirmations, prayer, or breathwork. The choice is yours.

6. WILL

What we put into our practice determines what we get from our practice. If we put in a meager effort, we get a meager outcome. If we give our best, we move forward at maximum speed.

Bring all of your heart, mind, might, and soul to your chosen method and desired qualities. This is single-minded concentration. It involves the totality of our being. Our conviction, dedication, and will are at full power, but we are not strained. The mind is at its best when it is calm and concentrated.

Longstanding patterns of thought, feeling, desire, energy, and behavior do not change overnight. There will be setbacks. When thrown off the horse, get back on. We learn by taking two steps forward and one step back. Resilience and perseverance mark the way of the spiritual seeker. With long-term spiritual practice, nothing can stop us.

7. GRACE

We have access to a vast intelligent healing power within and around us. We can tap into this power and get help with any type of suffering through work and grace. Our job in the healing process is to define the problem, pick a spiritual method, determine which spiritual quality we need to develop, and exert maximum effort for as long as it takes. This means putting our whole being into our work. When we do our part at maximum effort, ask for help, and endure the problem as long as it is there, grace follows.

We can conceptualize grace coming from a conscious God of Love or from the healing laws of the universe, which work for us when we cooperate with them. We can use whatever concept gives us inspiration and traction. The healing and transformation process works no matter how we label it.

Grace opens the gate to the field of Omnipotent healing energy. We have no control over the gate. The Keeper of the gate, a mysterious, intelligent force or law, opens the gate for us. The gate may or may not open for elimination of disease, disability, or other painful problems. However, if we do the work described in steps 1-6 of this method, the gate will always open to allow the expansion of spiritual qualities such as peace, Love, strength, courage, wisdom, and joy.

8.   EXPANSION OF SPIRITUAL QUALITIES

The expansion of spiritual qualities occurs in three stages. In the first stage, we experience nothing. There is expansion of Love, courage, peace, and strength, but the increase is subtle and imperceptible. In stage two, we feel these qualities expanding. This experience is tangible, concrete, and unmistakable. In stage three, there is a distinct transformation of consciousness. We experience unfathomable stillness, the changeless peace of the soul, ecstatic Love, pure joy, intuitive wisdom, cosmic sound, divine light, oneness with everything, disembodied consciousness, and other wonderful expressions of Spirit.

Although our experience is tangible in stage two and dramatic in stage three, the growth of spiritual qualities is slow. Do not expect results right away. There will be times when we think we are not moving at all. Sometimes we all slip backwards, but sometimes we have to go backwards in order to go forward, and all effort is progress. When we make the effort, we are advancing, even when we can't see it. If we keep going, we will eventually see progress. Each time we practice affirmations, meditation, prayer, mindfulness, service, or other spiritual methods, we are putting wisdom, strength, courage, and other currency in our spiritual bank account. When the time comes and credit is due, we can take them out.

9.   REPEAT STEPS 1-9

Spiritual work is lifelong and continuous. This is not something we do for a few weeks or months. Life is always school. The only question is whether we attend the classes, do the homework, and pass the tests. If we do the work, one by one our problems are contained, reduced, pulverized, or dissolved, and replaced by positive qualities and habits. Eventually we achieve mastery, a state of sustained superconsciousness in both meditation and activity.

10. MASTERY

Upon mastery, when our soul merges with Spirit, we enter and never leave the boundless Ocean of Love. We come to know the Changeless One as unlimited stillness, silence, spaciousness, and serenity. With this expanded consciousness, we can receive any condition without losing our equilibrium. Our reason expands to intuition, separation to oneness, and human love to unconditional Love. We are fearless, humble, strong, enthusiastic, and cheerful. Our faith is perfect. Our highly attuned intuition receives guidance and wisdom from Omniscience. We are awake, aware, and ready for anything! We give peace, Love, and joy in our words, actions, and vibrations to all we meet. Even-minded in all conditions, we serve humanity with Love, compassion, and kindness. We perform acts of courage and heroism, but most of our work is quiet and anonymous: acts of gentle, humble service. Liberated from the bondage of fear and insecurity, we watch the colossal cosmic drama with calm detachment.

Mastery, a sustained state of superconsciousness in both meditation and activity, is a very high state, difficult to achieve. Some think mastery is impossible, unreal, or too good to be true. To others, it seems inaccessible or overwhelming. It is not meant to be so.

Advanced sages, saints, and masters are simply people who have realized their potential. I have included their description of higher states of consciousness as part of the spiritual map to remind us of our potential. Their descriptions of infinity, eternity, immortality, imperturbable peace, fearlessness, pure Love, and ecstatic joy sound good and intuitively seem right.

I have experienced and verified some of the elements of superconsciousness, but I make no claim to mastery. I am a struggling student with many flaws, learning how to love. Nevertheless, I trust the teachings of the great ones. Throughout this work, I will describe the spiritual climb from beginning to end.

I suggest you find your place on the path and work from there. Begin your practice now, today, or if you have already started, march on. Persist and persevere through all obstacles. I plan to travel the distance. I invite you to join me. I am not a master, but I can become one, and so can you.

THE UNIVERSAL METHOD AND THE MYSTERY OF SUFFERING

For many people, the biggest barrier to beginning a spiritual practice is this question: If God is Love, why is there so much suffering and evil in this world?

Here are four possible explanations:

1. The mystery: There is a God of Love, but we cannot answer the question of why there is so much evil and suffering because His ways are mysterious. There are tests and trials but their purpose is beyond our understanding. God works in strange and mysterious ways.

2. Karma and reincarnation: Karma is the law of cause and effect, and reincarnation is the transmigration of the soul. There is free will and choice. Good choices lead to good consequences, and bad choices lead to bad consequences. As you sow, so shall you reap. The soul reincarnates until we work out our negative karma, the related consequences of sin, through meditation, Love, and service.

3. Agnosticism: An agnostic claims the existence of God is unknown.

4. Atheism: An atheist believes that there is no God and that events occur at random.

In any case, each of us has to struggle with the challenges life brings without fully understanding why. To grow spiritually, we don't need answers to all of our questions. Nor do we need theological constructs or dogma. We do need to discern our problems, develop a spiritual practice, and cultivate spiritual qualities. We can do this whether or not we believe in God, karma, or grace.

The centerpiece of this model is choosing a problem, method, and quality. Then we can add our concept of God, karma, and grace or float all questions in the mystery. Pain is the teacher and stimulant for the cultivation of spiritual qualities. We can cultivate Love, compassion, kindness, and courage in response to tests and challenges, without knowing answers to all of the questions. Whether or not we believe in God, we can always find problems, develop a spiritual practice, and cultivate spiritual qualities.

POINTS TO REMEMBER

- The ten-step method can help us accomplish the goal of spiritual work: the cultivation of spiritual qualities to help manage any issue, pain, or problem. This method is universal, applicable to anyone and every problem.
- We can respond to painful problems with any one or combination of 100 spiritual qualities. Spiritual qualities are healers and purifying agents. They are standard equipment, built into the body, embedded in the genetic code as our birthright. We can tap into these healing powers at any time in response to any problem, by practicing the spiritual disciplines described in this work.
- Events and our mental-emotional reactions to those events cause us to lose sight of the Omnipresent peace and wisdom of the soul. The spiritual methods described here help us reduce

our reactivity and move towards, and finally into, the peace of the soul.

- We may not be able to control everything in our environment, but we always have control over our will and thoughts. This is where the battle is fought and won. By choosing to practice a spiritual method, we can spiritualize any event. This means responding to life with a spiritual quality no matter what life brings.
- The formula for success in working with any pain or problem is:
  1. Apply maximum effort to a spiritual method for the cultivation of spiritual qualities.
  2. Accept and endure as long as the problem persists.
  3. Ask for help from a Higher Power.
  4. Grace comes on its own schedule. The result is the expansion of peace, Love, strength, courage, wisdom, and joy.

AFFIRMATIONS

- My spiritual practice is continuous and lifelong.
- I am always practicing a spiritual method.
- I am committed to spiritual practice for the rest of my life.
- I practice each spiritual method in the present, in the moments of my life.
- When I overcome difficulty, I expect new and more advanced challenges and tests.
- I practice with patience and perseverance. I never give up.
- I conduct all spiritual work with calm concentration.
- I give all of my heart, mind, might, and soul to the work.

EXERCISES

1. Define Your Higher Power

To get help from a Higher Power, we need an image that is accessible and comfortable. Will you pick a master such as Jesus, Mohammed, Buddha, the Bal Shem Tov, or Krishna as an embodiment of spiritual qualities? Will you go to the ocean of Love and find your guidance there? Will you observe nature and see in her the rhythm, harmony, beauty, and power that can carry you through anything? Will it be the mystery, the unknown, the absolute beyond conception? Will it be reason, morality, and the higher self? Is God like a Teacher, present in each event, person, and experience? Will you choose Love and service to humanity and surrender to the mystery, accepting God as unknowable? Whatever concept you choose, you will need your connection to it to be stronger than the worst pain, evil, or problem that arises. Then you can withstand the power of duality's brutal realities. What image works for you?

2.   Choose a problem, method and quality

The centerpiece of this work is the practice of a spiritual method to cultivate spiritual qualities in response to painful problems.

    a.   Review the list of problems described in the beginning of this chapter. Are you currently struggling with these or any other problems? Choose one or two on which you would like to focus.

    b.   Choose one or a combination of spiritual qualities that will help you manage these problems.

    c.   Choose one or a combination of spiritual methods that will help you cultivate your desired qualities. If you are not familiar with any spiritual practices, read the chapters on spiritual methods. Then return to this step.

Our differing, complex needs, capacities, and levels of receptivity require an individualized approach. There are as many pathways up the spiritual mountain as there are people. While all have some elements in common, no two paths are alike.

To best suit our needs, we can arrange and rearrange qualities and methods in any combination we wish. We can be flexible and individualize our program. If a method or quality seems too difficult, choose another. For example, if meditation is intimidating, try mindfulness and service. Later, the practice of meditation might prove less daunting.

3. Bring your mind to the best practice position: calm concentration

All of the spiritual methods described in this work require a calm, concentrated mind; but the mind loves to wander. It remains independent despite our best efforts to control it. In frustration, we fight back, but fighting mind with mind creates tension, taking us even further away from calm concentration. The way to prevent this frustration is to remain relaxed and non-judgmental when the mind wanders.

Begin your spiritual practice. Choose any spiritual method. Notice when your mind drifts. Do not identify with a particular stream of thought. Gently bring your mind back to its state of calm concentration.

This back and forth movement will go on for years. It is part of the natural process of spiritual work. The key is to accept the mind exactly where it is at the moment, because it could not be anywhere else. This will help you remain relaxed while you return the mind to its practice position.

Practicing concentration can be fun or frustrating, depending upon our frame of reference. If we remain gentle, compassionate, and accepting of ourselves, we can play the game of concentration as a sport.

4. Stay in the present

The next step in our spiritual development is here and now. Spiritual methods help us keep our attention and concentration focused on the present so we do not miss the opportunity to take the next step. We spend too much time dwelling on the past and future. We can learn from the past and plan for the future, however, the bulk of spiritual practice is in the seconds and minutes of our lives. When your mind drifts into the past or future during your practice, gently bring it back to the present.

5.　Start slow

We climb a mountain one step at a time. Similarly, we build our practice each day by applying a spiritual method one step at a time. Spiritual qualities grow slowly. Patience is necessary. By taking small steps and building our program gradually, we will have a strong spiritual foundation upon which to build higher floors.

You can start a practice such as meditation or mindfulness 5-10 minutes twice a day and gradually build up your time. If this seems intimidating, try starting at 30-60 seconds twice a day. Give your best effort. Your concentration will expand. Eventually you will learn to stay with a method at will throughout the day.

6.　Continuous practice

There is always spiritual work to do, whether life is smooth and stable or rocky and chaotic. If we practice the techniques when life is smooth, we can use them more effectively when it gets rough.

Advanced students try to practice one of the spiritual methods at all times. This is possible since some methods, such as meditation and contemplation, require solitude while service, practicing the presence of God, and mindfulness occur during activity. Slowly expand your practice until it is continuous.

7.　Pace yourself

Some individuals try to move forward on the spiritual path faster than is possible, but real spiritual growth occurs one day at a time. We need to relax and enjoy the day without adding undue pressure or stress by attempting to accomplish too much. We cannot do it all now. We can't live up in the penthouse when we haven't built the foundation or the floors in between. There are no shortcuts. We cannot skip any of the assigned classes. We need to do the homework daily. Then we can pass the tests and advance to the next grade.

It is a long climb up the mountain. When we try to climb too fast, we slip, fall, hurt ourselves, or get exhausted unnecessarily. When we climb too slow or not at all, we become bored or indifferent.

To find the right speed, focus on one or two problems at a time. Bring all of your heart, mind, might, and soul to your work of cultivating spiritual qualities but remain calm without strain or tension. When you find the right speed, you will experience harmony, balance, rhythm, and flow.

8. Do your best

Your ability to focus on your spiritual method and quality will vary from day to day. Do not worry about perfection. Just do your best and leave the rest.

Armed with the eight suggestions for starting a spiritual practice, the Serenity Prayer, and the universal spiritual method, you are ready for a detailed review of a variety of proven spiritual methods.

In the next section, you will study two techniques: the science of affirmations and habit transformation. Here you will learn how to change your destiny by changing your thoughts and habits.

Then you will learn five techniques that comprise a morning and evening spiritual program: progressive muscle relaxation, breathwork, contemplation, meditation, and prayer.

The final section describes five techniques you can practice while you perform your daily activities: mindfulness, practicing the presence of God, service, yoga, and the transformation of emotion.

Practicing these spiritual disciplines will heal and transform your consciousness. You will experience an ever-expanding feeling of peace, compassion, and joy expressed in acts of gentle, humble service to all of humanity.

PART THREE
CHANGE YOUR DESTINY

CHAPTER 10: AFFIRMATIONS

CHAPTER 11: HABITS

CHAPTER 10

AFFIRMATIONS

The Power of Thought

We can change our destiny by changing our thoughts. Thoughts, both negative and positive, have great power; they are magnetic and attract according to their vibrations. Negative thought attracts negative. Positive attracts positive.

The science of affirmations teaches us how to send powerful positive thoughts to our conscious and subconscious minds and to the cells in our body as chemical, electrical, and magnetic waves. Through a simple maneuver involving free will and choice, we learn how to deploy our own thoughts to break through limitations, transform bad habits, turn failure into success, and activate our healing powers.

Our thoughts have leverage in the inner workings of our cells having to do with transforming disease into health. By using affirmations to cultivate spiritual qualities, we stimulate healing power. When we align our thinking with such qualities as peace, compassion, and understanding, we set up harmonious conditions for the healing power to do its work. The right condition for healing is a mere thought away.

The discovery that we are both the problem and the solution in the intimate proximity of our own minds is of enormous importance. A new level of responsibility and work is assumed when we learn how to apply the power of thought to affect any need or condition.

Life is a battle between negative and positive forces. In the mind, this battle takes place between positive and negative thoughts. Following is a description of how practicing affirmations can help us transform our subconscious and conscious minds into a powerful, positive force.

AFFIRMATIONS AND THE SUBCONSCIOUS MIND

The subconscious mind is a vast storehouse of our memories, thoughts, and experiences. Most of us have experienced rejection, humiliation, abandonment, and the loss of loved ones. Many have had terrible trauma, abuse, accidents, or illness. These harsh experiences can lead to negative thought patterns or habits that cause unnecessary, ongoing pain. These patterns are stored in our subconscious mind and brain cells, in negative thought circuits that lock us into destructive ways of responding to the world. Some examples of this type of negative thinking are: "I am ugly, bad, guilty, and worthless. I am a helpless, weak, inadequate loser. I cannot change. I am doomed to suffer. I deserve punishment. I will never be able to get out of this problem. I can't beat this habit. No matter what progress I make, something will come along to take it away."

In response to life events, such negative attitudes emerge from the subconscious rapidly, automatically, and habitually. They often manifest in relentless repetitions referred to as ruminations or obsessions. The mind can get stuck in ruminations for minutes, hours, days, weeks, and longer. Some deeply embedded patterns can extend their influence over a lifetime.

We have a tendency to underestimate the mind's negative power, much of which is submerged beneath our awareness. The science of healing affirmations teaches us how to access the conscious and subconscious mind so that these negative patterns can be brought to awareness, rooted out, and replaced by positive new brain circuits and thought patterns. The result is a positive, calm, focused, and resilient mind, sharpened and ready for problem solving, managing life's harsh realities, and creating health, success, harmony, and joy.

Positive thoughts act like medicine released from the brain's own pharmacy. This thought-medicine cannot do its work, however, if negative ideas, beliefs, or attitudes neutralize its healing power. When a positive affirmation is stated, there is often an attack of negative thoughts or beliefs, which emerge from their storage place in the subconscious.

For example, you may be fighting low self-esteem because of prior abandonment. To change your self-image, you affirm, "I am good, beautiful, worthy, and strong." However, your subconscious mind sabotages your efforts to create a new positive identity by releasing the negative counter-thought, "You are an insecure, awkward, homely loser." This negative thought has had control of your self-image for years. It is a well-established thought circuit that does not give up its power so easily.

The effect of the countering negative thought is the same as if you wrote something with chalk on a board and erased what you wrote. The negative thought maintains its power unless neutralized by a stronger, positive thought force. The science of healing affirmations teaches us to use our concentration, will, feeling, and faith to infuse the positive thought with the necessary power to take hold in the subconscious mind.

With practice, eventually the positive thought will grow and associate with other positive thoughts such as, "I am a good person. There have been many victories. People actually do like me. I have a lot to offer." At some point, we can deploy an army of positive thoughts to rapidly and effectively neutralize the negative ones. Then, when the same provocative situation arises to test us, our mind stays positive, poised, and peaceful.

CREATING POWERFUL AND EFFECTIVE AFFIRMATIONS

Affirmations work, but they may not work for you if they lack the necessary potency to take hold and grow. Following are some suggestions for creating effective healing affirmations.

1. DEFINE YOUR PROBLEM

2. DEFINE YOUR GOAL

Focus on your solution rather than the problem. Do not think so much of where you have been as of where you want to be. You become and attract what you intend. Your goals will become your new habits.

For example, if you are working with disease, focus on health. For fear, invoke courage or bravery. For anger, try peace, patience, forgiveness, or gentleness. For weakness, try strength. For failure, try success.

3. PRESENT TENSE

State the affirmation in the present tense, as though the goal is already accomplished. You would not want to affirm, "I am going to be calm." You would affirm, "I *am* calm."

4. POSITIVE TERMS

State the affirmation in positive terms such as "I am calm," not the negative "I am no longer anxious."

5. INDIVIDUALIZE

Keep reworking the affirmation until it feels just right. For example, you may prefer "I remain even-minded under all conditions," or "even-minded no matter the condition," or simply a one-word affirmation: "even-minded." When it feels right, it will fit the rhythm of your being perfectly.

6. VISUALIZATION

We can reinforce the power of our affirmation by associating it with a mental picture or visualization. In this way we can think, see, and feel the reality of the affirmation. For example, we can all imagine circumstances that make us nervous, angry, or agitated. We can rehearse these scenes in our minds by creating thoughts and pictures of ourselves remaining calm despite provocation. The more we rehearse, the more likely the subconscious and conscious minds will help us stay relaxed when the actual stressful condition arrives.

7. PRACTICE

Practice and repetition are most important. Without repetition, there can be no progress. Deeply embedded negative thoughts, beliefs, and attitudes have been around for a long time in the subconscious mind. When the brain cells are loaded up with thought habits that have to do with disease and limitation, it takes time to form thought circuits that have to do with health and possibility. We need to repeat affirmations continuously for chronic deeply embedded conditions, and we need to ignore an unchanged or contrary condition as we repeat the affirmation.

Many people give up early, not understanding the effort required or unwilling to do the work. Some habits, patterns, or conditions may change with ease, while others may take a long time to heal or replace. We need patience: it may take months, even years, to transform deeply ingrained habit patterns of thought, feeling, desire, or behavior. Perseverance is the magic of spiritual work.

The more we use positive affirmation, the quicker change occurs for the better. With continued practice, the affirmation takes on a life of its own. It repeats itself by itself. The thought gains momentum and strength, eventually becoming powerful enough to become reality. Repetitious positive thoughts gradually replace and finally dominate the negative patterns of the conscious and subconscious minds.

8. INTENSITY

To be effective, we need to bring all of our attention and energy to our spiritual practice. Each method described in this book requires all of our heart, mind, might, and soul for maximum benefit. There must be sufficient intensity and concentration of feeling, thought, will, and faith to give the exercise--in this case, the affirmation--sufficient energy and power to make the necessary changes. If the affirmation is spoken without passion or planted in a restless, unfocused mind, it will have less power.

Muscles atrophy from lack of exercise. Similarly, those who have not been doing an inner workout weaken their powers of concentration and will, the tools necessary to break through the barriers of limitation into conscious possibility. With practice and repetition, our will power and concentration slowly grow.

As you strengthen your affirmation, be sure not to create tension by going too far. Calm concentration without tension increases the force of the thought. The goal is to repeat the affirmation as many times as you wish with calm concentration, deep feeling, and will. When you realize your attention has wandered, bring it back to the affirmation with as much focus as possible. Repeating the affirmation with increasingly intense concentration and feeling mobilizes healing power.

At first, our healing affirmations may be like sparks blowing in the wind with no apparent effect. With patient, persistent practice, these thoughts get stronger. They light healing power ablaze. Although it kindles slowly, if we keep adding affirmative fuel to the healing power, there will be a bonfire. Then the affirmation permeates our conscious and subconscious minds, every cell, fiber, molecule, and atom of our being, as well as surrounding space, eventually bringing into existence the very thing being affirmed.

9.   FAITH

Life energy, operating the bodily cells, tissues, organs, and systems, has within it the power of healing. This brilliant power heals our cuts, bruises, colds, and other ailments without our action. We can trust it, and there is evidence that the more we trust it, the better it works. Affirmations are more effective when practiced with faith and belief. Doubt and insecurity undermine the authority of the new positive thought, and work against the life energy and healing power. For maximum benefit, perform your affirmation with faith, trust, and belief in its power to heal.

WHEN TO DO AFFIRMATIONS

We can do affirmations any time: at rest, in meditation, or during activity. Affirmations are more effective when the mind is relaxed, opened, and less defensive, such as just before going to sleep or just after awaking. Its maximum benefit occurs when the mind is still during or after meditation.

We can practice affirmations before, during, or after a particular problem surfaces. For example, if we are struggling with anxiety, we can practice affirmations of peace while we are anxious. But we can also practice when we are feeling serene, which is a good time to fortify the subconscious for the tests of life that are sure to come.

THE TECHNIQUE FOR AFFIRMATIONS DURING PERIODS OF REST OR MEDITATION

We can perform this technique during periods of rest and before, during, and after meditation:

1. Sit
2. Breathe
3. Relax
4. Open
5. Affirm
6. Feel
7. Visualize
8. Repeat

1. SIT
Sit with the spine straight.

2. BREATHE
Take several slow deep breaths.

3. RELAX
Relax the body and calm the mind. Throw out all problems, restless thoughts, fears, insecurities, and doubts. Gather as much concentration and stillness as you can.

4. OPEN
Open yourself to the idea that affirmations work and that all conditions of the body, emotions, mind, and spirit are changeable.

5. AFFIRM
Choose an affirmation and repeat it with increasing intensity. With your will and concentration, eliminate all other thoughts. Hold the affirmation in the center of your being for several minutes. At some

point, notice the affirmation repeating itself even when you do not try to remember it.

6. FEEL

Feel the affirmation. Allow it to permeate your conscious and subconscious minds, every cell, fiber, molecule, and atom of your entire being and surrounding space.

7. VISUALIZE

Visualize yourself as you imagine yourself to be when the affirmation has become completely real.

8. REPEAT

When the mind wanders, bring it back to the affirmation.

THE TECHNIQUE FOR AFFIRMATIONS DURING ACTIVITY

We can perform this technique when we are engaged in activities that do not require our full attention such as walking, raking leaves, washing dishes, cooking, shopping, cleaning, or stuck in rush-hour traffic. We can also do this technique when our mind wanders into negativity, when we are upset, or when we want to change the direction of our thoughts for any reason.

1. STOP

Give your mind the command to stop.

2. FOLLOW STEPS 2-8 ABOVE

JAPA YOGA

Try practicing *japa* yoga. Japa yoga is the repetition of a mantra, affirmation, or chant resulting in attunement with the presence of God.

1. AFFIRM

Every thought sets up a corresponding vibration. When you repeat a word, thought, or chant reflecting the presence of God, you experience Her peace, Love, and joy. You can repeat any affirmation related to the presence of God such as "God, God, God," "My Lord, I love You, it is a blessed privilege to serve You," "I am immersed in the presence of God," or "I bow to the manifestation of my Divine Mother before me right now."

2. FEEL

Avoid mechanical or dry repetition. Feel the chant in your heart. When your repetition becomes mechanical, bring it back into your heart and infuse it with devotion and feeling.

3. REPEAT

Repeat the silent chant when you are working, cooking, shopping, cleaning, driving, walking, exercising, playing sports, or helping others. Repeat the affirmation with interest, attention, and devotion.

WRITING AND RECORDING AFFIRMATIONS

We can write affirmations on note cards and keep them in our pockets at all times. We can pull the card out during the day whenever possible, pick a relevant affirmation, and repeat it until the idea deeply ingrains itself in both the conscious and subconscious minds. We can also record affirmations.

HOW MANY PROBLEMS SHOULD BE ADDRESSED AT ONE TIME

We can work on one or many problems at the same time, but it is wise not to put too many affirmations into our program at first. It is better to concentrate on one or a few affirmations with intense concentration than to dilute our power by spreading ourselves too thin.

THE DIFFERENCE BETWEEN PRAYER AND AFFIRMATION

Affirmations and prayer are similar. In prayer, we seek help from our Higher Power. An affirmation is a statement of the prayer as though the result is already accomplished. For example, one might pray, "Lord, grant me even-mindedness under all conditions." The corresponding affirmation would be, "I am even-minded under all conditions."

Those who understand themselves to be co-creators and co-operators with their Higher Power can combine the use of prayer and affirmation. For example, it has often been said that God helps those who help themselves. When we work with affirmations, we are helping ourselves. Prayer is the request for God's grace as a means of getting help with the problem.

ONE-WORD AFFIRMATIONS

When we need to do some work in a particular area, we can affirm any spiritual quality with one word. For example, when we feel restless, we can talk to our body. It will take instructions. We can give the body a one-word command such as "relax," "harmony," "balance," or "rhythm." We can talk to our mind. Eventually it will listen. We can think, "patience," "peace," or "poise." When someone is giving us a hard time, we can affirm, "understanding," "compassion," or "forgiveness."

ACCEPTING THE THINGS WE CANNOT CHANGE

We can apply affirmations to get rid of any unwanted condition or to attain a desired goal. However, there is no promise of a cure or even improvement in simply doing affirmations. Some conditions will not change, no matter how long or perfectly we practice.

When healing occurs, if it is going to occur, is not up to the individual. Do not set a time limit. Desire for change is good but should not be confused with an expectation of results on our own schedule. Such expectations may create unnecessary tension, an attitude of entitlement, and disappointment.

Stay realistic and avoid magical thinking. Perform affirmations, prayer, and other spiritual techniques with the realization that the outcome is not up to us. If we improve, we are grateful. If we continue to struggle with our current problems, we can cultivate acceptance, strength, and courage.

It is natural to want a physical cure or to accomplish our goals in the external world, but this is not always possible. We can, however, always continue working with our inner being, seeking emotional stability, peace of mind, and spiritual wholeness. For most of us, there is more than a lifetime of work to do in these areas.

For those conditions that improve slowly or not at all, affirmations of surrender or acceptance may be of use. "I surrender to the will of God." "I accept the things I cannot change." "Pain is the teacher. I work with it. I learn from it. I am not afraid." Or you might try one word affirmations such as, "accept," "surrender," "yield," "open," "soft," or "silence."

EXAMPLE

Joe has a very difficult time accepting criticism without feeling rejected. When others are critical, he reacts with anger and fear. He loses control of his emotions, yells, and becomes verbally aggressive. Later, embarrassed by his immature behavior, he feels guilt, shame, and remorse.

Joe wants to change. He starts the practice of affirmations. He affirms, "I am at peace under all conditions. I remain calm when challenged. I am a warm, compassionate, loving human being. I am as good as any other person. I remain calm even if the other person is mean and wrong." With his imagination, he visualizes himself at peace no matter how angry others get. These pictures go into his subconscious mind.

Joe performs his affirmations and visualizations with calm concentration, will, feeling, and faith. His subconscious mind forms a new habit pattern of staying calm, just as Joe pictures himself to be when others get angry.

Later, an angry person confronted Joe in the street. Instead of reacting with anger and fear, he remained calm. He was even able to stay supportive of the other person and give him a kind word. He withdrew from the scene without adding oil to the other person's fire. Joe marveled at the power of affirmations to heal his long-standing problem.

Joe was also wise to the fact that his healing was not complete. From his study of the science of healing affirmations, he knew that his progress might not be in a straight line, that his record might not be perfect. He knew that he might not handle other situations as well and that negative thoughts of discouragement and insecurity would arise. Despite the inevitable setbacks, Joe continued his practice of affirmation with diligence, patience, and perseverance. Although he knew it would take time, he was confident that he would ultimately master his long-standing problem by calmly concentrating on his affirmations with all of his heart, mind, might, and soul. Eventually, Joe achieved mastery.

POINTS TO REMEMBER

- Nothing is closer to us than our own thoughts. It is in this realm that we can change our reality and our destiny.
- We look at the world through our thoughts as though they are glasses. Negative thoughts fashion a dark vision of the world. Change your glasses. Think positive thoughts rooted in Love.
- Spiritual qualities are the healers. When we align our thinking with such qualities as peace, compassion, and understanding, we maximize the chemical and electromagnetic forces that control healing. With affirmative thought, we can give ourselves inspiration and guidance, comfort and solace, transformation and purification.
- We can work on any problem by affirming any one or combination of 100 Love qualities. Choosing thoughts in alignment with Love lights the fire of healing power. In so doing, we make an immediate contribution towards the transformation and healing of the world by reforming ourselves.

- In each moment of our lives, we have a choice concerning our thoughts and attitude. As soon as we perceive a single negative thought, we can eliminate it with an army of positive thoughts. When feeling restless, affirm with peace. When judging others, counter with an affirmation of loving kindness.

- We compound our problems with our excesses. In response to the difficulties of the world, we respond with mental restlessness, high emotion, bad habits, and greed. Our selfishness gives us the illusion of protection while creating more fear and insecurity. Instead, we can respond with compassion, peace, and understanding ... powerful healers that neutralize all types of negativity.

- In a state of deep meditation, we can plant our affirmation and visualization in the subconscious mind. With continued practice, this thought-picture grows in strength and power until it has enough force to become a new habit.

- Love qualities are the gateway to higher consciousness. We can create the qualities we lack through concentration, will, thought, and faith. Pick a Love quality, breath it, affirm it, and practice it in your actions. Each time we align our thinking with Love or one of Her consort qualities, we move one step closer to spiritual realization.

- Applying the power of positive thoughts to heal life is simple, relaxing, and enjoyable. The results are of great benefit over time. Practice affirmations. You will be amazed when you see how the wonderful power of thought can change your life! Never underestimate the healing power of positive thinking.

- When we see something we dislike, we can affirm our vision of goodness and beauty. We can apply the scientific principles of healing affirmations to eliminate all traces of negativity.

- With continuous practice, life itself becomes an affirmation.

AFFIRMATIONS

FOR SUCCESS IN WORK

- I am successful in all aspects of my work.
- I focus on completing one task at a time.
- I am calm, efficient, and productive.

FOR SUCCESS IN RELATIONSHIPS

- I am in harmony with all people.
- I contribute to the health and welfare of everyone I meet.
- I am understanding and compassionate, even when others are wrong and provocative.

FOR CULTIVATION OF SPIRITUAL QUALITIES

- I am at peace no matter what the world does.
- Compassion and kindness permeate my thoughts, feelings, and actions.
- Love is the great healer. I give Love and kindness to all I meet.

HEALING

- The infinitely intelligent healing power permeates every cell of my body.
- The infinitely intelligent healing power cleans my cells.
- The infinitely intelligent healing power eliminates debris.
- The infinitely intelligent healing power creates antibodies against disease-causing microbes.
- The infinitely intelligent healing power generates new cells where needed.
- The infinitely intelligent healing power energizes my body.
- The infinitely intelligent healing power relaxes my body.
- The infinitely intelligent healing power melts disease.
- The infinitely intelligent healing power coordinates all the activities of my body.

EXERCISES

1. Review and study the nine guidelines for creating powerful, effective healing affirmations.
2. What is the difference between a prayer and an affirmation?
3. Describe how subconscious negative thoughts sabotage affirmations.
4. Describe and practice the technique for affirmations during meditation or rest.
5. Describe and practice the technique for affirmations during activity.
6. Describe and practice japa yoga.
7. As you repeat your affirmations, try writing down the negative thoughts that surface from your subconscious. This will demonstrate the nature of the negative images and attitudes that could be controlling you at this time. By doing this, you can find out what beliefs prevent realization of your intended positive thought.
8. Reflect on the brilliance of the healing power. Meditate on it. This will increase your trust in its magnificent intelligence. As you increase your faith, trust, and belief in your own healing power, your affirmations will be more effective.
9. Write out some affirmations on note cards and keep them in your pocket at all times. Pull out the card and practice these affirmations during the day. Select an "Affirmation of the Day."
10. Review the 100 Love qualities in the spiritual alphabet. You can use these as one-word affirmations. Let these one-word affirmations be your word of the day. These qualities will help you get through any physical, mental, emotional, or spiritual problem.

In the next chapter, you will learn how to transform bad habits into constructive meaningful activities, the habits of a seeker, and the habits of a sage.

CHAPTER 11

HABITS

How to Eliminate Bad Habits

The thought manifests as word;
The word manifests as deed;
The deed develops into habit;
And habit hardens into character.
So watch the thought and its ways with care,
And let it spring from love
Born out of concern for all beings.

The Buddha

A cocaine addict, a working person raising a family, a seeker practicing meditation and service, and a highly conscious sage all have the same motivation: the core drive. We all want avoidance of suffering and permanent Love, peace, and safety. What separates us is our habits. Habits rule destiny. Our life is a sequence of habits that determine our course and evolution.

We all have a mix of good and bad habits. Bad habits cause untold suffering. Good habits serve us in the cause of our liberation. To understand how we got where we are and how to change direction, we need to understand the formation and transformation of habits. The seeker will need to release the energy captured by bad habits and transfer this power to liberating good habits.

Any pattern of thought or action repeated many times results in a habit with a corresponding neurosignature, or brain groove. The brain is composed of approximately 100 billion cells, called neurons. A brain groove is a series of interconnected neurons that carry the thought patterns of a particular habit. Attention feeds the habit. When we give our attention to a habit, we activate the brain groove, releasing the thoughts, desires, and actions related to that habit.

The good news is that the brain is malleable. We can change our thoughts and behavior by recruiting new cells to form new brain grooves. Every thought and action is recorded within the interconnected nerve cells, and each repetition adds new depth to the brain groove. If we repeat a thought and action enough times, a habit is formed. Continued repetition strengthens the power of the habit. Inattention and lack of repetition weakens the power of the habit. These principles apply to the formation of both good and bad habits. Positive thoughts and actions create good habits. Negative thoughts and actions create harmful habits.

We can use these principles to eliminate and replace bad habits with good ones. We can gradually starve bad habits to death by not giving them our attention. As we pay more attention to forming a good habit, the new brain groove slowly gains power. Eventually, the new positive brain groove dominates the negative groove, and good habits drive out the bad. Without this transformation, spiritual growth is impossible.

When we are assigned painful problems in the school of life, we need to do the homework. All too often, however, we play hooky by escaping into the pleasures of a bad habit. If we repeat this behavior, at some point we get addicted. We end up with the original problem and a host of additional difficulties associated with addiction. Addiction leads to wild emotions, mental storms, paranoia, rage, humiliation, chaotic relationships, job loss, disease, and death. We can avoid this by doing our homework, by learning how to be good pain managers. Learning how to manage our suffering is critical on the spiritual path. However, most of us slide down the path of bad habits early in our lives in our attempt to avoid pain.

Bad habits include smoking, use of drugs or alcohol, excessive eating, compulsive gambling, compulsive shopping, addiction to the internet, computer or television, addiction to sex, money, fame, work, activity, power, or dependency on others at the expense of independence and individuality (a condition known as codependency or relationship addiction). Although bad habits are pleasurable in the beginning, their eventual evolution into emptiness and torment is inevitable as they force us to act in ways contrary to our true nature. We want to express Love, compassion, kindness, patience, and courage.

To begin the process of transforming bad habits to spiritual power, we must recognize that the pain of the bad habit is worse than the pain of healing. Cultivating good habits is difficult, but it is more difficult to maintain bad habits.

There are hundreds of good physical, mental, emotional, and spiritual habits. These fall into three categories:

1. Constructive activities related to health, work, relationships, recreation, or hobbies.
2. The habits of a seeker: the spiritual methods described in this and other spiritual books.
3. The habits of a sage: spiritual qualities such as Love, compassion, forgiveness, courage, strength, and others listed in the spiritual alphabet.

The time to create these positive habits is now. Every time we repeat a thought or action of a bad habit, it maintains or gains power. Procrastination weakens our will to the point that we think we cannot change. Before we know it, the habit has locked us in a prison of our own making. We may not even know if a habit already has enough power to imprison us for decades: we only discover its power when one day we try to stop it and find out we cannot.

> *Assume a virtue if you have it not.*
> *Refrain tonight,*
> *And that shall lend a kind of easiness*
> *To the next abstinence, the next more easy;*
> *For use almost can change the stamp of nature,*
> *And either lodge the devil or throw him out*
> *With wondrous potency.*
>
> Shakespeare, *Hamlet*

Following is a technique for replacing bad habits with good, spiritual habits:

1. Introspection
2. Avoid everything associated with the bad habit
3. Affirmations and will
4. Constructive meaningful activities
5. The habits of a seeker
6. The habits of a sage
7. Support
8. Solitude
9. Perseverance
10. Victory

1. INTROSPECTION

Make a list of the habits you would like to change. Examples of bad habits include smoking, substance abuse, gambling, compulsive eating, addiction to sex, computers, money, power, work, and codependency or addiction to people.

2. AVOID EVERYTHING ASSOCIATED WITH THE BAD HABIT

People, environment, routines, and our own thoughts are the breath that gives life to the brain groove of a bad habit. With continued stimulation, a bad habit grows, our will weakens, and we slide off the spiritual path. However, the neurocircuit for the bad habit remains dormant in the subconscious if we give it no thought or attention. We can gain power over a bad habit by avoiding exposure to everything associated with it. Stay away from the negative environment, people, and actions that supported the habit, until the new brain groove is strong. Avoid thinking about the bad habit as much as possible. We are subject to craving in an instant, if not careful. Even a passing thought or image of the negative habit can awaken desire. The more we let the idea play in our minds, the more at risk we are of recurrent addiction. Starve the bad habit to death by inattention.

3. AFFIRMATIONS AND WILL

Review the lessons on affirmations and will to see how thought power and will power can erase even the deepest grooves of long standing habits. The mind has the key that can unlock the door of a bad habit, as a single thought or visual image can stimulate craving. We need to choose our thoughts carefully. Thoughts associated with our bad habits do pass through our consciousness against our will, however. To prevent these thoughts from becoming action, we must work against them. As soon as we become aware of the unwanted thought, we can knock it out with will and affirmations. We can invoke our will at full power, deploy our favorite affirmations, and turn to good and spiritual actions. These include constructive meaningful activities, the habits of a seeker, and the habits of a sage.

4. ENGAGE IN CONSTRUCTIVE MEANINGFUL ACTIVITIES

Make a list of activities related to your work, chores, relationships, leisure, recreation, hobbies, and self-nurturance. These activities are a part of your repertoire of positive habits. You can use these activities to ward off the thoughts and impulses related to your bad habits. Such a list might include playing and watching sports, listening to or playing music, television, the Internet, movies, reading, writing, studying, exercise, arts and crafts, board games, crossword or jigsaw puzzles, gardening, paying bills, shopping, cooking, cleaning, taking a nap, getting a massage, and so on.

5. CULTIVATE THE HABITS OF A SEEKER

The habits of a seeker include any spiritual technique that leads to the growth of spiritual qualities. For our purposes, these are affirmations, will, surrender, contemplation, breathwork, progressive muscle relaxation, meditation, mindfulness, practicing the presence of God, service, prayer, yoga, and the transformation of emotion.

6. CULTIVATE THE HABITS OF A SAGE

The habits of a sage are the spiritual qualities listed in the spiritual alphabet. These include Love, compassion, understanding, forgiveness, courage, strength, endurance, peace, and joy.

If constructive meaningful activities, spiritual practice, and spiritual qualities keep the door of the bad habit locked, craving is kept at bay. We are safe. On the other hand, if despite our best efforts, the door of bad habits opens, the seductive music of craving may bring us to the brink of relapse. If this occurs, we must surround ourselves with people who will protect us from negative actions.

7. SUPPORT

We need to surround ourselves with people who support our spiritual goals. Friends and family associated with our bad habits often try to pull us back. When we move forward, they take it personally. Moreover, we are afraid of finding new people. We must get through this fear to create a supportive network of people with like-minded goals who act as our spiritual bodyguards, protecting us from ourselves in moments of vulnerability.

8. SOLITUDE

To heal completely, we need to practice discipline when we are alone. This is a tall order. Many of us are afraid to be alone and of the unknown. With continued practice, however, we will gain the necessary courage and self-control to resist craving even when we are alone. Then we do not need bodyguards. Eventually, craving ceases.

9. PERSEVERANCE

Change is difficult. Some strong bad habits may take years to break. Tests, trials, and temptations come. Setbacks occur. Back and forth movement between old and new patterns is a natural part of the process. *Do not give up.* When you slip and fall, be sure to create the mental habit of gentleness with yourself, while using the remorse, regret, or disgust you may feel as an incentive to push you on to greater efforts.

10. VICTORY

Keep feeding the positive habit to make it stronger and starving the negative habit to make it weaker. Give the best of your effort, concentration, and attention to the new habit until it takes over and becomes a natural, effortless, and automatic part of your repertoire. Keep battling and you will win. Craving ceases. Peace and strength deepen. Life becomes easier and more natural.

The ego, in its drive for immediate gratification, gets us into trouble with addiction and attachment. Not only do we lose pre-existing strength, but spiritual qualities cannot grow. On the other hand, our souls yearn for Love, and are willing to pay the price of work and patience. As we practice the methods of a seeker, we reinforce the neurocircuits containing spiritual qualities such as Love, compassion, understanding, strength, and courage, until these become unconditional habits. In the end, we realize our true spiritual identity by reconditioning our brain with soul qualities. We do not have to think about our practice. We express the habits of a sage, the Love qualities, automatically, naturally, and easily.

POINTS TO REMEMBER

- In the beginning of our spiritual work, it may be difficult to get traction. We can gain momentum by setting reasonable goals, taking small steps, achieving modest successes, and building from there.
- The next step in our spiritual development is in the immediate moments of our lives. However, when we do not like what is going on, we leap out of the moment and back into an unhealthy habit. We hypnotize and narcotize ourselves in order to avoid unpleasant feelings. Instead, choose constructive, meaningful activities and the spiritual methods of a seeker to develop the spiritual qualities of a sage.

- Break bad habits of thought, attitude, emotion, desire, energy, and action so you can emerge from the past and find yourself renewed: fresh, spontaneous, and in the moment.

AFFIRMATIONS

- I can eliminate any bad habit.
- I expand my will power through practice.
- With my expanded will power, I escape from bad habits.
- One by one, I eliminate all bad habits.
- Nothing can stand in my way.
- Nothing can touch my will.
- Nothing can shake my resolve.
- My will power grows stronger each day.
- My mind is set.
- Nothing can stop me.
- I will succeed.
- Old friends who would have me indulge my bad habits are out.
- With will and thought, I conquer every bad habit, one at a time.
- I am not my bad habits. My true self is free to be warm, compassionate, loving, and kind.
- I am stronger than any negative desire or temptation.
- No matter how many times I fail, I will rise and conquer.
- As I strengthen my body through physical exercise, I strengthen my will with mental exercise.
- With will and thought, I cast out this bad habit from the neurocircuits in my brain.
- With will and thought, I cultivate the habits of a sage: Love, peace of mind, compassion, and strength.

EXERCISES

1. Make a list of your good and bad habits. Which habits would you like to change now?
2. What barriers keep you from changing your bad habits?
3. Make a list of constructive, meaningful activities that you will use to avoid bad habits.
4. What spiritual methods would you like to practice?
5. What spiritual qualities would you like to develop?
6. What will you do when craving for a destructive habit returns?
7. Practice the ten steps for replacing bad habits with good and spiritual habits.
8. Keep a log. Each day you can inspect the status of your habits. Give yourself credit for your successes. Recognize your slips, but do not dwell on the bad habit; this only reinforces the associated brain groove. Instead, cultivate the mental habit of being gentle with yourself while you focus on the good habits you are creating.

In the next section, we will study five techniques that comprise a morning and evening spiritual program. These techniques are progressive muscle relaxation, breathwork, contemplation, meditation, and prayer.

PART FOUR
MORNING
AND EVENING
PROGRAM

CHAPTER 12

PROGRESSIVE MUSCLE RELAXATION

Energizing and Relaxing the Body

Progressive muscle relaxation is a method used to calm our mind and body through tensing and relaxing our muscles. An anxious mind results in a tense body. Progressive muscle relaxation calms the body, which in turn calms the mind.

This technique is effective for reducing anxiety, fear, panic, depression, insomnia, and fatigue. In addition, when the body and mind are relaxed, it is easier to practice other spiritual methods such as contemplation, mindfulness, and service. Many people use this technique to relax the body in preparation for deeper states of meditation.

GUIDELINES

1. Practice the entire routine described below in your morning and evening program for 10-15 minutes. You can also tense and relax specific muscles when stressed or fatigued.

2. Make this part of a regular routine including spiritual study, breathwork, meditation, and prayer.

3. Concentrate exclusively on tensing, relaxing, and energizing each muscle. Use your will and concentration to eliminate all other thoughts. This is not a time to worry, plan, fantasize, or solve problems. It is a time to relax and gain energy. When the mind wanders, bring it back to focus on tensing, relaxing, and energizing your muscles.

4. To reinforce your intention of energizing and relaxing your muscles, you can use an affirmation such as "energize" when you tense the muscle, and "relax" when you relax the muscle.

5. Tense each muscle at maximum strength but without strain for 3 seconds. Then relax for 3 seconds. The movements are smooth and continuous, not abrupt or jerky.

6. Repeat each exercise 3-5 times.

7. When tensing a particular muscle, keep the rest of your muscles relaxed.

TECHNIQUE

1. Position: Practice sitting, lying, or standing.

2. Eyes: Close your eyes and focus at the point just above and between your eyebrows.

3. Breath: You may breathe in as you tense and exhale as you relax each muscle, or simply maintain calm, natural, smooth, relaxed breathing in the background. When you inhale, imagine that you are inhaling energy. When you exhale, imagine exhaling tension.

4. Foot: Make several circles with your left foot in each direction. Then tense the left foot muscle by curling the toes downward. Repeat this exercise with the right foot.

5. Calf: Tense and relax the left calf muscle 3-5 times. Repeat this exercise with the right calf.

6. Thigh: Tense and relax the left thigh muscle 3-5 times. Repeat this exercise with the right thigh.

7. Buttock: Tense and relax the left buttock 3-5 times. Repeat this exercise with the right buttock.

8. Lower abdomen: Tense and relax the lower abdomen 3-5 times.

9. Upper abdomen: Tense and relax the upper abdomen 3-5 times.

10. Full abdomen: Pull your abdominal muscles all the way in and hold for 2 seconds, then relax your abdomen. Repeat this exercise 5-20 times.

11. Fist: Tense and relax the left fist 3-5 times. Repeat this exercise with the right fist.

12. Forearm: Tense and relax the left forearm 3-5 times. Repeat this exercise with the right forearm.

13. Upper arm: Tense and relax the left upper arm 3-5 times. Repeat this exercise with the right upper arm.

14. Chest: Tense and relax the left chest 3-5 times. Repeat this exercise with the right chest.

15. Lower back: Tense and relax the muscles in your lower back 3-5 times.

16. Middle back: Tense and relax the muscles in your middle back 3-5 times. You might imagine squeezing an orange between your shoulder blades.

17. Upper back: Tense and relax the upper back muscles 3-5 times.

18. Neck: Tense and relax the left neck muscle, then the right neck muscle, then the front neck muscle and then the back neck muscle. Repeat this exercise 3-5 times.

19. Head: Gently tense the muscles in your neck while you roll your head 3-5 times slowly in each direction.

20. Facial muscles: Notice any tension that you have here. Tighten your facial muscles by smiling wide, closing your eyes tightly, and wrinkling your forehead. Tense and relax each area 3-5 times.

21. Inhale and tense your whole body. Hold for a count of five. Exhale and relax, releasing the tension from your entire body.

22. Now take inventory of your body. Notice any lingering tension. Tense and relax 3-5 times where necessary.

23. Take several smooth, slow, deep breaths. On inhalation, imagine taking in life energy. On exhalation, imagine releasing any remaining tension in your body. Eliminate all negative thoughts. Concentrate on the peace and energy you have gained from these exercises.

24. Spend a few minutes feeling peace and energy spread to all parts of your body.

25. Open your eyes and feel awake, alert, and refreshed!

POINTS TO REMEMBER

- Practice progressive muscle relaxation slowly, with deep concentration. Eliminate all thought of problems, difficulty, and worry.
- Your muscle movement in these exercises should be smooth and continuous, not abrupt or jerky. It is important to tense each muscle to maximum strength without strain. Tense your muscle for 3 seconds, and relax for 3 seconds.
- Each time you tense and relax a muscle, you are energizing and relaxing that muscle. When you tense and relax all of your

muscles at the same time, you fill your entire body with calm energy.

- Tense and relax your whole body 3-5 times whenever you feel anxious or fatigued.

AFFIRMATION

- I permeate every cell in my body with energy and peace.
- I fill my body with energy and peace.

EXERCISES

1. Notice the contrast when you tense and relax any muscle. Muscle tension, followed by a conscious effort to relax the muscle, allows you to recognize the difference between tension and relaxation. Once you notice this difference, it is easier to induce relaxation.

2. Include progressive muscle relaxation in your morning and evening spiritual routine. It is easier to meditate when your body is relaxed.

3. Practice progressive muscle relaxation any time you feel anxiety or fatigue.

4. You can memorize the instructions for progressive muscle relaxation or make a recording, so you can listen to the instructions as you perform the exercises.

In the next chapter, you will learn how to use your breath to relax and heal your body, mind, and soul.

CHAPTER 13

BREATHWORK

Using Breath to Heal Mind, Body, and Soul

This chapter introduces breathwork, the second method of the morning and evening program. By learning how to breathe correctly, we can enhance our physical, mental, emotional, and spiritual well-being. For the body, breathwork results in more energy, better sleep and digestion, improved pain management, and lower blood pressure. For the mind, conscious breathing helps cultivate stillness, balance, concentration, and productivity. Emotionally, breath control helps us process anxiety, depression, anger, guilt, and other painful feelings into self-knowledge. When we learn how to breathe, we can find our calm center, a necessity for all spiritual practices.

Following are some simple, enjoyable breathing exercises. These exercises can be practiced anywhere, anytime, and in any position including sitting, standing, walking, or lying down. As with other methods, the benefits of breathwork develop gradually and cumulatively with daily practice.

ABDOMINAL BREATHING

To breathe correctly, we need to understand the difference between chest and abdominal breathing. Notice your breath. If you expand your chest or rib cage more, you are a chest breather. If you expand your abdomen or stomach more, you are an abdominal breather.

Stress causes rapid, shallow, noisy, and irregular chest breathing which in turn results in more stress, locking us into a negative cycle. Abdominal breathing, on the other hand, induces relaxation and has an immediate anti-anxiety effect. The heart rate slows, blood pressure decreases, and the mind and muscles relax. We regain our calm center and reduce the likelihood of getting stuck in a negative mental or emotional state. In addition to relaxation, abdominal breathing gives the body more oxygen, resulting in more energy. We should breathe abdominally when we feel well or when we have stress, restless thoughts, painful emotions, or fatigue. Following are several wonderful breathing techniques.

FOCUSED ABDOMINAL BREATHING WITH AFFIRMATIONS

1. Focus on your breath. Make a conscious effort to breathe slowly, regularly, quietly, smoothly, and deeply. Chest breathing, or holding your breath, is common when anxious or in pain. If this occurs, go back to slow, deep abdominal breathing.

2. Inhalation: When you inhale, feel expansion in your abdomen rather than your chest. An easy way to tell if you are doing this properly is to hold your hand over your stomach as you take a breath. When you inhale, your hand should rise; as you exhale, it should move back in. There is some expansion of the chest in relaxed breathing, but most of the movement is in the abdomen.

3. Exhalation: When you breathe out, exhale fully and completely. Squeeze all the air out of your lungs.

4. Affirm: Try any affirmation that makes you comfortable. You might affirm, "I relax my body." "I calm my mind." "Relax." "Peace." If the mind wanders, gently bring it back to the breath.

Breathe slow and deep five to ten minutes in your morning and evening program, or any time of day. You might try 10-15 quiet, deep breaths whenever you need to refocus and energize. If you feel light headed, stop for 20-30 seconds and then start again. With practice, abdominal breathing replaces chest breathing. The result is a relaxed body, peace of mind, and vitality.

THE CALMING BREATH

This breathing exercise produces a feeling of peace. Practice the calming breath when you are anxious, restless, or at any time.

1. Make a conscious effort to make your breath slow, regular, quiet, smooth, and deep.

2. Inhalation: Inhale fully to a count of eight.

3. Hold: Hold the deep breath to a count of eight.

4. Exhalation: Exhale fully to a count of eight.

5. You can count to 2, 4, 6, 12, or even up to 20. Choose whatever number you wish. Use that same number for the inhalation, holding it, and the exhalation. It does not matter how fast you count.

6. Repeat this 6-8 times in your morning and evening program, or any time of day.

THE BREATH OF FIRE

The breath of fire stimulates, energizes, and relaxes the body. Try it when you get up in the morning, or any time you are sleepy, fatigued, or anxious.

1. With mouth closed, breathe through your nose at a rate of 2-3 breaths a second. One breath includes inhalation and exhalation.

2. The inhalations and exhalations are continuous, smooth, and of equal length.

3. Practice this exercise for 15-30 seconds. Increase in small increments up to several minutes at a time.

THE BREATH AND
EMOTIONAL PAIN MANAGEMENT

Abdominal breathing helps us work through emotional pain. This allows us to experience the truth of our feelings. When we process anger, anxiety, depression, and other difficult emotions, we gain self-knowledge and peace of mind.

1. Notice what you are feeling.

2. Remind yourself that repressed feelings remain, while processed feelings dissipate.

3. Breathe right into the center of the feeling. Sometimes just breathing into the feeling clears it. If the feeling persists, stay with it and let it speak to you. When the feeling reveals its truths it moves on, and you gain self-knowledge.

Refer to Chapter 21, "Transformation of Emotion," for additional details on emotional processing.

POINTS TO REMEMBER

- We do not have to practice breathing for months or years to get results. The relaxation response occurs immediately.
- Breath is always available. We can use it at any time to get centered, calm, comfortable, and still.
- Abdominal breathing increases our awareness of our body, feelings, and the environment.
- Breathwork helps curb addiction and craving. Breathe right into the heart of the craving to make it disappear.
- Breathwork helps manage physical pain. Breathing into the pain helps to control fear and cultivate strength.

EXERCISES

1. Describe the benefits of conscious breathing for the body, mind, emotions, and spirit.
2. What is the difference between chest and abdominal breathing?
3. Describe and practice focused abdominal breathing with affirmations.
4. Describe and practice the "calming breath."
5. Describe and practice the "breath of fire."
6. Describe how breathwork can help you manage emotions.
7. Describe how breathwork can help you manage craving.
8. Describe how breathwork can help you manage your physical pain.

In the next chapter, you will study the third method of the morning and evening program: contemplation.

CHAPTER 14

CONTEMPLATION

A Sacred Technique for Spiritual Realization

"Contemplation for an hour is better than formal worship for sixty years."
Mohammed

This chapter introduces contemplation, the third method of the morning and evening program. The contemplation of wisdom is a special method of study that allows us to realize the powerful knowledge hidden in the great sacred texts. The *Bible, Bhagavad Gita, Koran*, and other sacred texts are loaded with pearls of wisdom that we can integrate into our being.

The aim of ordinary reading, such as a newspaper or novel, is the accumulation of knowledge and/or entertainment. For these purposes, we generally read straight through, without pause. Spiritual study requires a different type of reading as the goal is realization of soul qualities in the soil of our own consciousness.

Following is a method of spiritual study. With this contemplative technique, we slow down our reading so we can go deep into our consciousness, in order to convert the words into personal realization.

TECHNIQUE

The wisdom in sacred books reflects the soul qualities that already exist within us. To realize any soul quality, set aside some time and follow these steps:

1. Choose a topic
2. Study

3. Affirm
4. Act
5. Introspect
6. Mastery

1. CHOOSE A TOPIC

Pick an area where you would like to do some work, such as becoming more compassionate.

2. STUDY

Find a quiet place to study. Eliminate all distractions: Turn off the TV and unplug your phone. Find a passage in your sacred book, having to do with compassion. Read this passage to get the overall picture. Go back and read the material again, this time jotting down the important points. When written, the material is impressed much deeper in the mind and consciousness.

3. AFFIRM

Affirm one complete thought. This may be a sentence, a few lines, or a paragraph. An example of a thought on compassion from the Dalai Lama is, "The feeling of kindness, love, and compassion is the essence of brotherhood and sisterhood. This compassionate feeling is the basis of inner peace." Read it several times. With your will and concentration, eliminate all other thoughts. Place the thought in the center of your being and keep it there for several minutes. Allow its vibratory power to spread throughout your body. Visualize yourself spreading Love, compassion, and kindness with each action throughout your day. If you know a technique of meditation, you can include your affirmation and visualization before and after your practice. Affirmations are most effective when the mind is relaxed and opened, as during meditation.

4. ACT

Place note cards with affirmations related to compassion in your shirt pocket or other convenient places. Pull these cards out when you have a spare moment. Review these affirmations as a reminder of your theme for the day. You might give your mind a one-word affirmation such as "compassion." Remember to let compassion be the governor of every thought, attitude, feeling, and action. Notice how an oft-repeated affirmation will come into your conscious mind automatically. This is a sign that compassion is becoming a mental habit. Through repetition and practice, compassion slowly expands.

5. INTROSPECT

In the evening, you can review your performance that day with respect to your chosen theme. When you fall short—and you will—take note of it and keep trying. For most of us, such a great quality as compassion requires a lifetime of practice. There will be many setbacks. This is natural. Do not allow your ego to slow your progress by denying mistakes and blaming others. Instead, humbly accept your limitations as part of the human condition. This will help you be more compassionate with yourself as well as others.

6. MASTERY

After many years of daily study and practice, compassion slowly takes hold, eventually becoming a habit. It guides all of your thoughts, feelings, and actions. As compassion slowly expands, it surrounds, feeds, permeates, and saturates every aspect of your being. In the end, you become compassion itself.

Through contemplative practice, we convert the great ideas and spiritual qualities embedded in spiritual texts from shallow words in our heads to real vibrations that permeate consciousness and action. Without contemplation, the inherent healing power of sacred ideas remains locked up, waiting, if not begging, for liberation.

We have seen many preach about the enlightened life but come up short because they do not know how to transfer the life of the sacred written word into their daily lives. We can avoid this perilous trap by practicing contemplation. With this technique, we can crack open the shell of a pearl of wisdom to reveal its hidden secrets and release its soothing healing powers.

The contemplation of wisdom is in the hall of fame of spiritual practices. It converts such great qualities as compassion or any other spiritual quality or idea from the surface superficiality of mere words to experience, feeling, and action. Include this powerful technique in your spiritual program. Start your morning and evening program with a period of spiritual study. You will see that it not only works, but is supremely enjoyable.

POINTS TO REMEMBER

- The soul qualities described in sacred texts are within us. We can understand them better in contemplation and embody them through repetitive action. With practice, patience, and perseverance, we expand and express these virtues in our thoughts, feelings, and actions. We become peace, joy, kindness, compassion, courage, and strength. This is spiritual realization.

EXERCISES

1. What is the difference between ordinary reading and spiritual study?
2. Describe the six steps for contemplating wisdom.
3. Choose a spiritual quality you would like to develop. Follow the six steps for contemplating wisdom.
4. Describe how the ego interferes with the growth of spiritual qualities.
5. What is spiritual realization?
6. Why is introspection a necessary precursor of spiritual realization?

In the next chapter, you will study meditation, the fourth method of the morning and evening program.

CHAPTER 15

MEDITATION

A Technique for All Seasons

This chapter introduces meditation, the fourth method of the morning and evening program. In our culture, we are encouraged to surround ourselves continuously with stimulating activities. With work, relationships, recreation, the arts, radio, television, computers, the Internet, magazines, and newspapers, we have plenty to keep us busy. As a result, most Westerners have become activity junkies as we stay in motion the entire day.

In response to the barrage of continuous happenings of the outside world, the mind gets restless and hyperactive, getting no rest except in sleep. We crave peace of mind but have distracted ourselves from the tranquility that can only be found in the stillness and silence at the core of our being.

Meditation, an ancient technique currently undergoing a revival in popularity, brings such inner peace. In meditation there is a progressive slowing of the body and mind to the point of absolute stillness. When we connect to the stillness within by quieting the mind and opening the heart, we approach the soul, homeland of inner peace and all other spiritual qualities.

Stillness provides the opening for our next level of spiritual quest, the springboard for advanced spiritual development. It is much easier to grow spiritual qualities in the soil of our consciousness when we are still and quiet. We can more gracefully give Love, compassion, and understanding when the mind is calm than when it is restless and hyperactive.

When we get comfortable with the contemplative practices of the great traditions such as meditation, we learn to treasure our connection to the silence and stillness within. As we advance spiritually, we balance our active outer life with an inner life of tranquility. The benefits of adding the dimension of stillness to our spiritual program are profound.

There are five stages of meditation, each with a greater degree of stillness. The progression from one stage to the next is dependent on meditating longer and deeper. The stages are:

Stage 1: Meditation for the body: the relaxation response;

Stage 2: Meditation for the mind: a strong, positive, calm mind;

Stage 3: Meditation for the soul: no mind; a shift in identity to the soul; an expansion of spiritual qualities;

Stage 4: Meditation on the Higher Power: communion, guidance, protection, intuition, prayer, and further expansion of spiritual qualities;

Stage 5: Infinity: the full blossom of spiritual qualities; travel in the infinite ocean of Spirit.

Although these stages are progressive, they are not mutually exclusive. There is overlap. They are separated here for descriptive purposes only.

In ordinary consciousness, we identify with our thoughts, bodies, egos, and roles. The mind and ego rule the kingdom of consciousness and energy. The mind acts as sole arbiter of reality with its opinions, likes, and dislikes. The non-meditating mind is restless, hyperactive, and controlling. This is the active state from which we all start. The first step up from this level is meditation for the body.

STAGE 1: MEDITATION FOR THE BODY: THE RELAXATION RESPONSE

When we focus on a single point such as a word, phrase, or the breath, our thought process slows down. The heart, lungs, muscles, brain, and every other organ, tissue, and cell in the body relax. The heart rate, respiratory rate, and blood pressure decrease, as does the rate at which the body burns energy. This profound effect is called the "relaxation response," the easiest level of meditation. It occurs in a few minutes.

The relaxation response is good for health and healing: the trillions of cells in the body get a chance to regenerate, repair, and resist disease. Meditation helps improve chronic pain, insomnia, high blood pressure, and any condition caused or worsened by stress. For some, these health benefits are reason enough to meditate. For others, there are additional motivations such as strengthening the mind with positive thoughts and deeper peace.

STAGE 2: MEDITATION FOR THE MIND: A STRONG, POSITIVE, CALM MIND

In the first stage of meditation, there is no attempt to restructure thinking. There is simply a slowing down of the mind. In stage two, the goal is to slow the mind down further and replace negative with positive thoughts by using the technique of affirmation.

Affirmations are particularly effective during and right after meditation; the mind is more receptive at this time. Meditation helps clear the soil of our consciousness of hyperactivity so that we can plant new ideas and suggestions. When we restructure negative or distorted patterns of thought with affirmations, we reframe problems in a realistic, positive way.

You might review the lesson on affirmations and practice this technique during meditation. The combination of meditation and affirmations results in a strong, positive, calm mind. When the mind is peaceful and positive, it is better able to create success in relationships and activities, deal with painful problems in the school of life, and foster our enjoyment of life.

For some, the achievement of a positive, strong, calm mind is sufficient motivation to meditate. Others may be interested in the next phase of meditation, discovery of the soul. With longer and deeper meditation, it is possible to bring the mind to a position of complete stillness. This leads to the discovery of the soul and expansion of spiritual qualities.

STAGE 3: MEDITATION FOR THE SOUL: NO MIND

The goal in stage one is to slow the mind down and relax the body. The goal in stage two is to further slow the mind and replace negative with positive thoughts. The goal in stage three is to proceed with slowing the mind down to complete stillness. We transition from negative to positive thought, and from positive thought to stillness. Stopping the internal dialogue is referred to in Buddhism as "no mind" or "empty mind." To bring the mind to complete stillness requires longer and deeper practice.

The path of progressively greater degrees of stillness in meditation leads ultimately to the soul. The soul is always completely still, no matter what tempest is happening outside. The soul, also known as the witness, is our true identity and the home of all of the spiritual qualities. We can find the soul, the place of perfect peace, inside, through meditation, whether we are in a personal or impersonal relationship with our Higher Power.

To find the soul in the stillness of meditation is a valuable skill. It not only brings deep peace no matter the external condition, but also reveals our true identity. It is in this stillness that we see our consciousness not completely identified with our body, mind, ego, and the external drama of life. We can see that we are the soul, that we are warm, compassionate, loving, courageous, and strong. It is difficult to get to this state of higher consciousness. It takes years of daily practice.

On the way to progressively greater degrees of stillness, the mind continues to churn with all kinds of useless thoughts related to our concerns and insecurities. These thoughts come like waves, one after another. We are unable to stop them. However, we can counter them with our mantra, breath, prayer, affirmations, and visualizations. We can replace negative thoughts with positive thoughts. In addition, we can watch thoughts come and go from the witness, the place of stillness inside.

To reach the soul, we need to stop identifying with our thoughts as though they were the ultimate judge of reality. We must reduce the power of our thoughts so that we can give control of our consciousness back to the soul. We can do this in meditation by watching our train of thoughts without getting aboard the train. The mind will go on and on indefinitely, even after we start meditating. However, rather than being swept along with the movement on the train of thought, we can simply watch it go by, noting that thoughts are merely thoughts. They are not the whole of reality. They are not who we are. They are not in control of our lives. In this way, we can reduce their importance, their charge, their ruling power.

As meditation proceeds and the mind quiets, we have a chance to step back from the drama of life and view the story as if it were a movie or a play. We are still actors but now, rather than identify with the characters we play, we become the observer or witness. This detachment gives us a chance to relax in the face of our troubles. We gain perspective and objectivity as we begin to see that we are not our thoughts, ego, problems, or role in the drama. As we step out of the movie-mind and approach the soul, we realize that our ego and problems must be dealt with, but they are not who we are. We are the soul, a composite of the most wonderful qualities.

If we practice with diligence and discipline, if we persist and refuse to quit, if we give it our best over days, weeks, months, and years, slowly but surely the mind calms and is replaced by stillness. There are progressively greater degrees of quiet resulting in a state of absolute stillness.

When we enter and delve into this domain of stillness, we arrive at a state where we want to be, all the time. Here we find the peace that surpasses understanding, a Love that is pure, perfect, and unconditional, and a joy so intense that we call it ecstasy. This is a place of no pain and no problems, where nothing can harm us and nothing can touch us. This is the soul.

No weapon can pierce the soul; no fire can burn it; no water can moisten it; nor can any wind wither it. The soul is uncleavable; it cannot be burnt or wetted or dried. The soul is immutable, all-permeating, ever-calm, and immovable--eternally the same.

The Bhagavad Gita: Chapter II: verse 23-24. p. 221-223 Paramahansa Yogananda

When we stop the waves of activity from the world, body, senses, and mind and sit in the stillness and spaciousness of deep meditation, we absorb strength, courage, compassion, and wisdom. We become who we really are: compassionate, loving, serviceful human beings, capable of managing any problem or pain in the school of life. We enjoy the show in the theatre of life. We are ready for anything, including meditation at the next level, communion with our Higher Power.

STAGE 4: MEDITATION WITH OUR HIGHER POWER

There is an Omniscient, Omnipotent, Omnipresent Power that is in us, surrounds us, and extends outward endlessly in every direction. By making contact with this power in meditation, we can get help for ourselves, others, and the world. We can get guidance, healing, advancement in the development of any spiritual quality, and help with pain and problems.

Meditation is an ideal time for communion with our Higher Power; stillness promotes receptivity and attunement. For those who have a personal relationship with their God, this is a good time to pray, talk, share, listen, and feel. When the mind and body are still, we can send and receive with more clarity than when the mind is restless.

STAGE 5: INFINITY

This stage is reserved for highly evolved souls: saints, sages, gurus, and masters. After many years of deep and long meditation, prayer, and service to humanity, there can be a dramatic transformation in consciousness, sometimes referred to as liberation or enlightenment. This experience is like entering an infinite ocean of Spirit.

Think of life as an ocean. On the surface of the ocean are waves. At times, the surface is calm. Other times, the waves are variously choppy, turbulent, stormy, or dangerous. Beneath the surface, the ocean is deep, vast, still, ubiquitous, and immutable. Consider the deep part of the ocean as a vast repository of spiritual qualities.

Now think of the waves as change in life, and the underlying ocean as that part of life that is changeless. In ordinary consciousness, we bob about on the surface of the ocean, riding the waves of change. Our awareness remains tethered to the changing waves at the surface by our restless mind, volatile emotions, excessive material desires, attachments, hyperactivity, and egotism.

When we reach absolute stillness and relinquish our mind, our consciousness can slip beneath the changing surface waves of the ocean and merge into the depths of the vast Changeless One below. This results in a magnificent shift in consciousness: unity, infinity, and eternity replace limitation, division, and impermanence. In advanced yoga meditation, this is called Samadhi.

Entry tickets to this realm of superconsciousness are reserved for those who have achieved the egoless state of highly developed spiritual qualities. In this stage, the advanced meditator bathes in an infinite ocean of peace, joy, Love, power, wisdom, and other soul qualities. Some get to travel. The vehicle for travel in this neighborhood is fearlessness. The fuel is Love. The destination is other worlds.

Those who enter the greater world of Spirit return to the surface world of duality to share with us what they have found, not with words so much as through acts of gentle, humble service. They are able to manifest and express their soul qualities under all conditions. With calm and strong minds, powerful Love, and durable faith and courage, they are ready for anything.

The Love of such an advanced soul is palpable and tangible. If we are receptive, we can receive and feel their loving power through attunement. Many students try to spend too much time with such masters in order to receive their power, but the true spiritual adept will direct the student to practices that will allow them to gain these spiritual qualities for themselves. Meditation is one such method, a power tool of the ages and of great importance to our work in cultivating peace, Love, joy, power, and wisdom.

Presented below is one of many approaches to meditation. You can explore this or other methods until you find what works best for you. It may be of great value to have a teacher of meditation.

THE TECHNIQUE

1. Sacred space
2. Posture
3. Release all concerns
4. The breath
5. Prayer or affirmation
6. Mantra
7. Concentration
8. Absorption
9. Prayer
10. Closure and re-entry

1. SACRED SPACE

Go to a quiet place in your home. Try to return to the same place each time. This is your sacred space. You might want to build an altar. Turn off the phone and all other distractions so you can remain undisturbed for the duration of your meditation.

2. POSTURE

Sit on a chair with your back straight and make yourself comfortable. You may prefer to sit on a cushion on the floor with legs crossed, or in the lotus position. Close your eyes and lift your gaze to the point just above and between your eyebrows. Try to keep your attention fixed on this point throughout meditation. This is known as the third or spiritual eye. If you notice your attention has shifted to a lower level, gently bring it back up. There should be no strain of the eyes when you do this. Relax your body and all muscles. During the meditation, keep your body as still and relaxed as possible for as long as you can.

3. RELEASE ALL CONCERNS

Relax your mind, releasing all thoughts, concerns, and problems. Forget everything and everybody. Let go of the drama of life for the period of this meditation. Use your will to toss out the world and all its problems, cares, and concerns. Relax and surrender to the stillness and peace that is always present within you.

4. THE BREATH

Breathe slowly and naturally as you adopt a quiet, open, receptive state.

5. PRAYER OR AFFIRMATION

Start your meditation with a prayer, affirmation, or visualization that relates to peace and compassion for yourself and all people. In this way, the heart progressively opens.

6. MANTRA

Pick a word or brief phrase that comes from your belief system. Repeat it silently. Words such as "one," "ocean," "Love," "peace," "harmony," "Our Father who art in heaven," "shalom," or "Om" can be used. You might try focusing on your breath without the repetition of a mantra. If you try this method, make your breathing slow, quiet, and regular. Your mantra or point of focus will protect you from the turmoil of the world and the restlessness of your own mind.

7. CONCENTRATION

Try to maintain your concentration on the mantra. You will notice your mind wander off into its typical pattern of mental chatter. As soon as you notice that your mind has drifted off, bring it gently back to the mantra. This pattern of going back and forth between the mantra and the routine chatter of the mind is a natural process of meditation. Do not worry about how well you are doing. When thoughts return, gently return to the point of focus. Do not strain. The correct position is calm concentration without tension. Gradually, thinking slows and finally stops.

8. ABSORPTION

The ever-increasing stillness bred of meditation brings the body and mind to a state of deep peace, rest, and relaxation. When you stop the superficial waves of thought and are immersed in stillness, relax and feel the peace. Don't think. In this state of open, quiet receptivity and stillness, spiritual qualities grow, the ego shrinks, and problems burn up.

9. PRAYER

Toward the end of your meditation, you can commune with your Higher Power, seeking guidance, protection, or healing for yourself and others. You can close your meditation with a prayer for all who need help as well as for harmony and peace between all individuals, nations, races, and religions.

10. CLOSURE AND RE-ENTRY

Do not stand immediately when you are finished. Continue to sit quietly, enjoying the peace that occurs from slowing down your mind. Then open your eyes and sit for another moment before rising. You are now prepared to give the benefits that you have gained from meditation to all who need your help. Your peace, joy, Love, and other spiritual qualities grow in meditation. You will be able to offer these to your loved ones and all whom you meet.

Meditate for 10-20 minutes in the morning and evening. If this is too long, meditate for even one minute at a time. You can gradually extend this as motivation and time allow.

Some will meditate on a regular basis. Others will meditate whenever it feels right or fits into their schedule. Best results occur with regular, long, deep meditation. Advanced practice can be 1-2 hours, twice a day. Longer meditations of 3-10 hours are reserved for special occasions or retreats. You can increase your time in meditation slowly according to your desires and needs. The amount of time spent in meditation can vary depending on your level of responsibilities to family and work, and your desire to go inward.

RISKS

Meditation is not without risks. Some people become frightened rather than relaxed. Old wounds can be stirred up. You might experience a flood of emotional or mental anguish. Some find meditation useful in working through such periods of agitation or crisis. Others cannot meditate when in crisis but can meditate later when they feel better. If your meditation causes a frightening increase in inner turmoil or symptoms, stop temporarily and consult with an expert in mental health and meditation.

WHAT TO EXPECT

There are three common experiences in meditation:

- WORK: It felt like a lot of work and nothing special happened.
- PAIN: It was difficult and maybe even painful. The most common difficulties are restlessness, boredom, and frustration with the rebellious mind that will not quit thinking about everything. There may be physical or psychological discomfort. Many are afraid to look inward for fear of what they might discover.
- SPIRITUAL EXPERIENCE: We experience stillness, peace, beauty, joy, Love, compassion, light, energy, power, elation, or ecstasy. Often, however, these results are subtle. If we look for a big experience, we may miss the more refined changes in our vibration or consciousness. We want elation all of the time, but this is not possible. In order to get to the higher states, it is best to have no expectations, anticipating some of the meditations to be work, slightly difficult or painful, or nothing special.

RESULTS ARE SLOW, CUMULATIVE, AND LIFELONG

Think of the results of a meditative practice as a lifelong process of ever-increasing relaxation of the body, peace of mind, and opening of the heart. Do not worry about your progress, expertise, or whether or not you had a good meditation. Just practice.

In the beginning, you may not feel anything special. Although some may feel results immediately, for most it is likely to be difficult at first. Do not be discouraged. This is usual. Since the benefits emerge slowly, patience is helpful.

As with all spiritual practices, effort is progress. If you are meditating, you are making progress. You will succeed if you let the process unfold on its own schedule, have no expectations, and make no demands. If you persist, it gets easier.

In the beginning, you may not want to sit. Later, you will not want to get up.

REGULARITY

The key to success in meditation is regularity. Mastery is achieved through practice, as with any discipline or art. Think of playing the piano or any instrument. Without practice, there can be no progress. For best results, meditate in the morning and evening.

BRIEF MEDITATION

You can meditate for a few minutes, any time of day. Once meditation is part of your daily routine, try meditating briefly wherever you may be. Tense the whole body for a few seconds and relax your muscles. This releases physical tension. Breathe slowly and deeply, then focus on your mantra for a few minutes.

BURNING UP PROBLEMS IN THE STILLNESS OF MEDITATION

Many have a habit of thinking about their problems during meditation. This is very seductive; we think we are doing good work by facing our issues and working on them. To a degree, this is true. It *is* a good idea to set aside some time to reflect and learn from our experiences. The description of how to do this is in the lesson on transformation of emotion described in Chapter 21. This is self-knowledge born of introspection, not meditation. The purpose of meditation is stillness through concentration.

Thinking about problems is one of the tricks the mind will play on you, as it resists stillness by staying active. Your problems are important and require work and thought, but not in meditation. *What is important during meditation is getting beneath the thought waves on the surface and into the stillness below, for absorption of spiritual qualities.* In order to do this, you have to free your mind of all thoughts, including those related to problem solving. Whenever you become aware that you are thinking, return to your mantra. It is through concentrating on your mantra that you can attain stillness. Now, review step eight of the technique of meditation:

8. ABSORPTION

When you stop the superficial waves of thought and are immersed in stillness, relax and feel the peace. Don't think. In this state of open, quiet receptivity and stillness, spiritual qualities grow, the ego shrinks, and problems burn up.

In the stillness of meditation, we reach the deep healing power of the spiritual qualities. It is here, in stillness, that we slowly and subtly replace our problems with spiritual qualities. Spiritual qualities are healing powers. They have more power than our problems. In the stillness of meditation, Love burns up hate, kindness dissolves cruelty, courage defeats fear, and hope replaces despair. When we come out of meditation, the spiritual gems of Love, kindness, courage, and hope radiate their light through our thoughts, speech, and actions.

Bring deeper and longer meditation into your daily practice to speed up the evolution of your spiritual development. The mind, every cell in the body, and the soul crave the serenity bred of deep meditation.

POINTS TO REMEMBER

- The long-term practice of deep meditation results in ego reduction and the expansion of soul qualities.
- There may be phenomenal experiences at first, but meditation is not just joy. It is work. The results are cumulative, slow but sure. The more you practice, the more you feel the effects.
- Never strain during your practice. When you strain, you lose the goal of meditation, which is peace.

AFFIRMATIONS

- In meditation, I still my wandering mind and eliminate all thoughts.
- In the stillness of meditation, I discover a deep, permanent peace that has been with me all along.
- In meditation, soul qualities replace my ego. I become strong, calm, understanding, and patient.
- In meditation, I commune with God. I speak to my God with devotion. The still, small voice within shows me the way.

EXERCISES

1. Describe the five stages of meditation.
2. Practice progressive muscle relaxation before meditation. This relaxes the body, making meditation easier.
3. Review and practice the meditation technique described in this chapter.
4. The key to success in meditation is regular practice, just as with playing a musical instrument. Without regularity, you will still be a beginner in 20 years. Occasional practice does not work. We need to practice in the morning and the evening. Develop the habit of meditation for 10-20 minutes at the beginning and end of your day. If this is too long, start with 1-2 minutes. Expand from there in small increments.
5. One of the keys to success in meditation is balancing concentration with relaxation. Bring your power of

concentration to your mantra and relax your body and mind at the same time. Intense concentration does not require strain. The correct position is calm concentration without tension. When you learn how to do this, you will become progressively more awake, alert, aware, and calm.

6. What is the difference between self-knowledge born of introspection and meditation?

7. Describe how meditation reduces problems, shrinks the ego, and expands soul qualities.

8. Consider finding a meditation teacher and group. Group meditation reinforces individual effort and experience.

In the next chapter you will study prayer, the fifth and final method of the morning and evening program.

CHAPTER 16

PRAYER

Communion with Your Higher Power

This chapter introduces prayer, the fifth and final technique of the morning and evening program. There is a time for joy and a time for struggle. The brutal reality of death, suffering, and the unknown mysteriously loops its way through the show of our lives, making its appearance in a variety of costumes without apparent cause or reason. We do what we can to understand the mystery while we position ourselves in the drama. We work with will, thought, and action to achieve our goals. We use our inner and outer resources to work with and through our problems. Nevertheless, when we have finished our work, we remain vulnerable. Some problems linger. We suffer. We feel isolated, disconnected, and separate.

To get help, we pray. Prayer is a telephone call to our Higher Power as Friend, Counselor, Guide, Protector, Father, Mother, Beloved, Teacher, Healer, higher self, or higher states of consciousness. We seek counsel, support, knowledge, protection, solace, power, understanding, healing, forgiveness, and communion. We try to influence circumstances, conditions, and events in our immediate environment as well as in environments thousands of miles away.

Although controversy remains, there is scientific evidence that prayer works. Following is a description of some elements that may contribute to the effectiveness of prayer.

1. ONENESS: A unified field of consciousness and healing energy

In the spiritual realm, there is a vast field of intelligent consciousness, an Omnipotent Power that underlies and unites all. When we invoke this vast healing power, it helps us, those we are praying for, and all of creation. In prayer, we do not enter this field. We are already in it. It is already in us. There is no separation. All is one. We remind ourselves that this power is inside, outside, everywhere, extending forever in every direction, uniting all things and people.

2. HUMILITY

In ego consciousness, we feel separate from the vast healing power in and around us. In fact, were the ego to have its way, we would not even believe in the possibility of getting help from a Higher Power. Furthermore, the ego does not like to admit we have problems. To get help from a Higher Power, we need to identify our problems and know our limitations. This requires ego reduction. When we reduce our ego and accept our powerlessness, we create a channel for the flow of God's healing power. While we do all we can to achieve our goals and solve our problems, we ask for help from Omnipresent Intelligence.

3. INDIVIDUALITY

Prayer consistent with our individuality and belief system gives meaning and comfort. We can create our own ritual and pray with our own heartfelt words.

4. STILLNESS

Prayer is most effective when the mind is still. Some methods that promote stillness are meditation, progressive muscle relaxation, affirmations, breathing, mindfulness, practicing the presence of God, yoga, and will training. Stillness is essential during prayer, allowing us to make contact with higher, subtle, vibratory realms where we can follow the command: "Be still and know that I am God." By listening to the still, small voice within, we can be aware of new thoughts and feelings that come in response to our prayer. When still, we are more receptive to help, blessings, and guidance from God.

5. CONCENTRATION

In prayer, we open a channel of communication between the Omnipresent healing power and ourselves. The channel is most open when we focus exclusively on the perfect healing power of Spirit and the object of our prayer. All other thoughts should be eliminated. When we reach a high degree of concentration, we become one with the object of our prayer. The more we concentrate, the more powerful our prayer.

6. VISUALIZATION

In visualization, we imagine the desired goal of the prayer. The image should be as clear and specific as possible. For example, we can visualize a white healing light dissolving away disease, flaw, or imperfection.

7. DEVOTION

We can connect to the Omniscient, Omnipresent healing power through Love and compassion. Prayer is most effective when it comes from the heart, from our passion and from our pain.

8. WILL POWER

Will power is an essential element in prayer. Do not give up after one or two tries. Be patient and keep praying with intensity. Help does not come on our schedule.

9. FAITH

Doubt and disbelief undermine the power of prayer. Faith connects us with the infinite healing power of God and the possibility of getting help.

10. AWARENESS

Remain open and aware. Help comes in many ways, often subtle and different from our expectations. There may be a response through our thoughts, feelings, desires, or actions. We might hear the still, small voice within. We may see changes in other people, events, circumstances, or conditions. There may be guidance or protection, arrival of resources, lessons to learn, or an expansion of soul qualities.

11. SURRENDER

After we pray, we do all we can to solve our problem. Then we accept the outcome and surrender in peace to life as it is. We acknowledge pain and tragedy as part of the natural way of things. We resist the desire of the ego to be ruler of the universe. Rather than trying to control events, we gain an appreciation for the unfolding of the story, no matter which direction it takes. We must be willing to bask in the mystery, tolerate ambiguity, and face the unknown. We accept on faith that what occurs, including continued struggle, is best.

We align ourselves with what is, acknowledging that God knows what we need more than we do. We surrender to God's will through attunement and receptivity, believing there is meaning and order in the face of mystery and suffering. We trust that the healing power knows what to do. "God is the Doer, not I." "Thy will be done, not mine."

12. PEACE

While the reasons for the outcome improving, deteriorating, or staying the same may be beyond our understanding, acceptance brings tranquility of the soul. While there is a time for struggle and a time for joy, the ultimate lesson is to transfer the locus of control from outside to inside, where serenity is ever-present. When we completely accept the outcome, we contact our inner stillness and silence. In that quiet place, we accept all outcomes as part of the drama. When we make peace with life, the serenity that is always there begins to emerge. As this peace grows, the soul heals. Surrender takes us deep, to the domain of the soul, where we cannot be touched, hurt, cut, or burned.

TECHNIQUE

1. Invoke
2. Request
3. Act
4. Grace
5. Accept
6. Peace

1. INVOKE

With humility and reverence, invoke the presence of God. Bring in as much concentration, devotion, and stillness as you can. This sets up a channel of operations for the infinitely intelligent, healing power of God.

2. REQUEST

We can ask for:

- Essential needs such as safety, food, clothing, or shelter
- Help with work or relationships
- Success, wealth, or fame
- Healing or purification of body, mind, and soul
- Healing relationships between individuals, groups, races, religions, and nations
- World peace
- Peace of mind
- To become a better person by growth of any one or combination of spiritual qualities
- Forgiveness
- Receptivity to the help, guidance, and blessing that is always there
- The presence of God as peace, joy, Love, or wisdom
- Insight about the nature of our problems and ways to work with them
- Help and guidance for our problems
- Answers to our questions

- Alignment with God's will: In stillness and silence, we pray for the experience of God's presence without asking for anything but His will.

3. ACT

We use our will, thought, and actions to do what we can to change or remove a condition or circumstance. For illness, we may try medicines, surgery, special diets, or other healing practices. During activity, we can practice mindfulness or the presence of God to stay connected, attuned, and receptive to His guidance.

4. GRACE

There is a partnership between God and us. We do our part by exercising thought, will, and action. We maintain awareness of His healing presence and guidance, and we ask for help. God does His part. He determines the outcome, and we do our part by accepting it.

5. ACCEPT

Surrender to whatever the results may be. When we do not get what we ask for, we must trust that this is best and look for lessons in our not receiving.

6. PEACE

We gain serenity of the soul by accepting the outcome, whatever it may be.

POINTS TO REMEMBER

- Prayer is an expression of our unity with God and all people. In prayer, we connect to an Omniscient, Omnipresent power through the cultivation of Love and compassion. With this Love, we ask for help for others and ourselves.
- We can pray for something and get it. We can pray for something and not get it. We can also pray and not ask for anything. We just commune with our Higher Power. With an attitude

of complete faith, devotion, and surrender, we do not attempt to change the course of life's drama. With reverence, gratitude, and humility, we extract the lessons from life and enjoy life as it is. In prayers of gratitude and devotion, we express thankfulness for our many blessings, and give our Love to God.

- We can have a joyful conversation with God, or speak to God with a single word. We can also pray without words. God is in our hearts. He already knows what we need. There is great beauty in communing with God in silence.
- In our prayers for world peace, we can ask God to impact the hearts and minds of our leaders.
- We can change the world by changing ourselves. Pray to become a better person. Pray for wisdom, righteousness, and Love. This is the practical way to change the world.

EXERCISES

1. Describe the elements that contribute to the effectiveness of prayer.
2. Describe the six steps in the technique for praying.
3. You are now equipped with five techniques that comprise a morning and evening program. In the beginning, set aside 45-60 minutes and practice these techniques:
   a. Progressive muscle relaxation: 10 minutes
   b. Breathwork: 5 minutes
   c. Contemplation: 15-20 minutes
   d. Meditation: 10-20 minutes
   e. Prayer: 5 minutes

You have finished your review of the five morning and evening techniques. In the next section, we will study five techniques that comprise the daily activity program: mindfulness, practicing the presence of God, service, yoga, and the transformation of emotion.

PART FIVE
DAILY ACTIVITY PROGRAM

CHAPTER 17

MINDFULNESS

I am Awake

When the people asked the Buddha if he was a god, an angel, or a saint, he said, "No." "Then who are you?"

Buddha replied. "I am awake."

What is the Buddha trying to tell us? What is it that we are to awaken from? Why is it important to be more conscious?

This chapter will describe the importance of awakening from ordinary to spiritual consciousness and how mindfulness, a 2500 year-old practice taught by the Buddha, can help us with this transformation. Mindfulness is the first technique of the daily activity program.

ORDINARY CONSCIOUSNESS OR MINDLESSNESS

The field of awareness in ordinary states of consciousness is contaminated with a variety of negative patterns of thought, feeling, and reaction. We remain largely unaware of these negative patterns and how they prevent us from reaching higher states of consciousness. In mindless states of unawareness, we are hypnotized, functioning like robots on automatic pilot, sleepwalking our way through life.

The biggest culprit is the mind. The undisciplined mind disrupts our lives by taking us out of the present moment, where our life is at its fullest. The story of life is unfolding in the now, the place where we learn, enjoy, help others, find our courage, and experience inner peace.

The undisciplined mind reaps havoc on our peace. Repeatedly, the mind takes us out of our current moments when it does not like what is going on. It fights when angry, runs when afraid, competes when jealous, creates imagined calamities, and projects fantasies from its desires.

The mind is strongly attracted to the past and the future. While it is good to learn from the past and have hopeful plans for the future, the mind goes overboard in its replays and projections. We relive past hurts, resentments, and regrets, which only serve to recycle anger, depression, and guilt. Our projections of the future breed unnecessary fear and insecurity.

We build a rigid structure of selfish, dogmatic, overvalued thoughts, opinions, likes, and dislikes. We try to get our needs met by controlling and pushing events and people. However, the world does not conform to our egotistical desires; when things do not fit, we create new desires. Instead of working with what we have that is good, we escape into fantasy, to what we think we want next. The result is an increase in mental restlessness and turbulent emotions.

The mind is at its best when it accepts and works with one moment at a time. It is not set up for the excesses of attraction, aversion, high emotional reactivity, and the avoidance of problems ... all of which lead to restlessness and rumination, signs that the mind is overheated.

SPIRITUAL CONSCIOUSNESS

Mindfulness, an ancient technique of Buddhism, helps us manage our inner reactions to a turbulent and unpredictable world. We want to respond with poise and peace but all too often our thoughts and feelings will not cooperate. While there can be no respite from troubles and pain, mindfulness helps us receive the tests and trials of life in calm repose. Practice of this simple technique helps us increase our attention and awareness so we can be awake and ready for anything. By avoiding the destructive excesses of the mind and emotions, we can receive what life brings with even-minded tranquility.

In the transformation to spiritual consciousness, we can bring the mind under control by placing it where we want it to be: in the current moment, awake, attentive, and ready. It is in this alignment that we are most able to learn, solve problems, relax, serve, and enjoy. We can enter this state by cultivating the witness as an antidote to the restlessness and ruminations of the mind.

The witness is an aspect of the higher self from which we can observe the changes of life with calm neutrality. Change is not the objective of the witness. We do not add, subtract, delete, or edit. We accept reality as it is while we change our frame and attitude. We focus on the stillness and silence within and the outer present moment. As the witness grows through the practice of mindfulness, we can slowly bring the dimensions of spaciousness and serenity to the events of life.

In ordinary consciousness, we identify with the stream of negative and disruptive thoughts, feelings, desires, impulses, and fantasies that pass through our awareness. With the practice of mindfulness, we create a space large enough to hold the negativity. In this space, we do not identify with the rubbish and therefore do not need to repress or express it, both of which are destructive. Instead, we go to the compassionate witness of the true self and create a healing space within. This is a furnace of sorts: here we can burn up the junk thoughts, feelings, desires, and fantasies that keep our consciousness from rising.

Love is more powerful than any of the wayward forces that traverse our consciousness. By invoking and affirming Love and Her companion qualities, we create an inner atmosphere conducive to healing. As our compassion burns up the troublemaking negativity, there is a corresponding shift to peace and strength.

Aligning the mind and attention with the present is a crucial element in the healing process. The next step in our spiritual evolution is in these moments. They hold the continuity of our story, a story pregnant with lessons, entertainment, and opportunities to produce, create, love, and serve. In the lower state of ordinary consciousness, we miss these opportunities because we are preoccupied with other fields of awareness.

To practice mindfulness, there is no need to make any changes other than the placement of the mind as we go about our usual activities. With practice, the mind remains calm and poised no matter what occurs in the material world. We remain in balance. We get the rhythm of the story. There is no force in it. We are ready for anything.

A MINDFULNESS TECHNIQUE

Steps:

1. Stop
2. Breathe
3. Present moment
4. Frame:
   a.) Witness
   b.) School
   c.) Entertainment
   d.) Service
   e.) Warrior
   f.) Ritual
5. Repeat
6. One continuous sacred ritual

STEP 1: STOP

The mind lapses into one of its negative habit patterns, drawing us away from the opportunities of the moment. We go for a ride on the negative thought train. Because we identify with the negativity, we think this is who we are. When we become aware that our mind is wandering, we stop thinking and focus on our breath.

STEP 2: BREATHE

Take a breath and gently bring the mind back to the reality of the moment. By simply becoming aware of our breath, we can stop the rambling mind and return to the present moments of our lives. This simple maneuver of using our breath to control the mind helps us develop our power of concentration. We develop single-minded consciousness by continually bringing our attention back to our breath, every time the mind wanders. With practice, we can stay increasingly in the present, bringing our mind out of its aimless spin, back into alignment with the present moment.

STEP 3: PRESENT MOMENT

We give our full attention to each moment. We focus on the stillness within, the present moment without, and on what we are doing.

STEP 4: FRAME

When we use the breath to calm the mind and place it in the present moment, we have an opportunity to choose from a variety of frames of reference for life, as it occurs. We cannot control most of what is going on outside, but we can control how we respond. We can choose frames that inspire, heal, soothe, purify, entertain, and transform. We can create any frame we wish. In this lesson, we will review six frames: the witness, school, entertainment, service, the warrior, and ritual.

THE WITNESS

The silent witness observes without reacting. The witness watches events unfold from a position of stillness and peace. With a single breath, we can invoke the witness. Here there is serenity, space, and observation. With the breath as a means of centering ourselves, we can begin the process of disengaging from our identification with the negative patterns of the uncontrolled mind. Instead, we create a peaceful and compassionate space large enough to hold all. Breathe and refocus on the calm witness early and often to reach for the peace and enjoyment that resides there, inhibited only by our undisciplined mind.

SCHOOL

Life is school. Students in the school of life study their inner being to learn about the self and its complexities. Mindful introspection allows us to see the distracting power of the forces that control us. Through continuous observation of the flow of our thoughts, feelings, desires, aversions, impulses, and fantasies, we come to understand ourselves better. We can see how our desires, fears, and insecurities cause tension and how, with the technique of mindfulness, we can release ourselves into stillness, spaciousness, and serenity.

When life gets difficult inside or outside, we try to get away. We run and resist by going into unawareness or fantasy. But the school of life is merely presenting a lesson that we need to learn. The teacher and the lessons are found in the moments of our lives. We cannot move up the chain of awareness without learning from them, and we cannot learn if we are not in school: that is, awake, aware, and focused on the present.

Allowing your mind to wander is the equivalent of playing hooky from school. In mindfulness, we do not fight with the teacher or run. We pay attention, listen, and cooperate in order to graduate to the next level. Peace is not found by running away; rather, we find peace by facing the problem or difficulty and going through it. Through the breath, we can enter rather than run from unpleasantness. By entering deeply into the present, we can extract the lessons and move on.

The goal is to stay calm and suffer at the same time. We can do this if we create a healing space large enough to hold any problem or pain. Then we can allow our painful problems to exist in consciousness without the destructive aspects of denial, repression, or expression.

Denial and repression drive our painful problems into the subconscious and into the body, where they are stored as negative energy. The problem remains hidden and unresolved. Destructive expressions of our pain manifest in a variety of ways, including exerting power and control over others, irritability, anger, and aggression. In effect, we spread our pain and problems to others.

Alternatively, we can cultivate an internal healing space for the pain. We can do this by invoking affirmations related to Love, kindness, acceptance, and forgiveness for ourselves. We set up a favorable environment for healing; these soul qualities are more powerful than any pain or problem. By being patient, understanding, and gentle with the self, we can learn from our problem and diffuse its charge.

When we let our pain and problems play in an enlarged, peaceful, compassionate space, negative energy is released that has been repressed over the years within our subconscious and the body. By accepting pain and problems with compassion, we end the fear of releasing negativity. By stopping the fight within, the tension of repression dissolves.

There is a profound feeling of peace when we turn the table on our suffering by offering no resistance. By fully accepting the inevitable suffering of life without repression and resistance, we gain internal power. When we gently and courageously enter our pain, we gain the knowledge and strength that will help us take on the next set of problems or lessons. This is pain control through surrender. Additional details on how to process emotional pain into self-knowledge are described in Chapter 21, "Transformation of Emotion."

To shift gears from ordinary to higher consciousness, we need to think less, be aware of our breath, remain in the present, and accept pain as the teacher. Stay calm, be kind and gentle with yourself, and do the work. The result is strength, serenity, spaciousness, and stillness.

ENTERTAINMENT

The unfolding drama of life is not always about school and learning. Life is entertainment. Our stories are filled with beauty, joy, laughter, and fun. It is difficult if not impossible to see life as entertainment, however, if we are immersed in the drama, consumed by our problems and suffering.

By taking a step back from the role we are playing, we can take ourselves less seriously. We can do this by framing life as a movie or a sport. We are actors in a role, players in a game. By not identifying completely with our role, we gain distance and perspective. When we reduce our tendency to exaggerate the importance of events, we eliminate some mental restlessness and high emotional reactivity. When we calm the mind and create more operating space within, we can enjoy the show.

SERVICE

Mindfulness practice helps us escape the influence of negative thoughts and turbulent emotions. This helps us act with the consciousness of Love and service, fulfilling our innate desire to nourish all who come our way with peace, kindness and joy. Gracious, warm, loving service to all of humanity and creation is a natural consequence of the sustained practice of mindfulness.

WARRIOR

The practice of mindfulness slowly replaces unbridled thoughts, feelings, and desire with serenity and stillness. Mental reactivity and turmoil subside. With a more powerful and resilient mind, the difficulties of life are less likely to throw us off course. We can deal with whatever comes and hold our ground. We do not have to run or hide. We can stay in the moment, take a stand, and hold our position. We are awake, aware, and ready for anything including work, pain, change, the unknown, even death. This is the stance of a spiritual warrior.

RITUAL

We spend a lot of time in routine daily activities: eating, strolling in the park, chatting on the phone, standing in line, cutting the grass, running to the store, baking, washing dishes, brushing teeth, tying shoes …. There is meaning in any of these routines of life, but we miss it. Because we assume the mundane is boring, the mind wanders. We lose touch with the magic and miracles secreted in every moment, everywhere, outside and inside.

The practice of mindfulness brings awe back to the routines of life in focusing on our activities and creating a context of special meaning and importance. For example, we can appreciate the moments that might otherwise be lost in boredom by recognizing the Omniscience that is always with us.

Omniscience is the infinite intelligence that permeates our body and the entire universe. As we perform any routine activity, we can think of how the body follows our command when we tell it what to do. We can think of the unfathomable intelligence that creates and operates our vision and hearing as we go about our chores and tasks. When reading, we can think of the brilliance that allows us to understand these words right now. While eating, we can think of how the stomach and intestines digest food by breaking it into molecules that are sent to the right places in the body for energy, repair, immunity, and a host of other functions. When washing our hair, we can think about how the body responds to our commands.

The intelligence that creates and operates the body is phenomenal. We are magicians, performing astounding feats throughout the day but ordinary consciousness makes the miraculous mundane. To maintain awareness of the Omniscience that permeates the universe is part of capturing the wonder, magic, and mystery of being alive, in what might otherwise appear to be the humdrum of everyday routines.

We can start such a practice with any routine, anywhere, any time. By consciously looking for the positives inside and outside, we can find them. A blessing in disguise lurks everywhere; we must only work to uncover it. If we bring the full powers of a calm, concentrated, and positive mind to our routine activities, we can capture the blessings and make them our own. With breath, focused attention, and creative framing, we can extract the gifts of life: peace, joy, beauty, and the magic of being, from the most mundane activities.

STEP 5: REPEAT

It takes years to bring the mind under control. Expect it to wander from the present moment into its old negative habit patterns. Do not frame this as success and failure, as this will cause frustration and tension. When you go for a ride on the train of thought and find yourself back in a lower state of consciousness, remain kind, compassionate, and gentle with yourself. Stop, breathe, and reenter the moment with the frame of your choice.

STEP 6: ONE CONTINUOUS SACRED RITUAL

With practice, we can become increasingly aware, awake, and attentive in each of the moments of our lives. As our will power and concentration increase, we can begin to string the moments together. By maintaining our focus on what we are doing at all times, we learn to stay in the present more and more, even when life gets rough. We see that we can remain in reality whether it turns good, bad, or ugly.

When we recognize that all we have are these moments, that there is nowhere else to go, we gain strength and peace. When our concentration is highly developed, we can stay in the present and maintain harmony and balance no matter what life does. All of our moments become part of one continuous ritual in response to the truth of life just as it is, with all of its sorrow, beauty, and joy.

When we bring the unruly mind under control through mindfulness, we gain access to the calm witness, the student in school, the actor in the movie, the servant of humanity, and the warrior who is ready for anything. The witness remains even-minded under all conditions. When difficult or painful, life is school. We enter our pain to extract the necessary lessons. When life is entertaining, it is like a movie or a sport. When we frame life as a movie, we are observing the show or acting in a role. This gives us some perspective and protection from over-involvement. Playing with life as though it is a sport or game lightens our burden. We don't take it so seriously. We are in service when we help others. We feel peace and joy. The warrior is ready for anything. The ritual transforms the ordinary and mundane to sacred and special. When we rotate these frames, life becomes one continuous sacred ritual, offering up its knowledge and lessons, entertainment and joy, and opportunities to love and serve.

BENEFITS FROM THE PRACTICE OF MINDFULNESS

- An all-purpose increase in awareness
- Improves powers of concentration
- Enhances the ability to stay on task
- More present and calm
- Better at listening
- Removes debris and rubbish from our consciousness
- Purification and healing
- Helps us to accept the realities we cannot change

- Helps us get some distance from our trains of thought
- Stops the pursuit of negative thoughts
- More compassion, Love, and kindness to the self and others
- Reduces mental restlessness and emotional reactivity

POINTS TO REMEMBER

- We can practice mindfulness anywhere, anytime.
- To be fully aware of all of the elements of our lives, we need to pay attention. We can turn every action into a mindful meditative exercise by giving whatever we are doing our full attention. Mindfulness is a walking meditation, or meditation in action.
- The present moment is both the teacher and the entertainer. There are lessons to be learned and experiences to be enjoyed. Sometimes the lessons are painful. Other experiences are enjoyable and entertaining. Stay alert to get the most out of life, whatever the experience.
- Stay awake and aware in the present moment, since it is in the here and now that life offers up its knowledge and lessons, entertainment and joy, and opportunities to love and serve.
- The mind is geared to deal with the present. The past and future are too much to bear. There is more than enough reality here and now. Why add to the burden by leaning forward into the future or bending backward into the past?
- Mindfulness is an exercise designed to increase our concentration and attention so we can be awake and ready for anything, including work, pain, change, the unknown, or death.
- Highly developed intense concentration in the present moment results in a sense of flow, rhythm, harmony, and balance.
- Mindfulness is a part of the performance of all of the spiritual methods described in this work. Attention, concentration, and awareness are part of all spiritual practice.
- The peace, joy, Love, power, and wisdom we are looking for is right here in the moments of our lives. However, we must

be awake, aware, and focused; otherwise, restless thoughts, reactive emotions, and excessive desires will take us away.

- Rather than being negative, panicky, or agitated when life gets rough, ride the ups and downs like a rodeo cowboy on a bucking horse. With continued practice of mindfulness, the restless mind, hyperactive emotions, and excessive material desires will not bump you off the horse.

- Be compassionate, yet unencumbered. Give peaceful, joyful, loving service to all of humanity, and enjoy the show. With deep, sustained, long-term practice of mindful service and meditation, our inner space expands so that we can receive the harsh realities of life and maintain perfect peace and poise.

AFFIRMATIONS

- I calmly embrace the present moment.
- I invoke the witness, watching and observing.
- I invoke the witness, still and silent.
- I invoke the witness, patient and breathing.
- I invoke the witness, serene and spacious.
- Compassion is the fire that burns up my problems in the healing furnace inside me.
- By steady absorption in the moment, I get to flow and rhythm.
- I respond to the show with peace and poise.
- I am kind and gentle with myself under all conditions.
- I add Love and compassion to every moment of my inner life.
- I receive all events with gentle compassion for myself.
- I live fully in the present.
- I practice the presence of peace.
- I live fully in the present where change and healing occur.
- I am grateful for the blessings of entertainment and joy.
- I am grateful for the blessing of suffering for its cultivation of soul qualities.

EXERCISES

1. What is the difference between ordinary and spiritual consciousness?
2. Describe the six steps of the mindfulness technique.
3. Describe and discuss the six frames of reference listed in step 4 of mindfulness practice.
4. Can you think of any additional frames that might help you?
5. Life is school. How might the practice of mindfulness help you learn the lessons meant for you?
6. Life is entertaining. How might the practice of mindfulness help you enjoy life more than you do now?
7. When completely immersed in the turbulence of ruminative thoughts, feelings, sensations, fantasies, and impulses, remember the witness, that place inside where there is stillness, silence, space, and serenity. When you are in turmoil, try these one-word affirmations:
   - Stillness
   - Silence
   - Spaciousness
   - Serenity

   This may help you get through difficult times.
8. Be aware of your inner being, your body, and the sights, sounds, and feel of the environment. Look for the positives within yourself and in your present environment.
9. Always practice mindfulness with an attitude of compassion and understanding for yourself. Try this now.
10. To create a healing atmosphere for yourself, affirm Love and kindness. Try this now.
11. Meditation and mindfulness work in tandem. Both techniques reduce the excesses of the mind so it can be in alignment with the higher purposes of the heart and soul. Both techniques require one-pointed concentration. If you practice meditation and mindfulness, you will build a powerful control center at

the very core of your being. Events, the doings of other people, and your own reactivity will not ruffle you because you have more space and strength inside. This takes time to develop. Begin your practice now.

12. The Sacred is with you all the time. Relax, open, listen, attune, and receive. Can you feel it?

13. Every action, no matter how mundane, is a part of one uninterrupted holy ritual. Offer every action in service to humanity and God. Then you will have strength, and you will know peace.

You have completed your review of mindfulness, the first of five techniques recommended for your daily activity program. In the next chapter, you will study a similar technique: practicing the presence of God.

CHAPTER 18

PRACTICING THE PRESENCE OF GOD

A Personal Relationship

This chapter introduces the second technique of the daily activity program, practicing the presence of God. We can talk to God and get a response. We can have a personal relationship with an Omniscient Power whose nature is gentle, compassionate, loving, and wise, a living presence beyond philosophy or belief. Contact is not only possible, but this magnificent benevolent power knows what we need and wants to give it to us.

In order to give us the help we need, God performs one of His greatest tricks. He reduces Himself from Infinite Power to a number of aspects we can relate to: Father, Mother, Friend, Healer, Lover, Teacher, Guide, Protector, and Counselor. Then, through these aspects, He offers guidance, protection, friendship, healing, purification, and the expansion of soul qualities. As our Love qualities grow, we feel better, treat others better, and make the world a better place.

It seems too good to be true that such a wonderful relationship is available in the world of limitation and suffering, as we know it in ordinary consciousness. If it is true that an all-knowing, infinite power can mysteriously manifest at our level and enter our lives bearing priceless gifts, why don't we know Him? How can we find Him? And how can we keep Him in our lives?

This great invisible power bearing the gifts of friendship, peace, healing, and wisdom, knocks on the door of our consciousness, but we do not hear it. We have lost our connection to the subtle vibrations offered by the gracious Omnipresent Power, stuck as we are in the grosser vibrations of material consciousness.

We focus on the fascinating story and alluring objects of the material world. Tests and trials come. We get trapped in our thoughts, feelings, desires, habits, attachments, and egos. Separated, mired, and hooked by these limitations of material consciousness, we remain deaf to the Friend trying to help.

Material consciousness creates an invisible shield, a seemingly impenetrable defense against our experience of the subtle vibrations of compassion, kindness, gentleness, and warmth offered by the Grand Healer. We don't experience the next layer of reality just behind the veil of ordinary consciousness because we are not mindful of the possibility, and we don't know how to make contact. We need a technique to help us work through the limitations of material consciousness so we can contact God, prove His existence to ourselves, explore His nature, and partake of His wondrous gifts.

TECHNIQUE

Following is a technique for practicing the presence of God:
1. Stop
2. Breathe
3. Present moment
4. Frame: practicing the presence of God
   a. Any method described in this book: affirmations, habit transformation, progressive muscle relaxation, breathwork, contemplation, meditation, prayer, service, yoga, and transformation of emotion
   b. The sacred meaning of story
   c. Conversation with God
5. God responds
   a. Omniscient, Omnipotent, Omnipresence
   b. Healing
   c. Meditation
   d. Phenomenon
6. Hide and seek, find and keep

Notice the similarity between the technique for practicing mindfulness, and that of the presence of God. Both focus on our experience of higher states of consciousness. The difference is in the concept of a Higher Power. Mindfulness practice does not require a personal relationship with God. Practicing the presence of God presupposes the existence of God as a conscious power with whom we can have a relationship.

As in the practice of mindfulness, we need to employ our powers of concentration and awareness in the present moment, as we can know God best in the present. Follow the same steps as with mindfulness, but now, at step 4, the frame is practicing the presence of God through any of the spiritual methods described in this book, the sacred meaning of story, and conversing with God. Each of these spiritual practices results in a direct experience of God.

When the mind wanders into one of the many variations of ordinary consciousness, stop, breathe, focus on the present moment, and bring God to your awareness by choosing one of the frames listed in step 4. When we relapse and realize we are back in ordinary consciousness, refocus on the presence of God. As in meditation and mindfulness, we will forget and remember many times, for years to come; this is the nature of spiritual practice.

THE SACRED MEANING OF STORY

God's presence can be distilled from the sacred meaning of stories. We can experience the presence of God if we watch our personal and collective stories unfold from the point of view of God as our Teacher, training us to cultivate Love through a process of purification, the goal of which is perfection.

The Teacher is eager to train us in the art of Love, gratitude, reverence, humility, surrender, intuition, and faith. She sets up the entire universe of human experience as a training ground for the expansion of Love and Her associated qualities, until they become unconditional. She designs events and circumstances so that we can discover, remove, and replace our faults with Love qualities. Everything in our life experience is raw material to train us to be more loving in our thoughts, feelings, desires, and actions. To observe the story of life unfold from this point of view is to practice the presence of God.

God is untainted and unlimited peace, joy, Love, power, and wisdom. We are made of these same Love qualities in combination with our problems, flaws, and imperfections, which act as barriers between God and ourselves. When we slowly reduce and replace our imperfections by expanding Love qualities, we approach the gateway to Her presence: She is Love; it is her domain.

The Teacher does not care about our role, power, money, status, age, class, or religion. She only cares about what is in our hearts. Actions saturated with Love, kindness, humility, and understanding are pleasant in Her sight. Pick a quality such as peace, gentleness, sweetness, gratitude, appreciation, or surrender. Cultivate it with your will, through affirmation and meditation. Bring it to every thought, feeling, action, and event. Hold on to it and make it grow. This is practicing the presence of God.

We don't have to change anything in our life, except to respond to events and problems with God's qualities. When we respond to cruelty with kindness, to ignorance with understanding, to suffering with compassionate service, and to fear with courage, we practice the presence of God. In the end, when we have burned off our imperfections and become pure, we enter Her kingdom of unlimited peace, joy, Love, power, and wisdom, fulfilling the sacred intent and meaning of our life story.

CONVERSING WITH GOD

Prayer is formal, structured communication with God. We can also have an ongoing, spontaneous conversation with God. Some of us may find conversing with an invisible power strange at first. Because of our feeling of separation, we think no one is there. A few suggestions might help.

To make contact with God, we need a workable, accessible concept of who God is and who we are. We can speak to God's Omnipresent

Formless Form or to a more concrete aspect such as Teacher, Father, Mother, Friend, Healer, Counselor, Confidante, Beloved, Creator, King, Guide, or Protector. We can approach God as a babe, child, student, servant, witness, disciple, devotee, warrior, or simply a human being.

We can pick a concept based on our need at the time. If we need advice, we can call the Counselor. If we are lonely or need to share, we can call the Friend. If we need healing or purification, we can call the Physician. If we need forgiveness, we can call the Mother. If we need to extract the meaning and lessons from the events of our lives, we can call the Teacher. If we need wisdom, strength, or courage, we can call the Father. If we need Love, we can call the Beloved.

As in any relationship, we begin by starting a conversation. The conversation can occur at any point during the day, from the time we get up in the morning to just before sleep. We can be natural and relaxed as we would be with a friend, or formal and reverent. The communication should be honest, direct, and heartfelt.

We can weave God into the fabric of our daily lives by sharing our needs, goals, problems, joys, and successes. We can share what has happened in our day, what is happening in our lives, our feelings, idle thoughts, anything, and everything. We can be angry and argue. We can ask for guidance, protection, or support. We can ask questions. We can ask for help with our own problems and bad habits, and for aid in all that we do for others. We can express our desire to be closer to Him, to be more like Him. We can confess our embarrassing secrets and ask for understanding and forgiveness. It is liberating and healing to tell the truth to One who already knows what we have done and what is in our hearts.

GOD'S RESPONSE

We can initiate our communication with God through the sacred meaning of story, conversing with God, or through any spiritual method described in this work. How does God respond?

It is not easy to get a response from God. We cannot make contact with Him without intense, continuous, and long-term communication. We need to practice with all our hearts, minds, might, and souls until we get a response, however long it may take.

Most of us will not get a response in the beginning. As a result, many stop practicing. Some drop their practice because of indifference or boredom. Others give up when life becomes difficult. Some quit their practice when life becomes easy. However, if we take advantage of all our moments by practicing the presence of God and never giving up, we break down the invisible shield that we have built up between God and ourselves, experience God's response, and get the help we need.

God's response varies according to our individual predilections and our level of spiritual development. Following is a discussion of four ways that God may come into our lives: 1.) Omnipresence, Omniscience, and Omnipotence, 2.) Healing, 3.) Meditation, and 4.) Phenomenon.

OMNIPRESENCE, OMNISCIENCE, AND OMNIPOTENCE

Clues and evidence speaking to God's Omniscience, Omnipotence, and Omnipresence abound. God is a conscious intelligent power whose presence is ubiquitous. Her manifestation is ever-present in nature and in our consciousness. She occupies every millimeter of space, from the infinitesimal to infinity. She operates every level of reality, from microcosmic particles and waves to macrocosmic solar systems. Her unfathomable power keeps the whirling atoms, planets, and galaxies moving in harmonious balance with each other.

Her infinite intelligence and power creates, sustains, operates, and dissolves a seemingly endless parade of billions of forms, including us. The marvels and beauty of nature—birds, ocean, sky, sunsets, and flowers—are Her costume. The entire universe, all forms and every human body, are Her temple.

The entry point to Her realm is acknowledgement of the continuous signs of Her power, beauty, and intelligence. We need to remind ourselves that Her unseen, invisible intelligence is always sustaining and guiding atoms, galaxies, and us. God wants us to use Her boundless resources in our daily lives. We can get Her help if we remember to connect our thoughts, will, feelings, desires, actions, and all events with Her.

God's power and energy permeate every scene, in every moment, at every level of detail. By remembering Her Omnipresence, we can get help with any problem or crisis. No moment or detail is too small. Everything counts. It is easy to get tricked or fooled into apathy or boredom by quiet moments such as traffic jams or waiting in line. However, we can use these seemingly mundane events to see God in everything, and everything in God. If we persist in our practice, we will come to the realization that God is an unlimited source of power, Love, and wisdom that we can tap into at any time.

HEALING

God responds to our spiritual work by healing our mind, body, and soul. The mind becomes positive, calm, resilient, and strong. Destructive emotions and excessive material desires come under control. The healing power of the body is kindled. Soul qualities such as peace, gentleness, and understanding replace restlessness, aggression, and ignorance. As our Love qualities expand and our problems burn up, we get more space to receive the suffering of the world, so that we can respond with compassionate action, thus contributing to the healing of others and the environment.

MEDITATION

In meditation, God manifests as unfathomable stillness, the peace that surpasses understanding, ecstatic joy, pure Love, and intuitive wisdom. Some experience a breathtaking and thrilling, yet soft and gentle surge of power, a soothing embrace, or a feeling of safety. Advanced meditators experience samadhi, the ecstasy of complete union with God.

PHENOMENON

Some people experience phenomenon such as aura, light, visions, prophetic dreams, intuitive knowing, guidance, protection, answered prayers, synchronicity, healing powers, or entrance into the "zone," the experience of supreme flow, rhythm, and harmony.

HIDE AND SEEK, FIND AND KEEP

When we align ourselves with His will, God makes an appearance through:

1. His Omniscient, Omnipotent, Omnipresence
2. Healing body, mind, and soul
3. In the Love and stillness of meditation
4. Phenomenon

With continued practice, we gradually become more attuned and receptive to His will, guidance, and council. As we see His great healing principle at work in our lives, our trust in Him grows. However, as we go through our tests and trials, God disappears behind the veil of ordinary consciousness. We feel separate again, dry and seemingly alone as we struggle with our problems.

God's appearance and disappearance, His play of hide and seek, has a purpose: character development through the culture of unconditional Love. God is unconditional Love and its associated qualities. His wish is that we become like Him through a process of purification, through expansion of our soul qualities. During difficult times when God is hiding, our job is to seek Him through the pursuit of Love qualities until they become unconditional.

We can respond to events with manifestations of God's Love such as kindness, compassion, peace, and understanding, or with cruelty, hate, violence, and ignorance. When our response is one of the many forms of negativity, we need to work through it until we get back to Love and its companion soul qualities. God appears and disappears until such qualities become unconditional.

His play of hide and seek goes on indefinitely as we work through our pain and problems. He often hides as we work but eventually returns as the gentle Lover. We learn to trust His purification process, as He inevitably returns with infinitely creative versions of His sweet Love. The experience of even a trace of His sweetness is addicting. In our yearning for more, we avail ourselves to His healing process of purification; sometimes purification by fire. We learn to trust the process of His appearing and disappearing as we realize His intention for us: to become the tender gentle Love that He is.

Eventually it becomes impossible not to love Him intimately and deeply. He has given us the greatest possible gift: immersion in His presence, where we can contact the unconditional sweet Love of the Father-Mother, the perfect, ubiquitous guidance from the Counselor, the healing and purification from the Physician, the training from the Teacher, and friendship from the Friend. As this colossal, stupendous, multifaceted power plays hide and seek with us, we play find and keep with Him.

In the end, we find ourselves permanently immersed in His ocean. We see that everything is in Him, as fish swimming in water. Then we experience His Love no matter what difficulties life brings. Surrounded, fed, permeated, and saturated with His Love, we give only that to all we meet. Secure in the knowledge that we are always in Him and He in us, we bow in reverence and awe.

Think cosmic thoughts as you fold laundry and put the kids to bed. Instead of zoning out, realize that the Great One is always here, right now. Every moment is a manifestation of infinity, eternity, and immortality!

POINTS TO REMEMBER

- On the spiritual path, there is only one desire: the presence of God.
- To enter His realm, God expects us to learn how to behave. To behave properly, we need to become like Him, a composite of pure Love qualities. Then the all-powerful, all-knowing God

of the universe gradually, gently enters an intimate relationship with us by revealing His compassion and wisdom.

- To find God in an event, follow the Love. If you cannot find Love, bring it out from within yourself; wherever there is Love, there is God.

- God hides behind the veil of ordinary consciousness. We seek Him through the cultivation of unconditional Love in the present moment. When we fill our moments with Love, we experience the presence of God. God is Love. Love is our home.

- The Teacher wants us to respond to all events and people with Love qualities. The challenges are many. It is difficult to respond with compassion when we are insulted, provoked, or abused. However, the ultimate practice of the presence of God is responding with Love no matter what happens in our environment.

- Pain is a directive signal, telling us where we need to do some work. It is a stimulant for the development of spiritual qualities. We accept pain as necessary for transformation and purification of consciousness towards forbearance, endurance, courage, strength, humility, patience, or any combination of qualities. Pain is an opportunity to work in the direction of God.

- Practicing the presence of God is the same as practicing the presence of any spiritual quality. As we breathe, affirm, and grow a spiritual quality, we increase our experience of the presence of God. When we realize that we have lost our peace and our mind is restless, we can stop, breathe, focus on the present, and affirm any one or combination of the Love qualities needed at that moment.

- All of the spiritual qualities are connected and grow together. For example, if we choose to expand peace of mind, we will also grow in patience, compassion, and forgiveness. Thus, through the practice of peace, we connect our lives to God; it is His will that we permeate our thoughts with His peace.

- There are times when we have absolutely no control over the environment ... but we always have power over our thoughts and will. This is where the battle is fought. This is where we can bring God into every thought, feeling, and action. This is where we can make the relationship personal.

- Practicing the presence of God is a secret, sacred, silent act. No one knows.

- Selfless service to humanity brings us to the presence of God: this is His will.

- Selfless service to the environment brings us to the presence of God, which is also His will.

- As our spiritual qualities grow and our experience of the presence of God correspondingly deepens, our ability to serve God and humanity is refined and expanded. We become increasingly useful.

AFFIRMATIONS

- I come from and return to Spirit.
- I move, live, and have my being in Spirit.
- I am a fish swimming in the ocean of God.
- I love and serve in the Omnipresent temple of God.
- I worship the Lord equally in every body temple.
- I work with the God housed in my body.
- I work with the God housed in your body.
- I stay in the present, where I can know and feel God.
- Every person, form, and story serves as a reminder of His presence.
- I bow to the manifestation of the Divine Mother before me right now.
- I love the manifestation of the Divine Mother before me right now.

- I serve the manifestation of the Divine Mother before me right now.
- I am always in the mind of God.
- I am always in the heart of God.
- I am always on the throne of God.
- I am always at the feet of God.
- I am one with God.

EXERCISE

1. Why do we feel separate from God?

2. We can speak to God's Omnipresent Formlessness, or to a more concrete aspect such as Teacher, Father, Mother, Friend, Healer, Counselor, Confidante, Beloved, Creator, King, Guide, or Protector. We can approach God as a babe, child, student, servant, witness, disciple, devotee, warrior, or simply a human being. Can you think of any additional aspects? Which do you prefer?

3. Describe the six steps for practicing the presence of God.

4. What is the sacred meaning of story?

5. Describe the elements of having a conversation with God.

6. What are four ways that God can respond to the seeker?

7. Always check to see where you are. Where are your mind and feelings? Are you here and now or on automatic pilot? Of what are you practicing the presence? Is it God, a Love quality, or something else?

8. In ordinary consciousness, we find it difficult to believe that God is here with us right now. However, to practice the presence of God, we need to begin thinking, feeling, and acting as though we are in the temple of God at all times, because in reality we are, even though material consciousness hypnotizes us into thinking that God's presence is an illusion. How should we behave in the presence of the Lord of the universe? What would it be like to have thoughts, feelings, and actions consistent with being at the feet of God?

9. We do not need to change anything to practice the presence of God. Simply perform every action to please God no matter what the circumstances are. You might want to start practicing this right now. Practicing the presence of God is keeping our attention on God at all times. We can do this, since God is always present in one or more of His aspects. We can see the hand of God in events by watching for these aspects. Pick a concept, practice, and experience the results.

10. Begin your conversation with God. A conversation with God might go something like this: "I read about You in sacred texts. You are described in the most glowing terms. The saints say You are a gentle, loving, compassionate being. You come as peace, stillness, and joy in meditation. Some are given glorious visions, healings, or miracles. Where are You for me? I experience nothing but separation. When and how will You reveal Yourself to me?" After I pour my heart out, I wait for a response. She says, "I want you to be with Me, but first you must learn to behave. Look for the sacred meaning in the events of your life. Purify yourself by fostering Love qualities. Then you will know Me as your Teacher. Seek my guidance and council. Then you will know Me as Wisdom. Practice service, and you will know Me as the Giver. Practice meditation, and you will feel Me enter the temple of your body as the sweetness that you crave. Then you will know Me as your Father, Mother, Beloved, Friend, Healer, Confidante, Protector, and Guide."

You have now studied two techniques for your daily activity program, mindfulness and the presence of God. In the next chapter, you will review service.

CHAPTER 19

SERVICE

Adding our Light to the Sum of Light

I slept and dreamt that life was joy
I awoke and saw that life was service
I acted and behold! Service was joy.

Tagore

In this chapter, we will explore the third method of our daily activity program: service. The colossal suffering of the world takes many forms: ignorance, violence, poverty, homelessness, disease, tyranny, corruption, racism, unemployment, and injustice. We want to help. We want to heal the world. This natural compassionate drive is an expression of the soul, our true identify. Although we cannot influence the vast problems of the world as much as we would like, we can do our part, however small. We can add our light to the sum of the light. The world's religions would have us do just that.

True religions emphasize serving others in need. Spiritual giants like Jesus, Buddha, Krishna, Mohammad, Mother Teresa, and Gandhi name selfless service as the path to enlightenment. Masters in the art of service, they gave of themselves for the evolution of others and experienced the joy that comes as a result.

An example of the highest service is the *bodhisattva*. The Buddhists define a bodhisattva as one who vows to return to earth in as many incarnations as are necessary in order to relieve all human suffering.

THE BODHISATTVA'S VOW

Interpreted by the Dalai Lama

So long as space remains,
So long as sentient beings remain,
I will remain
In order to help,
In order to serve,
In order to make
My own contribution.

Masters, saints, and bodhisattvas model grand service to humanity. Although we may not have such a major role in the big picture, we can take some valuable lessons from their lead in order to be helpful in our immediate sphere of influence.

Small acts of gentle, humble service have impact. Wherever we are, we do what we can. Mother Teresa said, "I can't help thousands. I can help only the one who stands before me." John Newton added, "If two angels were sent down from heaven, one to conduct an empire and the other to sweep the street, they would feel no inclination to change employments."

It does not matter what role we play. What does matter is how we play it. We do not need to change anything. What we do need is to bring Love, kindness, and compassion to our work. It is our attitude that counts, whether we are postal workers, waiting on tables, health care professionals, bus drivers, or staying at home with children.

We can perform any task in a state of ordinary consciousness or in the consciousness of service. The difference is Love. Love converts an ordinary act to service. Service is Love in action. Service is giving inner and outer resources without attachment or expectation. Ordinary work generally focuses on external rewards and recognition. When we perform an act of service, giving our time, energy, and resources as an expression of our Love, the reward is inner peace, satisfaction, and joy. In this sense, service itself is selfish, since we do it because it makes us feel good.

Service is a universal healer, a potent medicine for individuals and the community. For individuals, it works as an antidote to the poison of guilt and as a powerful antidepressant. It takes us out of our tiresome self-ruminations, bolsters our self-esteem, and replaces feelings of insecurity with confidence. As service places us on the common ground with all of humanity, we grow in humility and equality. When we connect to others through service, our internal agitation is silenced.

Service is also a powerful medicine for the community. It works against those forces that tear us apart. Political, religious, sexual, racial, and national identities create division and conflict. Loving service, by nature expansive and inclusive, is the glue that binds us back together. Service is anesthetic to our troubles. It stops the internal wars, heals the divisions between us, and shows us who we really are.

Unfortunately, the very religions that promote service are often guilty of blocking its full expression. When a religion claims to be the one and only true way, it contributes to separation. All too often, when we think we are saved and safe, we become complacent and arrogant. Busy trying to convert others, we neglect the critical necessity of transforming ourselves. We hamper our ability to help others if we are not in an ongoing process of self-reform at the same time.

Self-reform is integral in effectively serving humanity. The work starts inside. We need to deal with our own issues before we can successfully understand and assist others with theirs. We can do the necessary inner work by practicing the spiritual methods described in this book.

Such practices as introspection, affirmations, meditation, and transformation of emotion are digging tools that can reach the deepest recesses of our being to root out all traces of negativity. It is only through rigorous inner work that we can eliminate our flaws and replace them with spiritual qualities. Then such jewels as humility, reverence, gratitude, and equality decorate our service to humanity.

Each of us has a unique way of expressing Love. With daily practice, we can find our distinctive service identity and personality. Next is a daily routine that may be of use in helping you discover your voice.

LOVE AND SERVICE: A DAILY ROUTINE

When we find our service voice and rhythm, our actions are naturally permeated with passion, focus, joy, warmth, and enthusiasm.

Try this daily routine:

MORNING PROGRAM

1. Progressive muscle relaxation
2. Breathwork
3. Contemplation
4. Meditation
5. Prayer

DAYTIME PROGRAM

1. Mindfulness
2. Practicing the presence of God
3. Service

EVENING PROGRAM

1. Progressive muscle relaxation
2. Breathwork
3. Contemplation
4. Meditation
5. Prayer

MORNING PROGRAM

The morning program is designed for self-healing. We start with progressive muscle relaxation and breathwork, which calm the body and mind. Contemplation converts spiritual ideas into reality. Meditation, affirmations, and prayer generate healing power that permeates every cell in the body. When we finish the morning program, we are aligned with Love and Her consort spiritual qualities.

DAY PROGRAM

We can maintain the momentum gained in the morning program by practicing mindfulness or the presence of God. These disciplines convert ordinary acts to service by introducing compassion to our actions. Without changing anything, we can focus on the presence of God, or perform each action mindfully.

If we pay attention to the details and the routine connections between us, we won't miss the myriad opportunities throughout the day to give and receive Love. We have all had experiences with waiters, doctors, teachers, or any worker performing their task with indifference or disdain. In the consciousness of service, we infuse the same tasks with kindness and joy. Spiritual qualities are the currency of service.

EVENING PROGRAM

After the day's activities are completed, repeat the morning exercise program. During the period of contemplation, review the day's activities with attention to successes, challenges, and ways to improve your ability to love and serve.

BALANCE

Many of us have a difficult time dealing with our own suffering, let alone the monumental pain of the world. We may try to avoid all suffering by denying problems and escaping into the distractions, entertainment, and pleasures of life. Some of us take on too much suffering of others, resulting in cynicism or burn out. How much is enough? Is there a way to find balance?

The daily routine described above offers a way to stay in balance while we help others and ourselves. The morning and evening programs are for self-healing. The day program is for helping others through mindful action and practicing the presence of God.

Through the spiritual practices of the morning and evening programs, we can withdraw from the pain and problems of the world and ourselves. In meditation, we leave suffering behind and enter a place of freedom, joy, peace, and beauty. We come out of meditation refreshed, ready to take on the next wave of problems. This is the full cycle of healthy spirituality, a way to stay balanced through renewal and regeneration.

Start by taking care of yourself. Then widen your circle of service to friends, family, and your community. Pick a cause. Transmit your gift of compassion for the victims of social injustice and inequality. Go on a campaign to lift the spirits of the sick and dying, or the poor and homeless. Volunteer at a soup kitchen. Read to a lonely senior. Fight religious and racial persecution. Stand up for fairness. Protect the meek and vulnerable. Be a big brother or sister to a neglected child. Talk to those shunned by others. Shop for a senior. Take a disabled person for a walk. Hold the door open for everyone. Let cars go ahead of you. Let someone ahead of you in line. Ask a sales person how their day is going. Thank the bus driver. Affirm loving kindness for everyone who goes by.

In service to humanity, we discover who we really are and what really helps. We come to know Love as the power that heals the self first and then others. As we change ourselves, we change the world. The healing power of Love is a magnet that draws to itself all good things.

I sought my soul, but my soul I could not see.
I sought my God, but my God eluded me.
I serve my brother and I found all three.

Anonymous

POINTS TO REMEMBER

- The goal of all spiritual practice is Love and service. Compassionate action is part of wisdom. When we apply the law of Love, we solve problems.
- In Hinduism, selfless service is karma yoga or right action. All actions are performed in the consciousness of Love in service to God, to please God. While there is an attempt to excel and

succeed, the results of action are left to God alone. We gain peace of mind when we leave the outcome to God.

- Our ability to serve improves with practice. People are complex. As we practice, our understanding is increased, so we can serve in a more refined and sophisticated manner.

- Who you are with at any given moment is the most important person in the world.

- Balance meditation and service for maximum spiritual growth.

- We can seek God's will in our routine meetings and relationships. As we start an action, we can silently ask God for guidance and direction. If we are calm and attuned, the still, small voice within shows us the best way to express Love in that situation.

- No matter what the world does, cultivate Love and practice service. Maintain a positive, calm mind and open, compassionate heart. Receive the good, the bad, and the ugly and return only good. The ones who make a difference bring anonymous, humble service to others. They are healers. They will quietly change the world.

- I may not be able to solve or fix your problem, but I will support you with compassion. I will be there and hear you, so you know that you are not alone. I cannot tell you what to do, but I can tell you what gets me through. I will help you do what you can. You have the power to get through any physical, mental, emotional, or spiritual barrier.

- Follow the law of Love, serve all of humanity, and keep your eyes open. You will find your place in the world. You will see healing and transformation. You will see expansion of Love and her sister qualities. You will experience ever-increasing joy.

- These are dangerous times. People are frightened, angry, and aggressive. No matter what happens, our job is Love and service. While we resist evil by whatever means necessary, we continue our work of ego reduction and the expansion of Love.

AFFIRMATIONS

- I serve others with Love.
- I am a peaceful servant of God.
- I help everyone.
- I am here to love and serve.
- I meditate on Love and give only that.
- I focus on Love and forget everything else.
- I fill every moment with Love.
- I fill every breath with Love.
- I fill every action with Love.
- The person I am with now is the most important person in the world.
- The person I am with now is God in disguise.
- I serve on the altar of the Almighty God within you.
- I serve as dust at the feet of the Almighty Lord within you.
- I think of others. I am sensitive to their needs.
- I give my time to others.
- I give what I can.

EXERCISES

1. What is the difference between an ordinary act and an act of service?
2. Describe the morning, daytime, and evening routine of Love and service.
3. How does the daily routine for Love and service help maintain balance?
4. Make a list of ways you already serve.
5. Do you have a desire to expand your service?
6. Make a list of ways you might like to serve in the future.
7. What are some of the barriers keeping you from expanding your service?
8. Anytime you feel bad and do something, however small, for someone else, notice the effect. You will feel better. It may be subtle, but it is there.

9. Most of us are comfortable serving those closest to us. It is natural to help family, friends, and neighbors in need. To expand our Love and service to those that we do not know can be more challenging.

   a. We can start by extending loving kindness affirmations, common courtesies, and thoughtful gestures to all who cross our path.

   b. We can formally volunteer in an organization that helps those in need.

   c. We can begin to see all people as members of one family, as brothers and sisters, as though they are our own.

   d. By practicing mindfulness, the presence of God, or karma yoga, we can transform ordinary actions and work into service by adding Love.

In the next chapter, we will explore yoga, the fourth method of our daily activity program.

CHAPTER 20

YOGA

A Way to Brahman or God

This chapter introduces yoga, the fourth method of our daily activity program. Yoga is a gift to the world from the Hindu tradition, a system of principles and methods designed to help us achieve a great reward: making contact and getting help from a compassionate, all-knowing power that exists just behind the veil of ordinary human experience. Yoga is a scientific body of knowledge with precise instructions to dissolve the layers of ordinary limited human awareness and discover that we are in reality one with the Grand Spirit known as Brahman, or God.

A yogi is one who practices yoga. The yogi learns how to break through the confining boundaries of ordinary perception to make the spectacular discovery that we are carrying with us at all times the promise of the core drive. Eternal peace, pure Love, and ecstatic joy—what we have been looking for in the external world—is a secret, buried treasure in the center of our very own being. What we really want is right here, right now, inside.

Yoga is God-realization through the union of soul with Spirit. We are created in the image of God. God implants His image in each human body as the soul, His representation of Himself in each person. The first stage of yoga is to make contact with the soul. Then the soul merges with Spirit. When we make contact with the soul, we experience expansion of peace, Love, and other spiritual qualities. In the end, when the soul unites with the Spirit, there is complete liberation from limitation and suffering, and entry into infinite, immortal, eternal peace.

In ordinary material consciousness, we do not experience the unlimited power of the soul and Spirit. Why? What is in the veil that prevents us from entry into the vast and eternal kingdom? How do we get through these barriers to make contact with the soul and Spirit?

The central problem is one of identification. We accept ordinary material reality as normal. We believe impermanence and change have ultimate power. We experience limitation because we identify with our body, personality, and role in the drama of life. We think we are our desires, habits, attachments, flaws, and problems. We identify with our ego, which causes us to feel separate from others, creation, and the Creator. Because of these identifications, our perception and experience is limited to the vibrational frequencies detectable by the ordinary mind and five senses.

The soul and Spirit, on the other hand, are vibrating at a frequency too subtle to detect by the mind and five senses. Any attempt to experience the soul and Spirit with the mind and senses is doomed to fail. This is where yoga enters the picture. Yoga offers a variety of methods to refine and purify our consciousness so that we attune to the more subtle frequencies of soul and Spirit.

To uncover our true self as eternal peace, pure Love, and ecstatic joy is a tall order. We need a set of spiritual practices that address everything which pins us down to the status quo, the level that we have come to know and accept as our home or "normal" consciousness. Because we cling to our current understanding and perception of reality, no matter how painful, difficult, and chaotic it might be, we cannot solve the cosmic puzzle and find the grand prize within. However, when we have finally had enough suffering, when we have a passionate, burning desire to change, when we are ready to do some work, yoga answers the call by helping us unplug from the material world as we know it, so we can finally enter the kingdom of Omnipresent Love.

FOUR PATHWAYS TO GOD

Love, service, meditation, and wisdom are basic to any spiritual path. Tapping our innate faculties of feeling, action, concentration, and reason, yoga offers four powerful techniques to help us plow our way through the multiple layers of ordinary reality to discover the God of the universe. The four techniques are:

1. Love, or *Bhakti Yoga*: the way of transforming feeling to devotion
2. Service, or *Karma Yoga*: the way of transforming action to service
3. Meditation, or *Raja Yoga*: the way of stillness through concentration
4. Wisdom, or *Jnana Yoga*: the way of transforming thought to wisdom

God can be known through Love, service, meditation, and wisdom, but not until we reduce the restlessness and excesses of the body, mind, emotions, desires, and ego by practicing one or a combination of these four yogas.

We can practice bhakti, karma, raja, and jnana yoga in a variety of combinations, depending on individual preferences and circumstances. Some practice all four methods daily in a balanced way. For others, one or two of the practices may dominate. These are not distinct categories. They overlap. It is a matter of emphasis. The common denominator of any combination practiced diligently over time is the gradual replacement of restlessness, hyperactivity, destructive emotions, and excessive material desires with stillness and peace, compassion and kindness, courage and strength.

BHAKTI YOGA: THE PATH TO GOD THROUGH LOVE AND DEVOTION

God is eternal Love and so are we. Everything else is *maya*. This is bhakti yoga, its purpose is cultivating an immutable union between the Love of the soul and the Love of God. Maya is a Hindu term that describes the impermanence, limitations, separation, and consequent suffering of the material plane. The bhakti yogi remains in the consciousness of Love no matter what troubles or difficulties arise in the world of maya. In bhakti yoga, we accomplish this by loving God with all of our hearts, minds, might, and souls, and our neighbors as ourselves. "It doesn't matter what happens, Lord. All that matters is that I love You, and You love me."

In bhakti yoga, we capitalize on the feeling of Love that is naturally in our heart by directing it toward God. We also channel likes, dislikes, emotion, passion, dependencies, and attachment in the direction of Love. We leave no trace of our being behind. We channel all to God as Love.

The bhakta strives to be within God's Love at all times. This is a difficult task, as stressful events often provoke a response of tension, irritation, annoyance, impatience, and worse. The bhakta wants no part of this, for a negative response is a return to the hypnotic sleep of maya. To be awake is to be aware that we are always in the presence of God's Love.

To remain in God's Love, the bhakta cultivates a real, intimate, personal relationship with the Divine. We can do this by choosing an aspect of God that arouses devotion. That aspect becomes a point of focus for the bhakti yogi's Love. God is both personal and impersonal. For most people, it is difficult to apply Love to an impersonal aspect of God, such as an incomprehensible, abstract power. However, we can form a personal relationship with God as the Father, Mother, Friend, Beloved, Teacher, or as one of the Divine incarnations such as Christ, Krishna, or Buddha. These aspects naturally evoke a loving response.

Loving God does not come easily or early on the spiritual path. In the beginning, we do not know God; it is not natural to love what we do not know. We can start the process by thinking about God. Then we can talk, share, and listen, as in any human relationship. With consistent meditation, service, and conversation with God, at some point She responds by revealing Herself as peace, joy, Love, power, wisdom, ecstasy, or some other manifestation. Then She goes back behind the veil, playing hide and seek. We return to ordinary consciousness and resume our spiritual work. During dry spells, we develop and mature our unconditional Love, surrender, devotion, trust, strength, and courage. How else would we develop our spiritual muscles?

Nevertheless, we yearn for God's return. Our heart's desire is to find and keep Her. We want more than just a taste of Her sweetness. If we persist in our spiritual work, God appears again, perhaps with the Mother's tender Love, warmth, and exquisite beauty. God may manifest as our unconditional Friend and Confidant, one Who knows, understands, and accepts us no matter what we have done. If attuned and receptive, we may know God as our infinitely wise Father, Guide, and Protector. When we are in pain, we can know God as the Teacher, giving us the experiences that we need for spiritual growth. As we get to know our Father, Mother, Teacher, and Friend, it easy and natural to love Her/Him in an intimate, ever-evolving, ever-new romance.

God is an infinite ocean of pure unconditional Love, an ocean we cannot enter until our Love is likewise pure and unconditional. In bhakti yoga, we accomplish this by applying all of our spiritual muscle to respond with Love to all people in every circumstance. We do everything with one intention: to love God. All we have to do is love God no matter what happens, and not worry about the rest. This is following God's will through attunement with His aspect of all-powerful Love.

We can apply God's Love, the most powerful healing force in the universe, to any pain or problem. When difficulties come and we find ourselves reacting poorly, we can find our connection to God's Omnipresent Love by going to the deepest part of our hearts, where He resides. By repeatedly returning to God's Love, we break our identification with maya and reduce our suffering. In our eternal romance with the almighty, gentle Father-Mother God of the universe, we get the peace-joy that we crave.

KARMA YOGA: THE PATH TO GOD THROUGH ACTION

Karma Yoga is union of the soul with Spirit through selfless action. Here we take advantage of our activity throughout the day. In karma yoga, we transform ordinary action to selfless action dedicated to God, service becoming the principle means of union of the soul with Spirit.

Every thought, feeling, and action is an offering in loving service to God. There is no thought of personal gain or impressing others. We surrender the results, outcomes, expectations, and rewards to God. "I work to please God alone." "Thou art the doer, not I." "Thy will, Lord, not mine." Every action is powered by His energy and will.

The ego is attached to outcomes. The ego derives its power in the battle for victory over defeat, gain over loss, and pleasure over pain. When the ego takes credit for success, it puffs up; when it fails, it grieves. In either case, it maintains its territory. To the yogi, however, the ups and downs of life are one and the same; the outcome is in God's hands. When motivated by the ego, we add to the separation between God and ourselves. The same act performed selflessly moves us closer to God. As servant to the King, the karma yogi claims nothing for the self, no matter what level of personal sacrifice.

In the practice of karma yoga, the sole intent is to follow God's will with every action. The Creator is the Author of the act. The yogi is the worker. Once the act is completed, the yogi disconnects from the results of the action, letting the story of life unfold as determined by God. When we surrender the results of our actions to God, we deprive the ego of consequences. The ego shrinks, allowing the soul to come into awareness.

We play our role, fulfill our tasks and responsibilities, and do the best we can. We strive for success in all endeavors but remain even-minded in any outcome. We perform each act with calm concentration and efficiency. Understanding that all work is God's work, we perform every act, however mundane or routine, with enthusiasm, gratitude, and humility. We avoid indifference, an aspect of laziness and selfishness.

Accepting difficulties as coming from God the Teacher, we learn and move on.

Wherever we are and whoever we are, we can turn this moment into serviceable action by dedicating it to God, humanity, and the greater good. Then every movement and action powers our way to God. It does not matter what we do. Our task may be simple or complex, routine or important, painful or enjoyable. What matters is that we hold the consciousness of God at all times and seek His guidance as we perform and give our best. Then all tasks merge into one continuous, sacred ritual of loving service to God.

By non-attachment to the results of action, we can enter the arena of worldly activity, serve with compassion and understanding, and remain calm even in the face of turmoil. The stillness of the true self remains constant in the midst of activity. The *Bhagavad Gita* refers to this as inaction in action. As stated by Paramahansa Yogananda in *Autobiography of a Yogi*, "I, the soul, watch the cosmic movie with calm detachment while at the same time I play my assigned role perfectly with zeal, ambition, and the supreme desire to please God." Karma yoga, meditation in action, is a source of joy. Joy is in the action, in service, in working for God and humanity. The outcome belongs to God.

RAJA YOGA: THE PATH TO GOD THROUGH MEDITATION

"Be still and know that I am God" is an invitation from the Bible (Psalm 46:10) to meditate. In meditation, we can achieve the motionless state which profoundly facilitates our ability to commune with God. Raja yoga describes the way to a direct experience with God in the stillness of meditation. Patanjali, an ancient master of yoga, outlined an eight-step model designed to achieve stillness and communion with God. By following the eight steps, we learn how to achieve stillness by stopping the world, body, senses, and mind.

To understand the eight steps, one must first understand *prana*, *pranayama*, and the *chakras*. Prana is the life energy present in the human body. We send prana outward towards the world for daily activities, and in and up the spine to the brain for God-realization. There are seven centers of concentrated prana in the spine and brain, called chakras. Yoga opens up the chakras, so that energy can travel upward into the higher centers in the spinal cord and brain resulting in God-communion. Pranayama is control of prana by reversing the outward flow of life energy, directing it to the higher chakras in the spine and brain. The result is expansion of peace, joy, and Love.

The eight steps of *Patanjali*:

1. *Yama,* or moral conduct: All religions have rules for moral conduct, such as the Ten Commandments. Yama refers to abstention from harming others, falsehood, theft, and greed.

2. *Niyama* is religious observance. Devotion, service, moderation, discipline, study of scripture, purity, and surrender, along with the moral conduct described in step one, provide a platform from which all else is built.

3. *Asana* is right posture. *Hatha* yoga is a set of body positions and exercises that prepare the body for meditation. In meditation, it is essential that the body is still and the spine straight.

4. *Pranayama* is control of prana or life energy. Energy directed outward in ordinary activity keeps us locked in the status quo of mundane consciousness. Pranayama reverses the flow of outward energy and directs it inward and upward, toward the spinal cord and brain. This stills the mind and senses.

5. *Pratyahara* is interiorization. Pranayama (step 4) results in interiorization of the mind, energy, and consciousness from outer attachments and bodily organs to the higher centers in the spinal cord and brain.

6. *Dharana* is concentration. The interiorized mind is completely still so it can concentrate on a single point, such as a mantra.

7. *Dhyana* is meditation. This is direct concentration on God.

8. *Samadhi* is union of the soul with God. This is the most advanced stage of meditation. There is complete union or merging with God.

When the mind slows and finally stops, consciousness and energy shift from the outer world, restless thoughts, and sensations of the body, to the higher centers in the spine and brain. In stillness, God reveals Himself on His schedule, through His grace, as peace, joy, Love, energy, light, wisdom, and guidance. We realize His beauty and power. When meditation is over, we manifest His Love and wisdom through service to humanity.

JNANA YOGA: THE PATH TO GOD THROUGH WISDOM

The path of jnana yoga capitalizes on our God-given gift of reason by transforming ordinary thought into wisdom. Through the practice of jnana yoga, intellect evolves to intuition, or direct knowledge of the truth. For those inclined to practice jnana yoga, thought is an enjoyable, stimulating, vibrant source of inspiration and realization.

In jnana yoga, we do not just think or theorize. We embody wisdom and become one with the truth through a process of listening, perceiving, and assimilating. The process starts with the study of scriptural truth. Then we bring the idea to contemplation and meditation for realization. We maintain this wisdom during activity, through affirmation, concentration, and will.

For example, in the beginning, we think the world as we know it in ordinary consciousness is the only reality. The jnana yoga thinker, however, is convinced of the oneness of Spirit underneath the complex surface of ordinary consciousness. Despite the appearance of complexity, the jnana yogi affirms God is One. S(he) maintains the affirmation of oneness in the face of the counter-pull of mundane thoughts and the senses which support the illusions of maya. The jnana yogi understands through discrimination that the nature of the world and its phenomena are illusory, and that only the oneness of God is real. This is union of the soul with God through discriminatory intellect and wisdom.

THE YOGI IN THE SCHOOL OF LIFE

In the practice of yoga, two key processes converge to accomplish the goal of union of soul with Spirit. These processes are:

1. The school of life: God sets up His school of life, where we have the opportunity to learn critical lessons for purposes of evolution of the soul towards Spirit. There are many classes, subjects, and tests. When we learn the lessons and pass the tests, we transform and heal. In a process of purification, the ego shrinks and spiritual qualities expand.

2. Pranayama: Bhakti, karma, raja, and jnana yoga similarly lead to evolution of the soul to Spirit. Practice of the four yogas slowly and progressively opens the higher chakras in the spine and brain. Consciousness and energy travel upwards through the chakras to higher centers in the brain and spine, eventually resulting in a tangible experience of God's wisdom and power.

Each person learns their tailor-made lessons in the school of life. Ego, problems, and flaws burn up in the fire of devotion, service, meditation, and wisdom. The higher chakras in the spine and brain open. Consciousness is refined and the soul evolves. With sustained practice, we reach a critical mass, tipping the scales in favor of the soul over the ego. In the end, when we conquer the ego, when the secret veils of maya lift, and when the soul dissolves in the one true reality, we find that God has hidden Himself as joy and peace in the human body temple itself. Then, in perfect attunement with God's will, we can follow the command of the sacred scriptures: to love God with all of our heart, mind, might, and soul and our neighbor as our self. Such a servant of the King can give patience, sweetness, kindness, and gentleness to all of humanity.

God's eternal peace, pure Love, and ecstatic joy are the highest states of consciousness, the beginning of all creation, the endpoint of evolution, and the ultimate grace. We are made of this pure and perfect, unending Love. We come from, move, live and have our being, and ultimately melt back into this sacred consciousness. This is yoga, evolution of the soul, and God-realization.

POINTS TO REMEMBER

- We are more than our egos, bodies, or personalities. We are not our problems, symptoms, flaws, or disabilities. We are made in the image of Spirit. We need to transfer our identity from our problems to soul qualities.

- We can experience what is just underneath the world as we know it when everything we understand as reality is reduced to zero in the absolute stillness of yoga meditation. This includes the ego, personality, body, senses, mind, personal story, world story, and fund of knowledge. When we escape from everything we think we are and enter the domain of stillness, we can experience the ecstatic joy of the soul and God.

- Yoga is not easy. It takes a lot of work and a long time to reach such superconscious states as the changeless peace of the soul, pure light, or cosmic sound. It is a long, arduous journey to Omniscient Love. Maya has great power. The way is paved with strife. Nevertheless, yoga works. Progress is slow but definite. Many quit because they want a quick fix. Practice, patience, and perseverance are prerequisites for success.

- The way to God is paved with unconditional Love. This is devotion, bhakti yoga.

- The way to God is paved with service to humanity. This is karma yoga.

- The way to God is through stillness. This is meditation or raja yoga.

- The way to God is through discriminative intellect or wisdom. This is jnana yoga.

- Bhakti, karma, raja, and jnana yoga work together. The practice of one feeds the other three.

- In the beginning, the goal of selfless service is not possible because of the ego. However, if our intent is selflessness and we do our best and continue to practice yoga, the ego slowly dissolves.

- Our service work is not about success or failure. The work is our responsibility. The outcome is not ours.
- The yogi cuts into the ignorance, suffering, and injustice of the world by adding compassion, humility, and understanding.

AFFIRMATIONS

- I conduct this act immersed in Your Love with the sole desire to please You.
- I am always at the feet of God.
- I am always on the altar of God.
- I serve every person as a manifestation of God
- I love unconditionally.
- Love is the only reality.
- God is one.
- God is stillness.
- God is in the stillness.
- God is beyond the stillness.

EXERCISES

1. What is yoga?
2. Why is it impossible to experience the soul with the ordinary mind and the five senses?
3. What keeps us locked up in ordinary consciousness?
4. Describe in detail the four types of yoga.
5. What are the eight steps of Patanjali?
6. What does stillness have to do with knowing God?
7. Describe how the school of life and the four yogas work together to advance the soul in its movement toward Spirit.

In the next chapter, we will study the fifth and final technique of our daily activity program: the transformation of emotion.

CHAPTER 21

TRANSFORMATION OF EMOTION

Converting Emotional Pain to Self-knowledge

THE GUEST HOUSE: RUMI

This being human is a guest house.
Every morning is a new arrival.
A joy, a depression, a meanness,
some momentary awareness comes
as an unexpected visitor.

Welcome and entertain them all!
Even if they're a crowd of sorrows,
who violently sweep your house
empty of its furniture,
still, treat each guest honorably.
He may be clearing you out
for some new delight.

The dark thought, the shame, the malice,
meet them at the door laughing,
and invite them in.
Be grateful for whoever comes,
because each has been sent
as a guide from beyond.

In this chapter, we will review the fifth and final technique of our daily activity program: the transformation of emotion. Often, we can successfully work through our painful emotions by practicing any one or a combination of the other spiritual techniques described in this work. Sometimes, however, these methods do not liberate us from the grip of painful feelings. In such instances, it may be necessary to stop all of these practices, stay alone, be with the pain, and let it teach. This involves introspection, or self-analysis. Introspection allows us to see our strengths and virtues, flaws and limitations, and the needs and desires that motivate our actions. Material for review includes attitude, thoughts, emotion, behavior, habits, conflicts, character flaws, relationships, and our ability to love, serve, give, and be useful.

Introspection is necessary for complete spiritual growth. There are times when we have to examine our pain and extract the necessary lessons in order to go forward. If we choose any other option, the pain lingers.

To succeed in introspection, we must learn to successfully navigate our way through painful emotions. Painful emotion is a teacher bearing the gift of self-knowledge. Self-knowledge is information gained when we explore our emotions. Most of us experience emotional pain daily. These feelings are normal, healthy, and intelligent. As reactions to ordinary daily events, emotions are intelligent, meaning they carry information. Within the painful emotion are problems, issues, and conflicts begging for recognition, work, synthesis, and resolution. When we extract the important information from within our emotions, suffering is contained. It is only when emotional pain is not processed that it causes us additional difficulties.

Anger, depression, fear, guilt, and other painful emotions are powerful energy forces that need to be managed wisely or they can overwhelm our defenses, cause us to lose control, and in the worst-case scenario, endanger ourselves and others. Yet most of us have had no training in emotional pain management. Because we don't know what to do with these feelings, we instinctively try to keep them from conscious awareness by denying their existence, drowning them in substance abuse, or pushing them into the subconscious and the body where they are stored in latent form.

When we resist experiencing pain, the unprocessed feeling energy remains in the subconscious and the body. The subconscious and body become carriers of suppressed, unresolved emotions and the unprocessed lessons embedded within them.

We attract events, circumstances, and people who elicit the painful feelings and problems hidden in the subconscious and body. These are setups. A setup is any circumstance that brings forth painful emotions. Setups come to reveal the issues requiring some work. The painful emotion, the carrier, tells us where to work.

If we do not do the work, the problem remains. When we miss the opportunity to get the necessary lessons, we continue to attract people and circumstances that bring out these suppressed feelings. We continue to attract similar circumstances until we learn the necessary lessons. For example, if we are codependent, we continue to attract codependent partners until independence is learned. We may remain stuck in a codependent relationship, or find new people and repeat the codependent pattern, until we sufficiently process the underlying, unresolved pain related to dependency into new knowledge and strength.

While in storage, these emotions can have a negative impact on our physical, mental, and spiritual health. We develop negative attitudes, distorted thinking, and behave in destructive ways. For example, unprocessed anger leads to judgment, criticism, blaming, and fighting with others. Instead of processing the anger into self-knowledge, we pass it along to others, making their lives more difficult.

The alternative to these negative scenarios is to learn how to extract the messages embedded within the feelings. We can process the emotional pain into a story with knowledge and lessons. Our feelings carry problems, solutions, and strategies that contribute to understanding life. To get this knowledge, we need a fearless, objective, honest introspective process. The ego is the greatest opponent to such a process.

The ego will try to tell the story solely from its point of view. Self-justification is one of its greatest tricks. It does not admit to mistakes. Since it lacks introspection on its own problems, it remains self-righteous while it treats others as scapegoats. It projects problems rather than taking responsibility. The ego is selfish, insecure, defensive, controlling, and self-important. In the face of criticism, it becomes frightened and aggressive. While it may accurately discover others' faults, it is blind to its own.

To combat the ego, we can turn to introspection guided by the soul. The soul is not afraid to look inward. It wants to find flaws and replace them with spiritual qualities. It is ready to look in every secret chamber of our consciousness in order to root out the barriers that prevent our full expression of Love. Our soul knows we will feel better when we do this work. It is willing to suffer any pain in order to rise.

The soul reviews our story, looking for the root of our pain. "What am I to learn from this? Where am I at fault in this story? Where can I improve? How could I have behaved more skillfully? How can I use this pain to find and replace my flaws with spiritual qualities? Where did I fail to express unconditional Love in thought, feeling, and action? Am I giving the best of my Love, humility, understanding and gentleness to everyone throughout the day?"

Upon introspection, the ego and soul fight for control. For example, when we are mistreated, we are quickly angered and name what the other person has done wrong and what the remedy should be. We take defensive actions, such as setting boundaries, deploying interpersonal communication for problem solving, and correcting injustice. Often, however, the wrongdoer is not cooperative, leaving us angry and resentful. It is easy to get stuck here; the ego tends to act like a self-righteous victim, defining the faults and weaknesses of others as the source of our discomfort. This prolongs our suffering, however, since we end up bearing the pain given to us by the wrongdoer.

The soul, on the other hand, assumes responsibility for any lingering pain as a stimulant for the development of spiritual qualities, even if the pain comes to us by way of injustice. The soul uses the transformative power of Love to counter any remaining anger and resentment. By responding to cruelty with strength, to ignorance with understanding, and to suffering with compassion, the soul spiritualizes our story, consequently giving us the peace of mind we seek.

The implications of the introspective process are profound. We stop blaming others for our problems. We abandon the victim stance and take responsibility for our emotions. We become more concerned with our own behavior than we are with another's. Regardless of whether others are right or wrong, we use our suffering as an opportunity to cultivate strength, courage, endurance, and peace.

Following is a systematic technique designed to help us extract the knowledge embedded in our emotional pain, so it becomes our ally rather than our adversary. Before reviewing the technique, please read the next section regarding risk.

RISK

Processing raw emotional pain into self-knowledge is not for everybody. Opening a dialogue with emotional pain can be frightening, requiring a dive into uncharted territory and facing the unknown. We must explore and even become friends with our fears. There is likely to be considerable resistance. We should never underestimate how frightful this may be. We should never push anybody into such a process.

Some cannot and should not engage in exploring their pain in such a manner without seeking professional help; it might flood their defenses, causing alarm or panic. In such circumstances, the individual can work with the other spiritual techniques described in this work. If you feel that processing emotional pain to gain self-knowledge is too intense, please avoid it at this point and consult with a professional counselor. For those ready to review the technique, the steps are outlined below.

PROCESSING PAINFUL EMOTION
INTO SELF-KNOWLEDGE

This technique applies to any emotion:

1.   Create a safe healing space
2.   Ask for help from your Higher Power
3.   Let the story unfold
4.   Spiritualize the story

1.   CREATE A SAFE HEALING SPACE

An honest look at character flaws can be threatening, even shattering to the ego. However, the goal is not to tear the self to shreds. The purpose of introspection is to discover those aspects that need to change, without causing unnecessary guilt, low self-esteem, or humiliation.

Sit quietly. Use your breathing and meditation techniques to bring in as much stillness as you can. Be gentle and compassionate with yourself. Remain calm and accepting. Rather than feel bad that you have problems, feel good that you have the courage to face them and the integrity to change for the better.

2.   ASK FOR HELP FROM YOUR HIGHER POWER

We are connected inside to an infinitely intelligent healing power whose nature is Love and compassion. We can ask for and get help from the Great Physician, the Healer within. Open yourself to the wisdom of your Counselor and Friend, asking for help understanding the nature of your suffering. Ask for the necessary courage and strength.

3.   LET THE STORY UNFOLD

There is a pressure inside of each emotion, pushing it to tell its story. Right or wrong, the feeling wants to be heard, accepted, and validated. We need to let our emotions tell their stories without judgment.

Go to your serene and spacious witness. In a relaxed, receptive state with your defenses down, observe your feelings. Feelings such as depression, anxiety, fear, anger, guilt, shame, jealousy, and abandonment may surface. Identify and label them. Feelings often overlap and merge.

It is possible to feel angry and sad or other combinations all at once. With practice and patience, you will be able to identify overlapping feelings.

Relax and breathe.

Feel each emotion fully. Let the feeling come through without resistance. Do not fight. Take full responsibility for the emotion. It is there for a reason. It is intelligent, pointing you in the direction of work that needs completion. When we experience the feeling and take responsibility for it, it releases the intelligent information it carries. In a context of compassion, gentleness, and understanding, let the emotion tell its story. It will tell us about ourselves.

In the story, we can find our strengths and faults. We can define the spiritual qualities we already have; however, we should not stop here. We can build on our strengths only if we define and work on our remaining problems and issues.

Introspection allows us to see the recesses of our mind that otherwise remain hidden. Without fear, go to the deepest, darkest places in your consciousness, to those recesses needing exposure and work. Take out your inner mirror. Turn on the light of introspection. Ask the pain, "Why are you here? What am I to learn from you? Show me why I repeat the same mistakes. What flaws do I have that contribute to my current problems? Show me anything and everything I need to learn to become a better person. Direct me to the work I need to do in the external world and within myself."

If we stay with our feelings long enough, we can determine the significance of our suffering. Our pain takes us to the root cause of our troubles. This is good news: Once we discover our flaws and attachments, we are en route to complete healing. But first, we must learn to spiritualize our story.

4. SPIRITUALIZE THE STORY

You can see how important it is to find your problems, for if you do not find them, you cannot improve. However, it is equally important to avoid reliving your problems. In this step, we replace our flaws with soul qualities. Guided by spiritual qualities, the story unfolds in the direction of Love.

Never identify with your weakness. Dwelling on flaws actually makes them stronger. Our flaws and problems are reinforced through the repetition of thought. The self becomes confused, identifying with negativity, thinking this is its nature. *Always remember: you are not your problems and flaws.* This is very important!

In order to avoid obsessing on errors or flaws and thinking that is who you are, discover the problem and construct its opposite positive spiritual quality. Focus on that quality. When you discover a negative quality in your nature, do not concentrate on it. Instead, direct all your energy to the cultivation of the opposite good quality.

For every negative quality, there is a polar opposite, positive quality. For anger, there is patience. For selfishness, there is Love. For anxiety, there is peace. For resentments, there is forgiveness.

You can do this by creating affirmations related to the spiritual quality you wish to cultivate. With this method, one by one, problems are contained, reduced, and dissolved, replaced by positive qualities and habits. The true self emerges as peace, strength, courage, and compassion, overwhelming all traces of negativity.

We learn many valuable lessons from our emotional pain as our life story unfolds. By completing an introspective process, our emotional pain exhausts itself and disappears, leaving in its wake new knowledge and strength. When we permeate our strategies for dealing with life's problems with Love and understanding, we spiritualize our story. In clearing and healing our emotions, we gain the peace of the soul.

AN EXAMPLE OF TRANSFORMATION OF EMOTION INTO SELF-KNOWLEDGE

Joe's wife has been complaining that he has been irritable with her and their children. He decides to see if she is right. First, he reviews the lessons in this book on affirmations, will, habits, and introspection. Then he finds some quiet time. He asks for help from his Higher Power. He looks inside with an attitude of honest, fearless compassion. Joe surrenders into his pain. He adopts an attitude of total acceptance to whatever story his emotions have to tell. As Joe lets the story unfold, he realizes he has indeed been impatient and angry with his family.

Further exploration of his feelings leads him to realize that he has been struggling at work. His boss treats him poorly. Colleagues are more competitive than cooperative. The work itself has become boring. Joe realizes that he needs to change his job, but until he can make that change, does not want to abuse his family. He fights off his ego's tendency to blame others and seeks to spiritualize his story.

Joe knows that there are times when he has absolutely no control over the environment, but always has choice about his will, thoughts, and actions. Joe decides to fight the battle against his anger. He consults the list of spiritual qualities. He finds a number of qualities that he can use to antidote his irritability. These include peace, patience, kindness, tenderness, gentleness, sweetness, understanding, compassion, forgiveness, tolerance, acceptance, openness, and surrender.

He writes affirmations on some note cards: "I am patient, kind, and understanding under all conditions. Sweetness of speech is the rule of the day. I accept the things I cannot change." Patience, kindness, understanding, and sweetness of speech are the watchwords he uses for every action. He practices these qualities in all of his actions throughout the day.

Joe finds it difficult to respond with spiritual qualities when the demands are great at work and at home. Nevertheless, with perseverance he sees slow but definite results. His family is happier. Joe gradually becomes more patient as he looks for a new job.

In allowing his emotions to tell their story, Joe discovered his issues and problems. He infused the story with Love qualities, realizing another degree of his true self.

POINTS TO REMEMBER

- How we manage painful emotion can make the difference between success and failure, health and disease, poverty or prosperity, Love and despair.

- Painful emotions are a part of the normal, natural, intelligent healing process. Without this reassuring knowledge, we are more likely to become frightened or overwhelmed, leading to loss of control.

- We can process feelings daily, or as they arise. If we wait too long, they add up and may become too hot to handle, forcing us to express them destructively.

- Emotions are a rich source of information. If we are able to experience sadness or anger without excessive use of alcohol, drugs, food, gambling, sex, or violence, we may discover why we are experiencing these feelings.

- Emotions tell a story. When we finish the story, it will not keep coming up.

- During introspection, the ego tells the story from its point of view. This is good. We can learn many things about ourselves by listening to the ego and seeing how it works. However, the ego tends to be self-righteous. It blames others, making itself into a victim. The soul, on the other hand, looks to replace our imperfections with spiritual power. It spiritualizes the story by bringing out our soul qualities.

- Emotions come in waves. Learn how to surf the waves. If you ride them, they dissipate, leaving behind a story packed with meaning, lessons, peace, and power.

- True self-analysis is essential for spiritual progress. Be honest with yourself. To have a clear conscience is one of the greatest joys.

- The ego keeps us tiny by inflating the importance of its story. When we reduce and finally replace the ego with the soul, we realize we are infinite and eternal.

EXERCISES

1. What is introspection?
2. What is self-knowledge?
3. Overwhelming emotions reduce our intellect, imagination, and choices. We become destructive. Describe the technique for transforming emotion into self-knowledge. How can you use this technique?
4. Can you think of some occasions where your emotional discomfort carried the lessons you needed to learn? How did you extract that knowledge from the pain?
5. How can you spiritualize your story?

You have completed your study of several spiritual methods, proven over the ages to be effective tools for cultivating soul qualities. In the next section, we will discuss how soul qualities help us manage problems. From the 100 qualities listed in the spiritual alphabet, ten are chosen for detailed discussion, study, and work.

PART SIX
SPIRITUAL QUALITIES

CHAPTER 22

INTRODUCTION TO
SPIRITUAL QUALITIES

The goal of all spiritual work is to cultivate soul qualities. These qualities are healing powers built into the body as standard equipment to help us broker and buffer the pain of life. Such healing powers as courage, compassion, understanding, and humility help us control our problems.

The qualities are related. They grow together. An increase in one leads to expansion of the others, and they all lead directly to Love and ultimately to joy. For example, if we improve our ability to be patient, we will automatically become more compassionate. If we listen more carefully, we will be more understanding. Gratitude leads to reverence, peace to Love, and when our Love is great enough, it transforms into joy.

Life is a school. Pain is the teacher. We learn to expand our spiritual qualities. We can expand any quality by practicing the methods described here. This work has no end. We can expand any quality indefinitely. Greatest expansion comes when we focus all our attention on the chosen method and quality, rather than our problem.

Our circumstances present us with the opportunity to cultivate any one or combination of 100 soul qualities. We always need more understanding, forgiveness, strength, and forbearance. We always need warmth, thoughtfulness, and sensitivity to the needs of others. There is always a need for justice and equality. We crave friendship, humor, fun, and laughter. These and other soul qualities help us manage anything.

Love qualities are the standard. They are the ideal. They guide us. They set the boundaries and pathway. We are either in or out of bounds, on or off the path. When our thoughts, feelings, and actions are not in alignment with Love, we have work to do. The work is to practice any one or combination of spiritual methods to expand our Love until it is unconditional. Soul qualities are the goal, the product, and the true measure of our success.

No matter what barriers would stop us, we can respond with soul qualities. These are our tools. These are the habits of a sage. In the next section, there is a discussion of how soul qualities help us manage any problem. We will now begin our review of ten qualities in detail. We will start with Love.

CHAPTER 23

LOVE

The Command to Love

Judaism: You shall not take vengeance or bear a grudge against any of your people, but you shall love your neighbor as yourself. Leviticus 19:17

Christianity: You shall love the Lord your God with all your heart, soul, mind, and strength, and your neighbor as yourself. Mark 12:28-34

Islam: Paradise will be occupied by those who love one another for God's sake, those who sit together for God's sake, and those who visit one another for God's sake. The Hadith

Buddhism: Whatever happiness is in the world has arisen from a wish for the welfare of others; whatever misery there is has arisen from indulging selfishness. A Buddhist proverb

Hinduism: O Arjuna, the best type of yogi is he who feels for others, whether in grief or pleasure, even as he feels for himself. The Bhagavad-Gita, 6:32

Taoism: The supreme good is like water, which nourishes all things without trying to. It is content with the low places that people disdain. That is like the Tao. Tao Te Ching, 8

Native American Spirituality: Whatever befalls the Earth befalls the sons and daughters of the Earth. We did not weave the web of life; we are merely a strand in it. Whatever we do to the web, we do to ourselves. Chief Seattle

THE COSMIC PURPOSE OF LIFE

The purpose of life is Love. The grand plan for each individual and the human race is evolution of consciousness toward higher realms of Love and service. The universe is set up as a school, our Teacher, the God of Love. The lesson plan is simple. *We are on this earth-school to learn how to love when we do not.*

God sets up Her school of life where we learn critical lessons that propel our evolution toward Love. The most important discovery is that God has invented a cosmic game of choice. We can use our free will to choose Love, or something else. Our troubles are the result of poor choices. We move in the right direction when we choose Love.

Lack of Love is the fundamental cause of all of our problems. The solution is Love. We are to follow the path of kindness and compassion, thereby becoming Love itself. When we learn how to love, we fulfill life's purpose. The entire setup of creation intends this to happen. All events point in this direction.

As described in step one, the core drive, we have an insatiable drive for unconditional Love. We *must* have it. In the beginning, we look to family, friends, and lovers to satisfy our craving for perfect Love. We all start here. However, human love can only satisfy a part of this need. Divine Love is the only experience that is completely fulfilling.

When we look to people for pure Love, we fail; human love is imperfect. We all have egos, flaws, attachments, and bad habits. These barriers impede our ability to manifest perfect Love. When our need for unconditional Love remains unmet, we get anxious. In frustration, we desperately seek Love in all the wrong places. We end up with codependency, multiple partners, addiction, and other such bad habits. The solution lies in the transformation of human love to Divine Love.

We can achieve this change through a process of purification towards perfection. This process requires discipline, effort, and ego reduction. It takes time and it hurts, so we are slow to enter the process; even when we start, we resist its completion. However, this is the purpose of life. We are here to learn how to love unconditionally. Until we begin the process of transforming human to Divine Love, there will be restlessness, frustration, and dissatisfaction. To eliminate this unnecessary suffering, we must expand and perfect our Love until it is unqualified. Until then, we cannot realize the core drive.

We can use our current relationships as a starting place. In our lives, we give and receive Love in a variety of roles, including as a parent, sibling, coworker, friend, neighbor, or romantic partner. In the daily grind of these relationships, problems inevitably emerge. Rather than be dismayed, we can use these as opportunities to expand and purify our Love. We can do some interpersonal work to improve communication and problem solving. However, the transformation of human love to Divine is ultimately about self-reform and self-mastery. It is not about others' behavior. It is about our response.

Instead of looking to others, we bring Love from within ourselves. Instead of trying to control and change others, which usually causes resistance, we learn how to be content and comfortable inside. There is no expectation, demand, or need for others to behave in a certain way. We give Love, no matter what. This higher Love gives complete satisfaction while setting up the condition for others to change when they can.

God's Love is Omnipresent, always available as the universal balm for any problem or pain. We can tap into Divine Love at any time; it is already with us, implanted in the bodily temple as the soul, or image of God. We already have the superconscious Love we are looking for. It is always inside, regardless of our outer condition. Through mindful introspection, we can identify any flaw that impedes the free flow of Love. Then we can apply a spiritual method such as mindfulness or meditation to cultivate the Love that is already there. We leave no stone unturned, working to remove all traces of negativity, however long that might take.

Most people have never experienced Divine Love. It is different than human love or any other experience. We cannot imagine it until we experience it. At first, it may seem unattainable. However, we can find it by purifying and expanding our human love. When our Love is strong enough, it eventually breaks into another realm described by saints, sages, and masters as ecstasy, the peace that surpasses understanding, bliss: nirvana. Here, words fail. The Love of God has to be experienced.

When we cooperate with the command to love and do our work, there is a radical transformation of consciousness. God's cosmic broom sweeps away junk thoughts, harsh emotions, and restless discontent. A flowing river of healing energy gently overpowers the ego. The veil of ordinary human consciousness lifts and separation ends. We enter the house of Love. Here we experience light, intuitive knowledge, unfathomable stillness, and ecstatic joy. We feel safe, secure, and immortal. The feeling is exquisite! We want to stay forever, but we return to ordinary consciousness, since there is more work to do. We are never the same, however: the memory of ecstatic Love marks our return. One taste of Divine Love is addicting. Hooked for eternity, we yearn for more forever. We are willing to do whatever it takes to get more until we become pure Love. Then we can return to our true home and stay forever.

Unconditional Love is the greatest force in the universe. It breaks down the barriers and walls between us. In its presence, over time, all that is not Love dissolves. It is the glue that binds together the fragments of our inner and outer lives. It eliminates anxiety, distrust, depression, indifference, apathy, frustration, and anger. It harmonizes our relationships and all of the events of our lives.

Everyone has a uniquely individual Love story. There is no end to Love's variety as it plays through each of our stories, leading us through trials to higher ground. As the story unfolds, we discover Love is the means and the end. Love is the way to God and Love is God.

We see the Teacher of Love calling us to cultivate compassion in response to all of the events in our lives. Every scene and every moment is a lesson from God, beckoning us to join Her in Her temple of Love.

Every person and thing is a window through which we can see God. When we are in Love, the universe reveals its secret truths and hidden magic. Love is the Mother of the Universe, the Healer of healers, the Power of powers. It can transform any problem into knowledge and wisdom. It gives us the necessary traction to move through our barriers. It is the healing force that can change the world. When we are in Love, everything falls into place. Love is the only religion. Where there is Love, there is God. This is the law of Love.

TECHNIQUES

We live in an infinite ocean of pure Love, an actual field of perfect energy. We are in it, and it is in us. It is in every cell of our bodies, in every atom, and in all space. In ordinary states of consciousness, however, we do not feel it. Our pain and problems cause us to feel separate.

Although we feel separate, we can access Love and use it as the universal balm for any problem. Following are some exercises that can help us connect to that Love. By practicing these and other exercises, we can prove to ourselves that Love is the most powerful force in our lives.

BURNING KARMA IN THE FIRE OF LOVE

The fire of Love is strong enough to move us through any barrier, if we love God with all of our heart, mind, might, and soul, and our neighbors as ourselves. To make Love an active force in your life, follow these steps:

1. Introspect
2. Invoke
3. Affirm
4. Visualize
5. Serve
6. Repeat
7. Transform

1. INTROSPECT

Following is a partial list of barriers that interfere with our ability to give and receive Love. See if you can recognize which of these have a negative effect in your life currently. At any point during your day, mindfully identify any obstacle that interferes with your ability to love.

- a. restless mind
- b. highly reactive emotions
- c. excessive material desire and attachments
- d. bad habits
- e. hyperactivity
- f. fear of being alone
- g. too dependent on others
- h. physical pain
- i. the ego and narcissism
- j. poor pain management
- k. denial of problems
- l. character flaws
- m. negative attitude
- n. feeling unworthy, guilty, ashamed, self-hatred
- o. feeling rejected, abandoned and humiliated
- p. hatred
- q. prejudice: judging others by their role, body, personality, age, race, religion, sexual identity, nationality, economic class, or disability
- r. indifference or boredom
- s. fixed false religious beliefs
- t. fear of the unknown and death
- u. other painful problems

2. INVOKE

Invoke the presence of God's Love. It is always available inside, outside, and everywhere as the universal balm for any pain or problem.

3. AFFIRM

"Love is the most powerful force in life." "I am in the ocean of Love." "I am all of the qualities in the spiritual alphabet." "The God of Love is one. The polarizing forces of hatred, conflict, and frustration cannot touch Her."

4. VISUALIZE

Visualize Love in your heart as a flame of light. Visualize the Love-light spreading to every cell in your body, to all people, nations, creatures, and ultimately to all creation. Picture the light melting every barrier. Feel the Love burn up all that is not Love inside, outside, everywhere.

5. SERVE

When you practice this exercise, your expanded and purified Love saturates your thoughts, feelings, and actions. Small acts of gentle, humble service are the natural result. You can give your Love in every action to all whom you meet.

6. REPEAT

We are either in Love, or something else: a large category filled with all kinds of problems that do not go away so easily. When anything shows up that is not Love, repeat steps 1-5 until you become Love itself. This is a lifelong project. Do not give up. Persevere and practice. The reward is great.

7. TRANSFORM

The reward is ever-increasing soul qualities such as contentment, harmony, and strength. When our Love is strong enough, it eventually breaks into the peace that surpasses understanding, pure light, and ecstatic joy.

EXPANDING LOVE IN MEDITATION

We do not love everybody all of the time. God does. We can improve our ability to love by communing with God in the stillness of meditation. Review the technique for meditation described in Chapter 15. Recall steps eight and nine.

Step 8: ABSORPTION: The ever-increasing stillness bred of meditation brings the body and mind to a state of deep peace and relaxation. When you stop superficial thought long enough to be immersed in stillness, relax and feel the peace. Do not think. In this state of opened, quiet receptivity and stillness, spiritual qualities grow, the ego reduces, and problems burn up.

Step 9: PRAYER: Toward the end of your meditation, you can commune with your Higher Power, seeking guidance, protection, or healing for yourself and others. You can close your meditation with a prayer for all who need help, and for peace between all individuals, nations, races, and religions.

Now you can practice the following exercise:
1. Meditation
2. Absorption
3. Prayer
4. Purification and expansion
5. Action
6. Repetition

1. MEDITATION

Practice your technique of meditation. Bring in as much stillness as you can.

2. ABSORPTION

In the ever-increasing stillness of deep meditation, think of the people in your life who are difficult to love. Include family, friends, neighbors, colleagues, strangers, and enemies. Place them and yourself in a bouquet. Offer the bouquet to God.

3. PRAYER

"Lord, purify and expand my Love. I cannot do it. You can. I need Your help, grace, and blessing. Create a space large enough in me to hold all. Eliminate all barriers that impede the flow of Your infinitely compassionate, all-understanding Love."

4. PURIFICATION AND EXPANSION

Relax, stay open, wait, and be patient. In stillness, you will experience your connection to the source of Love. Feel Love surround, permeate, and purify every cell and fiber of your being. Visualize Love expanding to include your troubled relationships, your family, friends, all people, and all of creation. Bathe in the sacred healing pool of Love as long as you can. Here, soul qualities replace all traces of negativity.

5. ACTION

Bring your expanded and purified Love to all you meet. Send affirmations of Love and kindness to your friends, family, strangers, and enemies. Let your generosity flow in every interaction. Help everyone.

6. REPEAT

In meditation, ego and problems burn up and soul qualities expand. This is a life-long process. Repeat this purification and expansion process until only Love is there.

LOVE EVERYONE EQUALLY

We place people in categories according to their roles in life, body type, age, race, religion, nationality, sexual identity, educational level, and economic class. We are attracted to some, repelled by others, and indifferent to the rest. In the spiritual world, everyone is equal. No one is above or below another. We can work against attraction, repulsion, and indifference by giving Love freely and equally to all. We cannot get to God otherwise; this is where She lives.

1. OBSERVE

Observe what qualities attract and repel you. Notice how body type, age, clothes, weight, size, race, religion, sexual identity, or nationality determine whether you are attracted, repelled, or indifferent.

2. AFFIRM

"I treat each person as God in disguise." "I respond to every person with even-minded Love." "I bow to the image of God within you." "I worship the Lord equally in every body-temple." "I bow to the manifestation of Divine Mother before me right now." "I serve the manifestation of the Divine Mother before me right now." "I see the face of God in every face." "I see the Cosmic Mother in every face." "I see the Cosmic Mother everywhere."

3. REPEAT

Repeat this technique until you can give your Love equally to all people.

THIRTY WAYS TO PRACTICE LOVE

1. Introspection: Avoid criticism and judgment of others. Instead, work at being a better person by reforming yourself. When you become critical of others, tell your mind to be quiet. Instead of judging them, work to reform yourself by cultivating Love.
2. The golden rule: Do unto others as you would have them do unto you.
3. Understanding: Slow down and go deep. Think about others. Try to understand why people do what they do.
4. Awareness: Be aware and sensitive to the needs of others.
5. Compassion: This includes compassion for others when they make mistakes, just as you would have in return.
6. Self-control: Learn to cool off your own emotions so you do not spread pain to other people in acts of unkindness or aggression.
7. Peace: Cultivate peace, the platform upon which Love is built.

8. Joy: Cultivate Love, the platform upon which joy is built.
9. Relationship: Be an unconditional friend. Friendship is a way to cement Love in our relationships.
10. Wisdom: Concentrate on the thoughts of saints and sages. Bring their wisdom into your life.
11. Spiritual practice: Jesus said that the Kingdom of Heaven is within. To find Love inside, practice mindfulness, meditation, and the presence of God.
12. Solitude: Learn how to be alone.
13. Balance: Create a balance between being with people and being alone.
14. Prayer: Give your energy to others through affirmations of Love and kindness during prayer.
15. Listen: Open your receptor sites. Reflect on what others are going through.
16. Surrender: Learn how to accept that which you cannot change with deep serenity.
17. Equality: Understand your true position as equal to all people.
18. Accountability: With Love as the standard, you are accountable for identifying and transforming bad habits, destructive emotions, excessive material desires, and the sly tricks of the ego, all of which disrupt your ability to Love.
19. Spaciousness: Spaciousness is expanding the room inside yourself to hold others in all of their folly. Understanding creates more space. This does not mean we accept negative behavior. We need to set limits when others violate our boundaries. We can set outer limits and create inner space at the same time.
20. Boundaries: Love includes protection. The bottom line is safety for the self and others. We defend the boundary of Love by setting limits.
21. Service: We can work against selfishness by thinking about how to improve our Love and service a little bit more each day. Connecting to others through service promotes healing.

22. Concentration: When we do not listen carefully, we are not in Love. A calm, focused mind repaired and healed by meditation and mindfulness helps us understand.

23. Intimacy: Love is holding on. Distance and detachment can be an excuse to avoid the suffering of intimacy. True learning occurs in the trenches. How else can we correct our flaws, if not in the daily grind of relationships?

24. Detachment: Love is letting go. Clinging and enmeshment stunt our growth.

25. Oneness: God is one. Love is one. Live as though there is only One Person here.

26. Soul qualities: Love is all of the spiritual qualities. If we cultivate any spiritual quality, our Love grows.

27. Pain management: We need to work with and through our pain to expand and purify our Love. The inner connection to Love and safety can only come if we face all of our troubles. Our suffering leads to inner strength and wisdom if we endure with courage.

28. Open: You love best when you are relaxed, opened, listening, and empathetic.

29. Communication: With good communication, we solve our problems. Everything falls into place.

30. Learn: Learning to love is a lifelong process.

THE WAY TO SUPERCONSCIOUS LOVE: AN AFFIRMATION

I am here to bring out my Love and the Love of other people.
I do not do this by working on others,
I do this by working on myself.
Love is about self-reform and self-mastery.
It is not about other people's behavior.
It is about how I respond to them.
I do not worry about others.
I do not expect or need others to behave in a certain way.

I do not try to get Love from others.
This is what makes me vulnerable.
I find Love within myself and give it to others.
This is what makes me strong.

In the end, I am Love.
I can give only that,
Free and content no matter the outer condition.
This is the way to superconscious Love.

POINTS TO REMEMBER

- The command to love is at the center of every great tradition. We are to love, serve, and give. We are here to learn how to take the high ground of understanding, compassion, and forgiveness, even when treated poorly.
- The command to love is as clear as can be. We are to love God with all of our heart, mind, might, and soul, and our neighbor as ourselves. Nothing is excluded. When something other than Love surfaces, it has to go. There are no exceptions or exclusions. This makes it both easy and hard. It is easy because the mission is absolutely clear, and hard because there is much within that we must eliminate.
- In response to any problem, we can cultivate Love. This gives us the necessary traction to move through any barrier. This is the law of Love. We can prove it through practice.
- We need the ego to establish ourselves in the world. At some point, however, we need to reduce the ego, think less about ourselves and more about others.
- When we look for Love on the outside, we are vulnerable: we may or may not get it. We already have what we need. When we learn how to love within ourselves, we are in a position of strength.
- We can use Love continuously as a powerful healing force in our lives.

- God is the Love that was there in the beginning and will be there in the end. It embraces all people, creatures, and creation. It is the cohesive force that holds everything together. The Love of God is here unconditionally embracing, understanding, and forgiving no matter what we have done. We come from, live in, and ultimately return to Her Love.

- Our bodies, personality, race, education, religion, sexual identity, status, role, flaws, problems, mistakes, and illness are but costumes disguising our true identity. Underneath all of these layers and identifications is our true self, the image of God, the image of Love. We are Love.

- Selflessness is selfish, since it gives the best feeling.

- Serenity, sweetness of speech, and compassionate acts of kindness are healing powers.

- For inspiration, we can go to church, synagogue, or mosque, listen to sermons, participate in rituals, sing, chant, meditate, and practice mindfulness. Then we need to translate our inspiration into acts of loving kindness and service.

- Every action is worship if done in Love.

- When we make an effort to bring more Love and kindness into the world no matter how the world treats us, we are making progress.

- To love God is to love Love.

- Love is built on truth. There can be no deception to others or ourselves.

- God reduces Her almighty power to the tender, sweet, gentle Love that She is. She gives me that. I give that in turn.

- We cannot get to God's Love with words. He is in the stillness. When we go there and come back, we find words inadequate to describe it.

AFFIRMATIONS

- I express God's sweet, gentle Love to all I meet.

- I am not seeking Love from you. I am in Love.

- No matter how the world treats me, I respond with Love and kindness.
- I live, move, and have my being in Love.
- Love permeates every atom, cell, and molecule of my being.
- Love is the guiding force of my evolving story.
- Love is the most powerful force in the universe.
- Love is greater than any pain.
- Love burns karma: mine, yours, and ours.
- Love, Love, only Love.
- I love myself, God, and others completely and unconditionally.
- I am a part of everything because I love.
- A boundless Love watches over me through all of life's experiences.
- I respond to cruelty with kindness.
- I respond to harsh words with sweetness of speech.
- I send Love and kindness to those who hurt me.
- I act in kindness to those passed up by others.
- Warmth is the word of the day.
- I love you as you are.
- I love myself as I am.
- I channel every word and act through warmth and gentleness.
- Show me the problem. I show you the Love.
- Love + Intelligence = God = Wisdom.
- I receive the Love of God. I give the Love of God.

EXERCISES

1. What is the command to love?
2. What is the difference between human love and God's Love?
3. Name the barriers that inhibit your ability to give and receive Love.
4. Describe and practice the following techniques:
   a. Burning karma in the fire of Love
   b. Expanding Love in meditation
   c. Love everyone equally
5. Review and practice the thirty ways to love.

CHAPTER 24

PEACE

The Changeless Peace of the Soul

We want eternal peace. We seek it in a world of people, places, things, and activities. However, our search for a lasting peace in the ever-changing external world is in vain. No amount of money, fame, or power will satisfy our inner craving for eternal peace. In our persistent effort to find peace in the external world, we develop bad habits which only add to our suffering. Furthermore, as described in step 5, the six tools that help us achieve a degree of peace in the world can cause us to spin out of control. The restless mind, reactive moods, uncontrolled desires, physical problems, hyperactivity, and egotism steal from our peace and deepen our troubles.

Our suffering causes us to seek and question. Our search takes us to the wisdom of the ages in sacred texts. Here we learn that the peace we seek is inside. God is an infinite ocean of peace; the soul, the reflection of God in us, is peace. Changeless peace is everywhere, all around us, and inside. It is the ground of all being.

We already have the deep, permanent peace we seek. It is always with us, inside. We can dwell there every moment of our lives. No condition of the world or body can touch it. To find this unlimited peace, we must look inside. If we do not find it here, we will not find it.

The permanent peace of the soul is our natural state, our true self, and our birthright. We can have soul peace no matter what condition befalls us; however, we must do some work. We must introspect, face reality, and solve our problems. We must conquer our bad habits, restless mind, reactive moods, excessive desires, and egotism. We must go beneath the superficial waves of the world, slow down, and go inside. We must love and serve. In short, to get the lasting peace of the soul we need to skillfully manage our suffering and develop a spiritual practice. If we do the work, our peace slowly expands until it becomes permanent. Following is a suggested pathway to the immutable peace of the soul.

TEN STEPS TO SOUL PEACE

1. Solitude
2. Introspection
3. Contemplation
4. Affirmations
5. Meditation
6. Mindfulness
7. Practicing the presence of God
8. Love and service
9. Grace
10. Peace of the soul

1. SOLITUDE

When we suffer, we turn to the world for support and relief. While it is obviously good to have the support of wise, compassionate people and meaningful activities, an important part of spiritual growth is shifting the locus of control from outside to inside. At times of crisis, the ultimate defense is the deep peace of the soul. To attain this, we need quiet time alone for introspection, contemplation of spiritual wisdom, affirmations, and meditation.

Our addiction to the outer life makes it difficult to retreat. Cultivating the new ground of solitude is akin to withdrawing from a substance of abuse like alcohol or drugs. When we retreat, we may feel anxious and crave our habitual pattern of activities. If we answer the call of this craving too quickly and fail to go through the rigors of withdrawal, we will not bring the critical element of solitude into our program. It may be difficult or impossible to find the perpetual peace of the soul unless we have periods of retreat for introspection, spiritual study, and meditation.

2. INTROSPECTION

Instead of running to our favorite escape such as television, the internet, radio, food, sex, shopping, or golf, we can sit in quiet solitude and look inside. If we stay with the feelings that come up, we discover what we have been avoiding: painful emotions, bad memories, flaws, mistakes, fear of loss, fear of the abyss, fear of death, and fear of fear. These painful problems arrive in the school of life to get our attention and show us where to work. We can work on these problems with any of the spiritual practices described in this book. When we do the work, we get peace. Peace is the ground of all being. It is on the other side of every painful problem.

In order to build durable peace, we must face all of our problems. We must go through whatever comes our way. We have to work through every layer of pain. If we avoid a problem, it continues to show up in different forms, directing us to necessary work. If we do the work, our peace slowly expands. Eventually, we can remain at peace under all conditions, including the transition to the great unknown: death.

Staying in the pain is not just a good idea. It is the bridge between attachment, dependency, and addiction, or spiritual power. When the going gets rough, we panic, drop the experience, and escape to one of our worldly habits. On the other hand, if we ride every wave of pain until it dissipates, our peace expands until it becomes permanent.

Attaining immutable peace is a tall order. We need some additional tools. Following is a brief review of contemplation, affirmations, meditation, mindfulness, practicing the presence of God, Love, and service. With these practices and grace, our painful problems eventually melt into the unlimited peace of the soul and Spirit.

3. CONTEMPLATION

Contemplation of sacred wisdom helps us manage the problems and fears we discover through introspection. Review Chapter 14 on contemplation. Study a passage from your favorite sacred book related to peace of mind under all conditions. Then practice even-minded peace throughout the day.

4. AFFIRMATIONS

In retreat and in activity, we can repeat affirmations of peace. The repetition or chanting of the affirmation helps us maintain peace of mind no matter what happens. Choose one or a combination of the following affirmations, or make up your own.

- I am calm.
- am poised.
- I am peaceful.
- I am patient.
- Peace is everywhere.
- I swim in the ocean of peace.
- Peace expands and fills my body and all space around me.
- Peace flows through every thought, feeling, and action.
- Peace flows through every cell in my body.
- I am a peace warrior.
- I stand serene in the center of life's storms.
- I never lose my peace.
- I am in the peace of the soul no matter what comes to me.
- Peace is in every movement of my body.
- All of my worries dissolve in the light of my powerful, peace thoughts.
- I choose peace in all situations.
- Peace is the order of this day.
- Peace flows through me like a gentle wind.
- Peace eliminates worries.
- Peace eliminates my mental restlessness.
- Peace vitalizes every cell of my body.

- Peace is inside and outside, left and right, above and below, in front and behind ... everywhere.
- I do everything with peace.
- I stay deep in the ocean of peace, below the choppy surface waves that try to bait me.
- No one can steal my peace.
- Nothing can touch me.
- Nothing can ruffle me.
- It does not matter what the world or my body does. I am at peace.
- The rougher it gets, the softer I get.
- I inundate my mind with constant inner thoughts of peace.
- I affirm continuous peace.

5. MEDITATION:

The ultimate retreat is in the stillness of meditation. Here we find the deepest peace. There is more peace here than in any worldly activity. To get to this peace, we must clear out the accumulated debris from the world such as restlessness, worry, and ruminations about our problems. The Bible says, "Be still and know that I am God." (psalm 46:10) The peace of the soul and Spirit is there, in the stillness.

We can commune with God in meditation and get His peace. When we detach from the choppy surface waves of His ocean and enter the deep stillness below, we know His peace as the foundation of the universe.

6. MINDFULNESS

We can practice the presence of peace in every waking moment of our lives. Practicing the presence of peace during activity is meditation in action, or mindfulness. When we are restless and distracted, we lose contact with our serenity. To counter this, we can use breathing and affirmations related to peace in response to all events.

When the chaotic world enters our life and we respond with a chaotic mind, we can follow these four steps:

    a.   Stop: the first step is to realize that our mind is in a chaotic or negative state.

    b.   Breathe: take several slow, deep, abdominal breaths.

    c.   Affirm: use one or several of the affirmations above to help return the mind to its natural state of peace and poise.

    d.   Act: We can perform every action in the presence of peace.

7.   PRACTICING THE PRESENCE OF GOD AS PEACE

God's peace is Omnipresent, eternal, infinite, and perfect. It is the underlying force behind all creation. We can get a glimpse of the harmonious operations of this cosmic power in the balanced movements of the planets and galaxies and in the beauty of nature: flowers, sunsets, oceans, mountains, and sky. We can align ourselves with this great power by practicing the presence of God as peace in every action.

When the mind is restless, follow these steps:

    a.   Stop: realize the mind is restless or negative.

    b.   Breathe: take several slow, deep, abdominal breaths.

    c.   Affirm: Affirm the presence of God as the Omnipotent peace that rules the universe and the beauty that infuses nature.

    d.   Act: Perform every action in the presence of that peace.

Omnipresent peace permeates every millimeter of space. The more we focus on peace, the more we will feel it in our lives. Eventually we stay deep in the ocean of peace, no matter what happens on the surface.

8.   LOVE AND SERVICE

Practicing selfless service reduces the ego and cultivates soul-peace. Our personal difficulties dry up and blow away in the face of Love and service. Where there is loving service, there is peace. This is divine law.

9. GRACE

God manifests changeless peace amid the most turbulent conditions. By Her grace, we can be in this peace. First we must do our part. In solitude, we can introspect, contemplate, affirm, and meditate. In activity, we can be mindful, practice the presence of God, love, and serve. With these practices, we purify our consciousness and help other people. With determination and will, we do our best and never give up. Slowly, peace expands.

To get to the perfect peace of the soul, however, we need help. As we do our part, we can submit our problems to our Higher Power, asking for inner calm. With practice, our peace slowly expands until it is strong enough to weather the trials of life. This peace, this stillness, is a gift from God.

10. PEACE OF THE SOUL

Buried underneath the rubble of our personal problems is the perfect peace of the soul. The soul is the witness. The witness is still, silent, spacious, and serene. Neither the world nor body can touch us here. No pain, desire, impulse, or fear can enter. This is our haven. It is always at the center of our being. We can take shelter here no matter what happens. Nothing can be more important than finding changeless peace within. When we know this place, we need not fear any condition.

We can slowly work our way to this peace by practicing retreat, introspection, contemplation, affirmations, meditation, mindfulness, the presence of God, and loving service. With these practices and God's grace, we learn how to live in the world and simultaneously maintain peace and poise. Then we are a force of peace in the world.

At mastery, we can stay deep in the ocean of peace, unaffected by the turbulence of the surface waves of change. We know God inside as perfect peace, and outside as the infinite peace that rules the universe. When we learn how to be quiet within, we can experience the Changeless One who underlies all creation.

PRAYER OF ST. FRANCIS OF ASSISI

Lord, make me an instrument of Your peace:
Where there is hatred let me sow love;
Where there is injury, pardon;
Where there is doubt, faith;
Where there is despair, hope;
Where there is darkness, light;
Where there is sadness, joy.

O Divine Master, grant that I may not so much seek
To be consoled as to console;
To be understood as to understand;
To be loved as to love;
For it is in giving that we receive;
It is in pardoning that we are pardoned,
And it is in dying that we are born to eternal life.

POINTS TO REMEMBER

- There are three layers: events, our ego's reaction to events, and the perfect peace of the soul. The middle layer, our reaction, is very powerful. We need to take away its power and give it to the soul. All of the spiritual methods described in this work reduce egotistical reactivity and expand the peace of the soul. We can cultivate soul-peace in response to problems by practicing solitude, introspection, contemplation, affirmations, meditation, mindfulness, the presence of God, and loving service.
- Peace is the platform upon which all other spiritual qualities are built.
- We can dwell in the peace of the soul no matter what happens. It is our home in pain and pleasure, success and failure, health and disease, life and death. This elevated state of consciousness is accomplished through surrender or acceptance. We can use every event to bring us closer to our soul-peace. In this sense, everything is a blessing.

- God is peace. If we perform an action in peace, we are with God.

- We can train our minds to remain calm under all conditions.

- When we have inner peace, we are more skillful, successful, loving, understanding, and receptive. We worry less, enjoy more, have better health, and get along better with others. We are more perceptive, make better decisions, and solve more problems.

- The God of peace is trying to show you deeper levels of peace than you have ever known. However, He cannot speak when you are restless. Meditate. Stop the world, body, senses, and mind. Be still and know Him as the peace that surpasses understanding.

EXERCISES

1. Popular media promotes fast-paced reality based on consumer spending, material consciousness, hero worship, youth, sex, power, money, and violence. These images enter our consciousness, speed up our minds, and undermine our common humanity. Take a break from your usual routine. Do a media fast. Reduce or eliminate television, the radio, magazines, newspapers, and use of the computer.

2. Reduce your addictions. Review the lesson on habits. Use these principles to reduce your addictive behaviors to drugs, alcohol, food, cigarettes, television, power, people, sex, money, and work. These habits and attachments may help you avoid your problems and give you a false sense of security. However, these same problems will return later to haunt you with more force and vigor.

3. Take some time for retreat and reflection. In solitude, ask yourself what you are running from.

4. Practice the ten steps to soul-peace or design a similar program for yourself. Practice daily. Keep going. Realize ever-deeper levels of peace.

CHAPTER 25

HUMILITY

The Mother of All Virtues

We are tiny, infinitesimal specks in the universe. The ego puffs up that speck to make it look like the grandest thing that has ever happened. Confusing its little story with the whole of reality, the ego leads us into the blind alley of self-importance and arrogance. We can counter this by learning humility, the greatest of all spiritual virtues.

Humility takes us to our true identity, the soul connected to Spirit. The true self is compassionate, kind, and courageous. However, the false god of ego blocks our awareness of the soul, keeps us separate from Spirit, and prevents us from experiencing higher states of consciousness. To become who we really are, we must reduce the ego by cultivating humility. The antidote to the ego, humility, is the key that unlocks the door to the soul and God. Without it, there can be no entrance.

In this lesson, there is a description of seven routes to humility: self-reform, Omniscience, equality, service, Love, darkness, and knowing our place.

THE WAY OF SELF-REFORM

The only way to advance to higher Love is to find our flaws and fix them. The ego inhibits this work, trying to be right and look good all the time. It is afraid to look within and uncover imperfections. It is unable to give up its power without embarrassment and humiliation. Nevertheless, what we give up in egotistical power we gain in spiritual power. The spiritual way is ego reduction and the expansion of soul qualities.

To reduce the ego, we stop blaming, criticizing, judging, and trying to change others. We understand that the best way to change others is to reform ourselves. We become students, always ready to learn. We listen to feedback from others and from our conscience. We identify our mistakes and flaws, but they do not define us. Our problems are simply signposts on the road to the soul and Spirit. The work is cultivation of spiritual qualities.

Life teaches humility when we open to the lessons. It takes courage to look inside and make the necessary changes. When we do the work of introspection, the humiliation of the ego transforms into the humility of the soul.

THE WAY OF OMNISCIENCE: INTELLECTUAL HUMILITY

Intellectual humility is knowledge of our true and rightful place in the universe. God is vast. We are tiny but not insignificant. We are made in the image of God. We are co-creators. We have power, free will, and a role to play. Our job is to manifest and express God's greatness by ridding our consciousness of its egotistical impurities and cultivating His qualities.

To gain perspective, drive your little bus of knowledge to the border of the infinite unknown and look out the window. There you will find countless illustrations of the intelligent power that runs the universe. For example, imagine the earth rotating on its own axis every 24 hours at 1000 mph, around the sun at 60,000 mph, while moving as part of our galaxy at 600,000 mph. The earth travels in mathematically precise harmony, rhythm, and balance with the other planets and stars. The ride is smooth. There are no bumps. We don't feel any movement. The ocean's water does not spill into space. No matter where we are on the planet, we think we are on "top," yet those on the "bottom" do not fall off.

The creative power of the universe is Omniscient. It is inside, outside, and everywhere. It operates on every level of creation. It permeates every centimeter of space. It runs the cells of our body while holding the universe together. We move, live, and have our being in this infinite ocean of intelligence. Although we cannot be outside of its presence, neither can we plumb its depth: our human intelligence can take us only so far. Even the IQ of a genius is puny in comparison.

No matter how much knowledge we accumulate, what we do not know remains infinite. The sum total of everything we know individually and collectively remains infinitesimal compared to the infinite knowledge of God. God's knowledge will always be infinitely beyond our grasp. God knows everything. We know very little. Yet the ego persists in projecting its tiny speck of knowledge as the nature of reality.

To combat the ego and maintain a humble stance, we can focus on God's infinite intelligence. Omniscience permeates atoms, galaxies, and us. All we have to do is remember. Even when we forget, we are only a thought away.

The self-important ego gets us into trouble by overestimating its knowledge. However, we can view the world with one eye on our knowledge and the other on the unknown. In this way, we remain at the actual boundary of our current knowledge and the mysteries of life. With this receptive stance, we recognize when we do not know the answers. When we know our true place in this mysterious, infinitely intelligent universe, there can be but one response: humility.

THE WAY OF EQUALITY

In the world of roles, there are divisions with status determined by wealth, education, position, age, power, race, religion, or sexual identity. Our egos get caught up in competition. As we surf the waves of success and failure, we develop feelings of superiority and inferiority. The perception of superiority is associated with arrogance, pride, and domination. Feelings of inferiority breed insecurity, anxiety, and doubt. Some people suffer from both states. Equality and its partner, humility, are healing powers that cure these ills. We approach true humility when we see ourselves as equal to others, not better or worse.

In the spiritual world, all are equally included in the circle of Love. Role and status have little importance. We look neither up nor down but across, eye to eye, squarely, honestly. The realization of our equality in God's Love gives us humility, a source of deep peace and strength.

THE WAY OF SERVICE

The ego strives for greatness in the world. The way of the soul is simple acts of humble service to humanity. In humility, we make no distinctions, equally serving the mighty and the meek. Small, anonymous acts of service mark the true path of Love. Humility grounded in unselfish Love is the mother of all powers. Without it, no virtue can grow. The way to God is paved with acts of selfless service.

THE WAY OF LOVE

As we advance on the path of self-healing through ego reduction and the cultivation of soul qualities, the mind and heart become increasingly quiet. Patience, kindness, and gentleness expand. We have more space inside. We are content, receptive, understanding, and forgiving.

Progressively anchored to the soul, we are able to accomplish something very difficult and profoundly needed: an ever-increasing ability to tolerate the problems and provocations of other people. We find ourselves reacting less to what other people do. We are more gracious in the face of their limitations. We yield to opposing views, insults, condemnation, even malice. We have no need to defend ourselves, even when we are right, because we do not feel threatened.

Humility does not imply enabling others to be abusive. We continue to give feedback, set limits, and maintain boundaries. However, we are often unnecessarily reactive. The highly volatile ego defends its territory at the slightest provocation. The soul knows when to react and when to absorb.

We can make a small contribution to healing the world by accepting the pain of others without reacting. Steadfast and firm in the face of provocation, we can transmute our own and others' pain with our

Love. When we refrain from adding fuel to their fire, others have a better chance of successfully dealing with their own problems. When we respond to other people's problems with patience, kindness, and understanding, we reduce the suffering of the world and fulfill the destiny of the soul.

THE WAY OF DARKNESS

On the way to spiritual knowledge, some of us pass through the cave of darkness, a place of severe pain where we face the unknown, death, and/or evil without immediate answers to our questions. War, ethnic cleansing, racism, domestic violence, rape, child sex abuse, and other horrific conditions can bring us to this cave of darkness. Here our spiritual belief systems come under their most rigorous challenge. This is a critical place: If our sacred knowledge holds here, it will hold anywhere.

There are many classrooms in the school of life but none like this. The training here is fierce. The cave is dark. All evidence of spiritual life is gone. The world seems to be against us. There is no solace from our usual sources of family, friends, work, the arts, or recreation. Sometimes even going to church, synagogue, or mosque brings no relief. We feel alone, separate, powerless, and frightened.

In the face of major crisis, we ask the big questions. Why are we here? Is this a moral, benevolent universe? If God's Love is Omnipotent, why is there so much suffering and evil in the world? Do good and justice ultimately triumph? Life on the physical plane does not give easy answers to these questions. Some believe in karma and reincarnation as the explanation for ultimate justice. Others remain mystified. In any case, we need something to hold on to as we go through our trials and face the abyss.

We need something that can get us through these conditions, however long or severe, something more powerful than the worst scenarios life can bring. But what if harsh reality challenges and ultimately strips away our illusions and belief, leaving us in despair?

Who can we turn to if we experience only turmoil and questioning? Does God's Love exist in the cave of darkness?

While we may not understand why there is so much suffering and evil, we can accept horror and tragedy as part of the mystery. We can accept our current condition as the next step in our spiritual development. We can have faith that God wants us to transform our suffering into spiritual power. We can accept pain as a teacher and stimulant for the growth of spiritual qualities. Though we are not sure where we are going, we can ask for help from the God of infinite compassion and wisdom. We can follow the path guided by Love. We can trust that He knows what He is doing.

To work our way through extreme conditions, we will need to build an infrastructure of patience, courage, strength, and endurance. We can do this by developing and maintaining our spiritual practice. No matter how rough it gets, our job is to persist. If we do the work, eventually the Light of Spirit enters the cave of darkness bearing gifts of peace, joy, and wisdom.

In the cave of darkness, we lose our illusion of control and safety. We fall through the cracks in our belief system and hit what seems to be the bottom, a spiritual ground zero where we experience fear associated with the unknown. Although we may feel helpless, we persist in our spiritual practice. We yearn, work, search, and persevere. Because of our efforts, strength grows and grace follows. Omniscient Love, bearing gifts of protection and peace, comes to our rescue. Through our work and God's grace, we discover that the ground of all being is not the unknown and terror, but Omniscient Love and peace.

This is the way to humility through the cave of darkness. It cannot be taught. It must come from experiencing the transformation of suffering and powerlessness to serenity and security through grace. God comes to our rescue by resurrecting our feeling of safety. Then we know that our peace is a gift from the mysterious, wonderful power of God; we are nothing but for His grace. Jesus said, "Of myself I can do nothing. The Father who dwells in me, He does the work."

KNOWING OUR PLACE

In humility, we know where we are on the spiritual path. We have a realistic view of our strengths, progress, limitations, and the work that remains. This may not be as easy as it sounds. All too often we use our spiritual belief system to provide all of the answers. Thinking we have discovered the truth, we elevate ourselves above others and become arrogant. Identifying ourselves as special, chosen, or children of God while others are excluded, we deny our problems and delude ourselves into thinking that we are already complete.

We can invoke the image of God as our true self, but not at the expense of losing awareness of our limitations. We should not think that we are complete just because we have joined a religion or walk on a spiritual path. We do not have all the answers, and we do not need them. We embrace the unknown as a source of wisdom, strength, and peace. Change is a slow process. We understand our relationship to God. We know that we cannot move a finger, take a step, breathe, see, think, or digest food without Her power. In humility, we ask for help in becoming free of the ego, which prevents us from knowing God.

God cannot get into the body temple when it is filled with junk products of the ego such as selfish desires, volatile emotions, fear, pride, or the denial of problems. To create a channel for the flow of God's power, we need to reduce and ultimately eliminate the ego and replace it with soul qualities. Then, in the stillness and quiet of meditation, we can hear the sweet voice of Love whispering, "Welcome. You are at the brink of eternity. Become nothing and nobody. Then you will be one with Me, with everything, and everybody. This is the power of humility. Ask for help in all you do." Grace cannot flow without humility. Know where you are on the spiritual path.

THE PRAYER OF AN UNKNOWN CONFEDERATE SOLDIER

I asked God for strength that I might achieve.
I was made weak that I might learn humbly to obey.

I asked for health that I might do greater things.
I was given infirmity that I might do better things.

I asked for riches that I might be happy.
I was given poverty that I might be wise.

I asked for power that I might have the praise of men.
I was given weakness that I might feel the need of God.

I asked for all things that I might enjoy life.
I was given life that I might enjoy all things.

I got nothing that I asked for, but everything I hoped for.
Almost despite myself, my unspoken prayers were answered.

I am, among all men, most richly blessed.

POINTS TO REMEMBER

- God cannot get into the body-temple when it is filled with a restless mind, reactive emotions, and egotistical desires. We can experience the gentle sweetness of Her grace when we are soft and yielding, surrendered and meek. Bow down. Get low. Be still and empty where the grace of God can flow.

- We can counter pride, arrogance, and entitlement with humility and gratitude. We can endure injury with a patient, quiet heart. We can counter criticism and judgment with acceptance and support. We can counter condemnation with forgiveness. Soft is more powerful than hard.

- In spiritual reality, we do not actually own anything. All of our possessions are gifts on temporary loan from on high. Everything is a gift. We own nothing. Recognize the blessing and be grateful.

- The ego builds its empire on a foundation of control and power. The soul knows that the foundation of a spiritual life is Love and service. There is no place to go and nothing to do but Love and serve. The humble servant goes everywhere, helping everyone indiscriminately.

- Humility is patient and kind, tolerant and understanding, meek yet firm.
- The one you are with is the most important person in the world, the image of God, nay, God Herself.
- All of the lessons of life teach humility, but we must be awake. Otherwise, we miss the lesson.
- The quiet, lowly places are where we can find the peace of God. Most look for it in the high places. Spiritual experiences are possible there too: they can occur anywhere. However, if you graze in the lowland, stop and listen for a time, you will discover the peace and sweetness of humility. Humility is the mother of all virtue.

AFFIRMATIONS

- Humility is my temple, the cradle of wisdom.
- Equality brings peace and strength.
- I am nobody in particular.
- I let others discover my good qualities without my help.
- I find peace and contentment in humility and equality.
- I am a beginner every single moment.
- I progress because I know what I do not know.
- I ask to become a better person, not for more things.
- I ask for nothing more than inner contentment.
- I follow the lessons of life, all of which teach humility.
- Humility gives strength and serenity.
- Humility gives contentment and satisfaction.
- Humility brings me closer to God and humanity.
- Humility is Love.
- Humility is the path to Truth.

- I am learning humility under all conditions of life: success and failure, health and disease, wealth or poverty, the highs and the lows. This is the way to serenity.
- I am not high or low. I am equal.
- I serve all equally.
- I serve the mighty and the meek with the same Love.
- I strive to remain humble at all times.
- I counter pride, arrogance, and entitlement with humility and gratitude.
- I endure injury with a patient, quiet heart.
- It is not about me. It is about service.
- I am nothing. God is everything.

EXERCISES

1. Describe the seven routes to humility.
2. Why is humility the mother of all virtue?
3. What is the connection between humility and other spiritual qualities?
4. Think of everything you know and compare it to what you don't know. You will see that your knowledge is infinitesimal, while the unknown always remains infinite. The more you know, the more you realize what you don't know.
5. What did Jesus mean when he said, "The meek shall inherit the earth"? Think about the power of "soft over hard." Where is gentleness needed more in your life?
6. A middle-aged, mildly retarded African American man dressed in old tattered clothes was waiting in the hall of my clinic. "How are you?" I asked. "Sad today," he said. "Why?" I asked. He replied, "I wish everybody good luck and happiness." From his sadness, he prays for others. This man teaches humility. Can you see how this applies to your life?

CHAPTER 26

FAITH

Proof of Things Unseen

*"Now faith is the assurance of things hoped for,
the conviction of things not seen."*

Hebrews 11.1

A belief is an idea that remains untested. Faith is proof of things unseen. We may like an idea, but we cannot know if it is true until we prove it. Then we have faith. To test the reality of a belief, we need to develop a spiritual practice. Then, through direct personal experience, we can see for ourselves if it is true. In this way, we can discriminate spiritual law from fixed, untested belief.

Spiritual laws are universal truths that apply to all people, transcending history, culture, and conditions. These laws outline the nature of reality and the governance of the universe. Spiritual laws cannot fail. They operate with precise accuracy, just as surely as the laws that govern the physical universe.

Saints and sages discover, live, master, and teach the workings of spiritual laws. They advise us to follow these laws to make our lives more effective. We can follow their lead, but we cannot have faith in metaphysical truths until we prove that they work in our lives. We must operate the laws ourselves. Then we have faith.

Faith, an eternal power that springs from the soul, cannot be touched or destroyed. Doubt and insecurity can temporarily overwhelm our faith, but it recovers. It is incomparably resilient. The magnificent power of faith does not come easily, however. Though it is an inherent quality of the soul, it lays dormant until exercised.

Following is a method for cultivating faith by converting belief to truth, through direct personal experience. This method helps us determine if a spiritual concept or method is empty or an immutable truth deserving of our faith.

1. Test
2. Hypothesis
3. Practice
4. Experience
5. Faith

1. TEST

Faith cannot grow without tests. A test can be any pain or problem. We all experience loss, pain, and tragedy. Some of us have to face the darkness of barbaric crime or catastrophic violence. All of us must eventually leave our possessions, loved ones, and bodies behind. At death, each of us must face the abyss, the mysterious infinite unknown.

2. HYPOTHESIS

Religions and spiritual teachers give us advice on how to handle the painful problems of life. The advice is massive, complex, confusing, and contradictory. To decipher spiritual fiction from fact, we need to convert fixed beliefs or dogma to hypothesis requiring proof. To do this, we transfer authority from others to ourselves. We should not blindly follow religion, teachers, or masters. Our own experience is the ultimate criterion for determining truth.

We can test any concept or method: Does the body-temple harbor the soul and the God of the universe? Are karma and reincarnation true? Is unconditional Love the key to the kingdom of heaven? Does meditation work? Does compassionate service to humanity give us peace of mind and strength? We can put these profoundly important questions to the test of direct personal experience in the laboratory of life. The experiment may take years. On the way, we stay receptive. We do not accept or reject the theory. We just do the work by developing a spiritual practice.

3. PRACTICE

We can practice any one or combination of spiritual methods.

4. EXPERIENCE

Discovering truth through personal experience is called spiritual discrimination, or discernment. Direct personal experience is the teacher and ultimate authority. If a method or concept works, we keep it. If not, we discard it. We trust our ability to tell the difference.

5. FAITH

We prove to ourselves that a concept or method works in our lives, thus converting untested belief to faith through experience.

We can apply this 5-step method to any spiritual practice or idea. Following is an example of how to apply the method to prove the existence of the soul and God.

PROVING THE EXISTENCE OF THE SOUL AND GOD

1. TEST

A painful problem arrives. It disturbs our peace and indicates an area in need of work.

2. HYPOTHESIS

We can test steps 7-10 of this model. Pain management (step 8) and spiritual practice (step 9) lead to the discovery of the soul and God (step 7) as the peace, Love, and joy we crave (step 10). We have a soul made of Love qualities, which we will discover if we practice spiritual disciplines in response to life's problems. When we do the work, we experience a progressive growth of courage, peace, forgiveness, and other wonderful spiritual qualities. With continued practice, God reveals Himself as a loving Friend whose aid arrives in many forms, with reinforcements, on His schedule.

3. PRACTICE:

The arrival of a painful problem indicates we have homework in the school of life. We must accept our current condition as the next step in our spiritual development. We pick any one or combination of spiritual methods that fit our problem, and we accept our pain as a teacher and stimulant for the growth of spiritual qualities. Pain is an intelligent teacher who will lead us to our greatest spiritual asset: Love.

Pain is the purifying agent that transforms negativity into spiritual power. When we enter the pain, it reveals the lessons we need to learn. The lessons always have to do with learning how to cultivate soul qualities. Through introspection, our pain informs us of the nature of our problems. Through transformation, we respond to our problems by cultivating Love, compassion, understanding, and forgiveness. This is the work of the spiritual path.

When overwhelmed with difficult problems, we may be tempted to give up our spiritual practice. To avoid this, we need to be patient and persevere. There will be dry periods where we feel there is no progress. When we think we are not growing, remember that effort is progress and good results are accumulating. Faith does not come without tests and work. When we do the work, God responds in His way and on His schedule.

4. EXPERIENCE

We are in a relationship with God. Our job is to practice spiritual methods. When we do this, spiritual qualities slowly grow. To give us additional assistance, God enters our lives as Friend, Father, Mother, Guide, Protector, Teacher, Healer, or Counselor. We experience ego reduction, pain relief, healing, guidance, and protection. When we contact God, there may be an unmistakable change in consciousness. We experience changeless peace, ecstatic joy, pure Love, intuitive knowledge, or light of the soul.

Whether we understand our suffering as karma or as part of God's mystery, we do our part to work on our problems. As we progress on the spiritual path, we become increasingly aware of how grace operates in our lives. We see how God appears and disappears in an apparent play of hide and seek. In the beginning, we cannot hold on to God all of the time. However, with practice, we are able to find and keep Him more and more. Each time He reappears, our faith grows. Faith is the knowledge that He is there and will be back. Then, even if we feel separate or empty, we know that we have not been abandoned.

As we go through tests, we may continue to experience turbulence in the form of fear and doubt. Nevertheless, we learn through experience that when we do our part and wait with patience, grace comes in the form of direction, relief, inspiration, courage, forbearance, or protection.

Gradually, we come to understand that God's grace is continuous, even during the most difficult times. He is always right here, right now, helping, and guiding. No matter what the world or our bodies are doing, God is present.

5. FAITH

As our experiential faith grows, it slowly replaces and finally eliminates doubt. Then we know that we have a Friend who is always with us, helping and guiding. We know the ground of all being is His Omniscient Love, greater than any pain. We know He will never fail us in our hour of need, and that we get what we need when we need it. We know our work and His grace combine to reduce our egos, melt our problems, expand our soul qualities, and get us through any barrier. At mastery, when we know the immutable peace of the soul, the fiercest conditions can not shake our faith. When we know our soul is eternally safe and protected, we remain fearless even in the face of death. This is perfect faith and perfect surrender.

To know the soul and God is to have the power that faith intends, a power that lights the way, moving us forward in the face of darkness. While earthly conditions may be fierce, faith directs us to our spiritual home, a place where there is no loss.

POINTS TO REMEMBER

- Faith arises when evidence is lacking. It starts with hope and possibility. It ends with experience.

- Faith is the bridge between the material world of limitation and insecurity and the spiritual world of immortality and peace.

- Blind belief is weaker than faith proved by direct experience.

- The brain has a pharmacy that can send healing chemicals to the cells of our body. Thoughts of faith have healing power. Send faithful thoughts to heal the body, mind, and soul through chemistry.

- Faith is a dynamic healing power that can get us through any trial.

- We can grow when life is smooth, but our greatest progress may come when we face difficult problems. It is at these times that we need faith the most. If we continue our spiritual practice, we gain strength and endurance. Eventually our burden lifts and peace comes. We prove to ourselves that we can get through any trial if we persevere.

- The answer to pain and evil would be Love even if God did not exist, but He does. There is a God of Love. Respond with Love, and you will see Him respond to you.

- We learn through experience that Love is greater than any problem. Moreover, each victory of Love over pain expands our faith.

- Faith is the knowledge of our inner connection to the river of Divinity, the infinite source of compassion.

- God's grace is continuous. She is Love, compassion, and peace no matter what the world is doing.

- A solution is forthcoming to any problem. When we do our part and wait with patience, grace comes. Never doubt the infinite grace of the Creator.

AFFIRMATIONS

- I get what I need when I need it.
- Every test is the next step in my spiritual development.
- I transform my suffering into spiritual qualities.
- I do my part by cultivating strength and courage.
- God has set up His school of life. He knows what He is doing.
- I get help from the God of infinite compassion and wisdom.
- God is my Friend, Protector, Teacher, Counselor, and Healer.
- God is always right here, right now, helping, and guiding.
- God's great healing power knows how to transform my suffering into spiritual power.
- My work and God's grace can get me through anything.
- Love is greater than any pain.
- Nothing can stop me.
- I never give up.
- Nothing can touch my faith.
- I am the immutable peace of the soul.
- I remain fearless even in the face of death.

EXERCISES

1. Following is a list of ideas that can serve as a basis of faith. Review the list to see if any of these ideas are already a part of your faith system. We can have faith in:
   - Ourselves
   - Our Higher Power
   - Other people
   - A connection to something larger than ourselves
   - Higher meaning and purpose
   - The meaning inherent in our story
   - The positives of life
   - Beauty, truth, goodness, and Love
   - Our own strength
   - Our ability to contribute

- Each has a special gift to give
- Our ability to respond to problems
- The healing power of the soul
- The power and intelligence that runs the universe
- What comes to us is the next step in our spiritual development
- Pain as the teacher and stimulant for the growth of spiritual qualities
- All of our experiences teach us soul qualities
- The existence of a plan for each of us and the world. The plan is good.
- Our ability to respond to negative with positive

2. What is the basis of your faith?
3. What can you turn to when tested with loss, abandonment, rejection, disease, disability, poverty, sickness, trauma, or failure?
4. Is there a central organizing principle in your belief system that cannot be touched?
5. What is the definition of faith proposed in this chapter?
6. Describe the five-step method for cultivating faith by converting belief to truth through direct personal experience.
7. Review the following four categories. Where do you stand in this continuum?
   a. Atheists dogmatically assert the non-existence of Spirit. Their logic stems from their lack of spiritual experiences.
   b. Believers dogmatically assert the existence of Spirit often without spiritual experience to back up their beliefs.
   c. Agnostics do not know. They are willing to test truth and wait. They ask the cosmos questions. The cosmos says, "Test me." This is the most scientific stance. It depends on direct experience. There is a transfer of authority from religion, leaders, and books to the body temple. Ideas and methods are tested in the laboratory of human experience.
   d. Faith is proof of things unseen based on direct personal experience.

CHAPTER 27

COURAGE

The Bridge Between Fear and Peace

Change and loss mark life on the physical plane. We will ultimately lose everything, including our loved ones, possessions, and ultimately, the body. At death, we must face the abyss, the infinite unknown. Fear, a natural and intelligent response to these changes, has two key functions. It identifies the nature of the dangers we face, and it helps us fashion the best strategy for survival.

Fear becomes a problem itself, however, if we avoid it. If we run, it takes on a life of its own. Although we may temporarily gain comfort by pushing our fear into the subconscious, it does not remain dormant. Rather, it infuses the conscious mind with fearful fancy, chronic worry, and doubt. It may escalate to panic or terror. Irrational fear ties up energy, impairs judgment, adversely affects health, and obstructs psychological and spiritual growth.

Fear is often difficult to detect: we design all kinds of creative disguises to avoid it. If we dig deep enough, however, we can find our fear hiding behind anger, jealousy, addiction, dependency, self-importance, and rigid beliefs. To master fear, we must first strip it of its many costumes, experience it directly, and face it with courage.

Courage is the bridge between fear and peace. When we courageously work through our fears, new levels of peace and strength slowly emerge. If we face it until it is gone, we eventually reach the grand prize, the fearless peace of the soul.

In ordinary consciousness, we feel insecure, knowing that we can lose what we have at any time. In spiritual consciousness, we feel safe, since there is nothing to lose. The soul is conscious, immortal peace. Nothing can touch the soul. It is eternally protected and safe. With sustained spiritual practice, we can shift from the fear and insecurity of the material plane to the permanent peace of the soul.

The key to maintaining peace is the mind. Everything that happens is perceived by the mind. The mind, in turn, determines the body's response. The mind is conditioned to respond to events with fear or tranquility. If the mind reacts with fearful thoughts, the body responds with an elevated heartbeat, sweat, shortness of breath, butterflies in the stomach, dry mouth, and a feeling of impending doom. If the mind stays calm, the body stays relaxed.

By practicing the spiritual methods described in this work, we can recondition the mind to remain calm in frightening circumstances. Ordinarily we use a small percentage of our concentration, our minds thus remaining susceptible to thoughts of fear and insecurity. A concentrated mind maintains its focus on the peace of the soul, no matter what. In effect, our work is to change thoughts of fear to those of peace by practicing mindfulness, meditation, the presence of God, affirmations, yoga, and other techniques. With sustained practice, the mind remains calm, positive, strong, and focused under all conditions. Eventually, we can achieve the superconscious state of fearless peace.

There are three stages of fear. In stage one, we try to avoid fear. This makes it grow. In stage two, we face all of our fears with courage. Slowly, peace replaces fear. In stage three, we reach the permanent peace of the soul.

Fear is an enemy only if we run and hide. If we ride its waves until they dissipate, it will give us its power. The following process offers a way to help us achieve mastery over our fears:

TECHNIQUE

1. Introspection
2. Spiritual practice
3. Grace
4. Mastery

1. INTROSPECTION

To gain soul-peace, we need to identify our fear whether it presents itself directly or in disguise. We may experience fear directly as an increase in heart rate, respiratory rate, tremors, butterflies in the stomach, dry mouth, or a feeling of impending doom.

Fear can also manifest indirectly as anger, rigid beliefs, self-importance, domination, aggression, or addiction. To get to deeper states of peace, we need to face these hidden fears. We can start by unmasking our defenses through introspection. Then we are in direct contact with our fear.

To unmask the defenses that cover your fear, retreat to a quiet place. Practice deep breathing and meditation to achieve stillness. Go deep. Ask your subconscious and Higher Power to guide you to your hidden fears. Be patient. Listen for the soft voice within. Let nothing stand in the way of the truth. Eventually, you will realize that fear is hiding behind your many defenses.

2. SPIRITUAL PRACTICE

Fear is a difficult emotion to master, but we can do it. We can become masters of fear if we face it. We must stand our ground, step into the fear, and stare it down. This is difficult, painful, and requires long-term practice. With persistence and perseverance, we can slowly reduce our fears, expand our peace, and eventually reach the permanent peace of the soul. As soon as you become aware of fear, practice one or a combination of the following techniques:

    a. Breathe: Practice deep abdominal breathing.

    b. Progressive muscle relaxation: We can tense and relax our muscles as described in Chapter 12.

    c. Affirmations: We can affirm the existence of the immutable peace of the soul even if we do not feel it. We might also practice affirmations related to strength, courage, heroism, endurance, faith, trust, belief, confidence, power, and immortality.

d. Visualize: We can picture ourselves in fearless peace even as we go through our trial.

e. Mindfulness: Mindfulness practice helps us surrender into the moment, take a stand, and hold our ground. We are awake, aware, and ready for anything. This is the stance of a spiritual warrior.

f. Meditation: In the stillness of deep meditation, the peace of God dissolves all traces of fear.

g. Activities: When afraid, we can distract ourselves by engaging in constructive meaningful activity, such as recreation, socialization, the arts, and hobbies.

We can practice these or other methods described in this book in any comfortable combination. We persevere, fight our battle with courage, and do our best. While we do our part, we can get additional help by turning to our Higher Power, a bottomless source of strength. To make contact with our Higher Power, select an image, practice the presence of God, pray, and have faith.

h. Select an image: We can choose an image such as Father, Mother, Buddha, Krishna, Christ, and so on. The image is symbolic of God's benevolence. We can make our attachment to the image stronger than the fear that confronts us. We can apply all of our will, thought, feeling, and concentration to our image. We hold on to the image as the waves of fear move through our being. If the image is swept away, we bring it back.

i. Practice the presence of God: God is Omnipresent peace. In the face of our fear, we can practice the presence of God as the immutable peace within ourselves. It is there, just underneath the stormy weather.

j. Prayer: We can talk to God and ask for help. We can tell Her that we want to experience the changeless peace of the soul.

k. Faith: We can have faith in the Omnipotent healing power of God. She is there, helping and guiding. She cannot fail.

3. GRACE

When we do our part, grace flows. We realize God is here, helping, protecting, guiding, and caring. God's power is infinitely greater than our fear. On Her schedule, she comes to our rescue. The turbulent waves of fear subside. Peace comes.

4. MASTERY

When fear returns, we continue our spiritual practice. Slowly, we gain confidence and trust as we realize our effort, combined with God's grace, can get us through anything. At mastery, we move forward fearlessly because we know God is there, taking us to safety. Here nothing can touch us, nothing can harm us, and nothing can ruffle us. We are fearless peace.

POINTS TO REMEMBER

- Fear is only the enemy if we do not face it.
- We are afraid of what we cannot control. However, when we cannot change bad outer conditions, we can respond with courage. Courage is the bridge between fear and peace. Eventually, we reach permanent peace.
- Most worry focuses on the future. We can break the habit of worry by learning to focus our attention on the present, living one day or one moment at a time. Focus on the present by practicing mindfulness, breathing, and affirmations. The current moment is all you have to work with, and it is all you need. When you begin to worry, feel insecure, and become afraid, use your will and thoughts to bring yourself to a state of faith, trust, belief, and positive thinking. You can learn to respond to any event with even-minded courage.
- Despite the variety and excitement that the future offers, we resist and fear change and the unknown. When afraid, affirm unconditional peace. Even if you do not feel reassured,

affirm peace with faith and concentration. Peace is inside, waiting to come out, if you will only battle with courage and perseverance.

AFFIRMATIONS

- I am fearless peace.
- I look fear in the face.
- I embrace fear with courage.
- I am calm.
- Courage and faith dissolve my fears.
- I have lived through many difficult problems. I can take the next thing that comes along.
- I am steady and even-minded in the face of trouble.
- I rise up every time I fail.
- Love and faith give me courage.
- I endure. I persevere. I have courage.
- I stay in the fear one minute longer. My courage grows.
- I stay in the fear five minutes longer. My courage grows.
- I stay in the fear until it ends. My courage grows.
- I have grace under pressure.
- I will take whatever life gives.
- I face pain, the unknown, and death.
- God is peace. Wherever I am, God is. I am peace.
- Effort is progress.
- Peace consumes anxiety.
- My Love is stronger than fear.
- I stay deep in the ocean of peace, away from the turbulent surface waves that try to ruffle me.
- I am fearless peace.

EXERCISES

1. Discuss fear as a natural and intelligent response to life on the physical plane.
2. What happens if we do not face our fears?

3. What disguises does fear wear in your life?

4. Describe the relationship between fear, courage, and peace.

5. Describe the peace of the soul.

6. Discuss the importance of the mind in dealing with fear.

7. Describe and practice the four steps of the fear management process.

8. Face your fear. Step into the middle of it. Stand your ground. Stare it down. Practice affirmations, breathing, the presence of God, mindfulness, yoga, and other spiritual methods with will, intensity, and concentration. Persevere and endure. Practice these methods throughout your life. Continue your fight as long as you live. In the end, when your soul exits your body, hold on to your image of God to help you withstand the thrust into the unknown.

CHAPTER 28

FORGIVENESS

The Peace Medicine

The quality of mercy is not strain'd;
It droppeth as the gentle rain from heaven
Upon the place beneath: it is twice bless'd:
It blesseth him that gives and him that takes.
Tis mightiest in the mightiest;
It becomes
The throned monarch better than his crown...
It is an attribute to God Himself.
And earthly power doth then show likest God
When mercy seasons justice.
Shakespeare, The Merchant of Venice

One of the greatest teaching acts in history is the crucified Jesus Christ forgiving his tormentors, "for they know not what they do." It was one thing for Christ to preach Love for all, including enemies, but quite another for him to demonstrate mercy while experiencing exquisite agony at the hand of those enemies. The forgiving Christ on the cross is the ultimate symbol of the healing power of compassion and understanding. While suffering unimaginable pain, he expressed selfless sympathy for his adversaries. This supreme act of unconditional forgiveness, arguably the most difficult aspect of unconditional Love, is beyond the reach of ordinary mortals. Nevertheless, we can learn how to forgive on a smaller scale and build from there.

All of us suffer the provocations of other people, and each of us has acted poorly towards others. On a small scale, we are confronted daily with minor incidents: disagreement, misunderstanding, or frank rudeness. And most of us at one time or another experience major problems from physical, mental, or sexual violence, infidelity, betrayal, rejection, abandonment, and unjust treatment.

Our natural reaction when provoked is anger and fear. These emotions are part of the fight or flight response, a built-in survival mechanism. Anger and fear are good defenses, but difficult emotions to manage. They seem to have a life of their own. Instead of intelligently guiding us to protection and safety, these feelings often become the problem. They stick to us, feed on themselves, and infiltrate our identity in counterproductive ways.

Anger smolders as resentment or expands into all-consuming rage. Unresolved anger stays in the body causing health problems, fatigue, and depression. When it becomes a tool for vengeance and punishment, it leads to escalating cycles of violence and the perpetuation of danger. Fear spirals into painful panic attacks or paranoia. In addition, painful memories and replays of traumatic events often dominate our thoughts. To rid ourselves of the pain, we may turn to self-destructive behaviors such as promiscuity or addiction. Some of us become abusive ourselves, passing our pain along to others. It seems like the wrongdoer injects us with a painful toxin, and we make it worse by responding with our own toxic thoughts, feelings, and behaviors. There appears to be no remedy.

At some point, however, we begin to realize that we are suffering not only from the original trauma, but also from our own reactions. Though we cannot control what has happened to us, we can control our response. Forgiveness, a spiritual practice taught by the great religious traditions, provides us with the antidote to the poisonous effects of the original trauma and our own toxic reactions.

Forgiveness transforms anger and resentment into understanding, compassion, and loving kindness. Forgiveness, an aspect of the soul and

God and an expression of unconditional Love, is itself unconditional. It is applicable to any degree of offense or abuse.

The main reason to forgive is to rid ourselves of recycled pain resulting from the original trauma, so that we can reclaim peace of mind and enjoy life. Without forgiveness, we may stay locked up in our own emotional prison indefinitely, thus perpetuating the original insult of the wrongdoer. Fortunately, we have the power to neutralize the toxins injected by others with the medication of forgiveness. When we choose forgiveness, we give ourselves a precious gift: the return of our peace of mind.

Forgiveness does not imply weakness or passivity, nor do we deny or minimize what has happened. An evil action remains what it is: terrible, repulsive, or simply obnoxious. We do not tolerate or condone injustice, and we hold people accountable for their actions. We should not trust the wrongdoer or remain in dangerous situations. Forgiveness is managing our inner life while taking action for safety, protection, and justice in the outer world. While we heal and integrate traumatic memories inside, we take corrective action outside.

Forgiveness is not reconciliation. Reconciliation is the repair of and return to relationship with the wrongdoer. Forgiveness is the healing of the self without involving the offender. We can gain the inner peace of forgiveness without reconciliation. We cannot reconcile without some degree of forgiveness. Just as forgiveness is a choice, so is reconciliation. We do not have to reconcile.

Forgiveness is a powerful healer, greater than anger or even murderous rage. It soothes and quiets other emotions, including depression, anxiety, shame, and guilt. Forgiveness nullifies the noxious power of the offender and releases us from the prison of past trauma and our own toxic emotions. When we bathe our cells, tissues, and organs with the peace-medicine of forgiveness, we reap the benefits of the relaxation response, and our healing power expands. When we forgive, we gain strength, courage, compassion, and joy, our relationships improve, and we become more skillful at solving our problems.

Despite these benefits, forgiveness is controversial. Religions and individuals vary in their approach; there is no one correct way to deal with it. Each person must choose to forgive or not, a choice involving complex, intimate questions. Some choose not to forgive. This decision should be respected. Forgiveness is not for everybody.

Those who choose to forgive will need a process; simply intending to forgive is not enough. We need to learn how to swim upstream, against the torrent of emotions which demand revenge. This very difficult spiritual task requires strength, courage, and skill, since it is much easier to respond in kind when mistreated. Following is a ten-step method designed to guide the reader through a process of forgiveness. This technique can help us manage small, daily challenges as well as major life crises.

Before beginning, please be aware that the forgiveness process is not without risk. The process may release intense emotions that become overwhelming. If this occurs, stop the process, take a break, and engage in pleasant, comforting activities alone or with friends. Then return to your forgiveness work. If your pain is severe and unrelenting, you may need to consult with a mental health or spiritual counselor. Generally, the criteria for seeking professional consultation are a loss of sleep or appetite, an inability to complete daily tasks, thoughts of harming yourself or others, or any symptom of concern.

A METHOD FOR FORGIVENESS

1. Action
2. Let the story unfold
3. Spiritualize the story
4. Affirmation
5. Visualization
6. Meditation
7. Grace
8. Service
9. Self-forgiveness
10. The forgiving character

1. ACTION

When provoked or violated, we need to take the necessary external corrective action for self-defense and protection. The focus is on safety for our loved ones and ourselves. If the abuser is still present, we may need separation and an order of protection. If a crime is involved, we need to press charges and seek justice. When we are physically safe, we can retreat for the extended inner work of forgiving.

2. LET THE STORY UNFOLD

Review the chapter on the transformation of emotion. Remember, emotions are intelligent messengers carrying information about our problems and solutions. We can ride the waves of anger, depression, fear, guilt, and shame until they dissipate. If we surrender to the pain, we get the necessary lessons, solve our problems, cultivate spiritual qualities, and move on. Initially the process involves letting the story unfold.

The first step is to remember the facts of the event. Then experience and feel the emotions associated with the event. We should not be surprised to find multiple layers of emotional pain requiring weeks, months, or years of work. There are deep pockets of hidden emotion that block the flow of healing energy.

It takes time to remove all of the debris. We need to accept and absorb the pain as it comes. We must work our way through the many layers of anger, one at a time. The process may seem finished when more anger appears, years later. Process whatever emotions arise until there are none left. Because of intense pain, you may tend to avoid some, moving through the process too quickly. Take your time. Do not rush. Let the story unfold completely.

To let the story unfold, let each emotion surface and speak its truth, whatever that might be. Emotions seek understanding and validation, not value judgments. If we allow our emotions to speak freely at this stage, we will often hear a story about injustice, unfairness, loss, humiliation, insecurity, and revenge. There may be questions about good and evil, why we suffer, and the role of God in the story.

The value of letting the story unfold freely is that we get our emotions to move out of their hiding places in the body and the subconscious. However, if we stop at this stage, we recycle a story based on self-righteous anger, smoldering resentment, and vengeful fantasy. Unless we give the story higher meaning, we may remain locked up in the prison of our own painful emotions indefinitely.

The transition to the next stage, spiritualizing the story, is difficult. In the face of severe anger, the idea of adding anything positive to the story such as understanding or compassion for the wrongdoer seems ridiculous. When anger is very strong, we may have to wait before proceeding to the next stage.

When you are ready, make a firm commitment to the process of forgiveness. Stop telling your story to other people, to reduce some of its momentum, and begin working steps 3-7. As you work through these steps, you may experience additional turbulence, swimming as you are against the current of your raging emotions. Take your time and pace yourself. If your reaction is too disturbing, you may not be ready to proceed.

3. SPIRITUALIZE THE STORY

We can continue to tell ourselves a story driven by hate, pain, and despair, but then we remain victims of the abuser and suffer unnecessarily. To mobilize ourselves out of the position of victim, we transform anger into peace and strength by spiritualizing the story. Spiritualizing the story includes understanding the offender and separating the soul of the offender from their bad behavior.

To understand the offender, we can look at the developmental causes and conditions that led to the hurtful act. Sometimes, it is not clear why the wrongdoer acted out. Often, however, we find offenders are deeply troubled victims of neglect, abandonment, and abuse themselves. There is a lack of Love, moral guidance, education, meaningful employment, and self-knowledge. Although this does not excuse wrongdoing, it helps us understand and respect the problems confronting the offender.

Some actions are so barbaric, however, that no degree of understanding can neutralize our outrage and disgust. In these circumstances, we can still separate the soul from the evil action to realize our common humanity. On the spiritual plane, we are all the same: human beings with a soul. We can maintain this vision by seeing the good in everyone, even when it is not immediately apparent.

Looking at the perpetrator's history and separating the soul from the wrongful behavior lay the groundwork for a gradual shift from anger to respect and compassion. This transition takes time. It is a difficult part of the process. Anger, fear, and resentment are polar opposites of compassion, Love, and kindness. These emotions fight with each other. The experience can be tumultuous and overwhelming. It is easy to get lost and quit. For additional help with this difficult process, we can affirm, visualize, and meditate. With these techniques, we gain access to a wider pool of healing energy.

4. AFFIRMATION

Forgiveness affirmations bring us into alignment with the healing power of unconditional Love. Practice the following or similar affirmations no matter what others do. Eventually, these thoughts become your reality.

- Everyone is a child of the same Father/Mother God.
- _____ is a child of God, equal in Her sight.
- I see the humanity and soul of _____.
- I drink the peace-medication of forgiveness.
- I drink at the fountain of understanding and compassion.
- I establish myself as a center of understanding and compassion.
- Understanding and compassion radiate throughout my entire being.
- Love and kindness fill my body-temple and radiate to all beings.
- I see the beauty and goodness of every soul.
- I am concerned for others as I am for myself.
- The soul remains uncorrupted behind our mistakes and flaws.

- I am the soul, the image of God within, pure Love.
- The Love I feel for all beings remains the same despite provocation.
- I forgive others.
- I forgive myself.
- I am willing to forgive_____.
- I make peace with family, friends, strangers, and enemies alike, for therein lies my peace.
- I love family, friends, strangers, and enemies alike.

5. VISUALIZATION: THE LOVE-LIGHT HEALING EXERCISE

Sit in a comfortable chair in a quiet place. Close your eyes and take several slow, deep, abdominal breaths. Concentrate on your spiritual eye, at the center of the forehead just above the eyebrows. Relax and focus on the warmth and sense of well-being in your heart. Ask God for help in feeling Her Love for the soul of the wrongdoer. Now visualize the one who has harmed you, immersed in the healing Love-light of God. Imagine the light dissolve and replace the imperfections of the wrongdoer with peace and harmony. Then immerse yourself in the light. Visualize the healing light dissolve and replace your anger with peace and harmony. You might also visualize the forgiving Christ on the cross, or another image that would help you dissolve the pain given to you by others.

6. MEDITATION

We can get additional help with forgiveness from meditation. In the stillness of meditation, we reach the deep healing power of Love and Her consort qualities. It is here, in stillness, that we slowly and subtly replace our problems with spiritual qualities. Spiritual qualities are the healing powers. They have more power than our problems. In the stillness of meditation, Love burns up hate, kindness dissolves cruelty, understanding breeds compassion, and compassion melts anger. Instead of remaining a victim of other people's problems and our own recycled painful emotions, we cultivate peace and strength. When we come out of meditation, we give Love and kindness to all whom we meet.

7. GRACE

We do the work as described in steps 1-6 above, but we are not strong enough to do all of the work of forgiveness on our own. Fortunately, we have access to God's infinite ocean of all-forgiving Love. We can tap into Her vast powers of compassion and mercy by asking for Her help and grace.

Retreat to a quiet place and make contact with your Higher Power. You might pray, "Divine Mother, You know I cannot forgive on my own. I need Your help. Bless me with Your grace. Help me build a story based on understanding, compassion, and forgiveness. Give me Your Love and forgiveness that I may give it to others."

When we do the work and ask for Her help, on Her schedule and by Her grace, the gate to Her infinite healing power opens. She sweeps away anger, resentment, shame, guilt, humiliation, and other such emotions, replacing them with peace, forgiveness, and harmony.

8. SERVICE

With our work and God's grace, Love qualities replace harmful emotions. We channel our expanded understanding, compassion, and peace into universal service. We can express our service to humanity as a quest for justice, human rights, or any action that benefits others.

9. SELF-FORGIVENESS

All of us make mistakes that hurt others. We become aware of our mistakes when others give us feedback or from introspection. When we see that we have hurt someone, we feel guilt. This is good. Guilt is intelligent. It helps us become responsible for our flaws, and it deters us from repeating the same mistakes.

Guilt becomes a problem, however, when we are too hard on ourselves. Excessive guilt leads to low self-esteem, which can become self-hate. We lose our peace of mind. The flow of Love between our self and others is blocked. The antidote to excessive guilt is self-forgiveness.

To forgive ourselves, we can follow the same steps described here in the forgiveness process. By following these steps, we can learn to be gentle, patient, and understanding with ourselves even when we make mistakes. In addition, we must do what we can to change our behavior, apologize to the one we hurt, and make amends.

10. THE FORGIVING CHARACTER

Forgiveness is a skill we can learn through study and practice. We can start with forgiving a small event or a single person and expand from there. The more we forgive, the easier it gets. We think forgiveness. We intend forgiveness. We tell forgiveness stories. We practice forgiveness until it becomes a habit, part of our character. Eventually, when our forgiving muscles are very strong, we can forgive unconditionally and instantaneously. Then we have a great gift to give to the world! Instead of revenge and retribution, we give understanding and compassion. Instead of transferring the pain others inflict on us, we return kindness. When we learn to give ourselves unconditional Love, we become our own best friend. When we absorb the pain of others and transform it to peace and harmony, we reduce the pain of the world.

GENERAL RULES FOR THE FORGIVENESS HEALING PROCESS

1. The forgiveness healing process works, but it takes time. It is slow, painful, and difficult. It may take weeks, months, or years. There is no timetable. We cannot control the speed. The process must be allowed to unfold on its own time. We need to work with each step, however long it takes. We should not try to rush or force our way through the process. There are no short cuts.

2. Although we all heal at different rates, forgiveness generally takes longer if the hurt was deep.

3. There may be times when we experience pain without relief. This is part of the process. Do not give up. Forgiveness is a life-long discipline. A breakthrough can occur at any time. With practice, it gets easier. Be gentle with yourself and persevere.

4. We can only do a little bit of work at a time. When the pain is too intense, we need to take time out.

5. If the forgiveness process becomes overwhelming, seek professional consultation with a mental health or spiritual counselor.

6. Whenever we experience new waves of anger or resentment, we can rework the steps. Eventually, we completely transform our anger into peace and strength.

ADDITIONAL POINTS TO REMEMBER

- Forgiving helps us deal with major problems such as physical or sexual assault, infidelity, abandonment, injustice, and cruelty. It also helps us with smaller, daily challenges when we conflict with others. It is easy to judge others who are insensitive. However, even mild resentment infiltrates our consciousness, stealing our peace of mind. We must become more aware of the subtle, insidious forms of anger and resentment that occur in response to the provocations of daily life. Then we can refine our consciousness by responding with the healing power of forgiveness. We need a lot of forgiveness; the daily challenges are many.

- When we make mistakes, we want forgiveness. It helps to remember this when we are doing the difficult work of forgiving those who have harmed us. They want forgiveness, too.

- Anger is a poison. Forgiveness is the antidote. The karma of the criminal is between them and God. The attitude of the criminal is irrelevant to our healing process.

- Martin Luther King, Jr. said, "The chain reaction of evil—hate begetting hate, wars producing more wars—must be broken, or we shall be plunged into the dark abyss of annihilation. Love is the only force capable of transforming an enemy into a friend. By its very nature, hate destroys and tears down; by its very nature, love creates and builds up. We love every man because God loves him. At this level, we love the person who does an evil deed, although we hate the deed that he does."

- We do not accept evil. We fight for safety and justice. This does not necessarily heal our inner being, however. For this, we need forgiveness.

- Forgiveness is a skill we can develop. It is a good tool to have. No one is immune to the daily challenges of life or to a major attack, but if we know how to forgive, we can maintain our peace of mind and strength.

- Forgiveness heals individuals, families, religions, and nations. There is no end to the expansive power of Love. How great it is that we can reduce our pain, the pain of others, and the pain of the world with the healing power of forgiveness!

EXERCISES

1. Describe the ten-step forgiveness process.
2. Review how your belief system addresses forgiveness. What are some of the ways that it supports or inhibits forgiveness?
3. Forgiveness is a choice. Describe the pros and cons of forgiveness. This may help you decide if forgiveness is a good idea for you. If you are clear about the benefits of forgiveness, you will be more likely to persist when the process becomes difficult.
4. When a negative person causes us to react negatively, we get mired in negativity. The negativity inside is composed of two layers: the input of the offensive person, and our reaction to it. With gentle compassion, we can dissolve this complex. Try directing compassion to the offender and to yourself.

CHAPTER 29

TRUTH

Four Pathways to Truth

Jesus said, "You shall know truth and the truth shall make you free." This chapter outlines what this truth might be and how to find it. Following is a discussion of how four dimensions of truth work together in the cause of our liberation: scientific truth, spiritual truth, personal truth, and the truth of the spoken word.

SCIENTIFIC TRUTH

We want to know how the world works, and we want to get it right. We can do this on the physical plane through controlled experiments where scientific laws emerge as immutable facts of life: water freezes at 32 degrees every time. Such measurable certainty is not possible on the spiritual level. Here, too, there are absolute truths and laws, but no controlled experiments, blood tests, or x-rays to help us discover their precise nature. Nevertheless, recent advances in health care research reveal a relationship between spirituality and healing. We know people who have a spiritual practice have better outcomes in medicine, surgery, mental health, and in fighting addiction. From these and similar studies we can infer, but not prove, the nature of spiritual truths.

METAPHYSICAL OR SPIRITUAL TRUTH

Great religious traditions and their teachers attempt to outline for us the laws and principles that govern the universe beyond the physical plane; hence the term "metaphysical truth." We cannot measure metaphysical truths with precision. For example, there is no absolute proof by scientific means for the existence and nature of God. This leaves room for interpretation and disagreement. In the vast array of spiritual books and teachers, we find a variety of conflicting ideas and beliefs. How can we determine the nature of spiritual truth?

To verify spiritual truth, we accept no idea on blind faith. Instead, we decide for ourselves via experimentation. The laboratory is human experience. The test tube is the body. Our tools are the built-in equipment of the body: consciousness, energy, reason, feeling, intuition, and direct personal experience. We use these tools when we practice any of the spiritual disciplines described in this work.

Consider the method of spiritual study described in Chapter 14. Contemplation is a powerful tool for determining truth. We can see which ideas work for us by realizing them through practice. In this lesson, we learned how to realize a spiritual idea through the following six steps:

1. Choose a topic
2. Study
3. Affirm
4. Act
5. Introspect
6. Mastery

For example, we might want to explore whether compassion and forgiveness heal anger and depression. By practicing the six-step method of contemplation, we can test this theory.

Testing a new idea is like trying on glasses to see which lens gives us the clearest vision. If an idea fits, we have better eyesight and can see life more clearly. However, some ideas will not prove plainly true or false for years. For example, the Hindus and Buddhists speak about karma and reincarnation. Christ recommended unconditional Love as the ticket into the kingdom of heaven. These are very powerful ideas that may or may not be true. Rather than accepting or rejecting them, we might put these ideas on as one would glasses, and over time see if they help us see more clearly or create blurred vision.

Each of the spiritual methods described in this work give us an opportunity to test new ideas in the laboratory of personal experience. We can prove or disprove a new idea by developing a spiritual practice.

PERSONAL TRUTH OR SELF-KNOWLEDGE

In the chapter on transformation of emotion, we learned how to find our personal truth or self-knowledge through introspection. As in the metaphysical realm, there is no blood test or x-ray to help us determine personal truth. Nevertheless, we can succeed in discovering the truth of our lives by learning how to introspect. In introspection, we learn to work with and through our painful problems. Pain is the teacher bearing the gift of truth or self-knowledge.

Please review Chapter 21, the transformation of emotion. This chapter teaches us how to extract the important information hidden in our pain. Pain is the teacher of the lessons we need to learn and the spiritual qualities we need to develop. When we stay with our pain, we get to the truth.

The greatest barrier to the discovery of personal truth is our desire to avoid suffering. The truth often hurts. When we deny or suppress the painful truths about our lives, we create distortion and self-deception.

Although we think we know what is going on as the story of our lives evolves, all of us have distorted thinking. The mind, however marvelous and amazing, is not always precisely accurate. Bias, prejudice, and fixed false ideas result in our holding unrealistic ideas about ourselves, others, and life.

Distorted thinking occurs especially during times of high emotion. All of us have had painful experiences with associated thinking patterns that color later experiences in negative, distorted ways. Some people have experiences that appear to be real but are actually delusions or hallucinations. We cling to irrational or frankly delusional ideas as though they were true, to the point that they interfere with our functioning or safety.

Following is a process that can help us use suffering to discover the deeper truths of our personal story. In this process, we go within to seek guidance from our Higher Power and soul, the center of truth within ourselves.

1.   CREATE A SAFE HEALING SPACE

Sit quietly. Use your breathing and meditation techniques to bring in as much stillness as you can.

2.   ASK FOR HELP FROM YOUR HIGHER POWER

Ask for guidance from the infinitely intelligent power that is truth itself. Open yourself to the wisdom of the Great Teacher. Ask the Teacher, "What is the meaning of my suffering? Direct me to the lessons I need to learn. What mistakes have I made that need correction? What flaws do I have?" Ask for elimination of all that is untrue and illumination of the truth.

3.   LET THE STORY UNFOLD

Bring your pain to awareness. Accept the pain as an honored guest and teacher. It carries valuable information about your life's meaning and purpose. Gently enter the center of the pain and let it tell its story. Let the story unfold in whatever direction it naturally takes. Do not resist, fight, repress, or deny anything. Observe your thoughts, feelings, and bodily sensations. Avoid nothing. Do not rush the process. Accept whatever shows up, precisely as it is.

The purpose of this exercise is to find the truth about ourselves, no matter how uncomfortable we may be. This may be difficult at first because of the ego, which we have already learned resists change and clings to outmoded ideas.

The soul, on the other hand, is willing to go through a process of fearless introspection for the sake of the truth. It is not afraid to be wrong or to change. It wants to find and correct flaws and mistakes in order for us to become better people.

Acknowledge the ego's version of the story. Although incapable of introspection, it may give you some valuable information. For example, the ego may be right when it finds fault with others. However, the ego gets stuck in self-righteous anger. We become prisoner of our own emotions and miss opportunities for growth.

It is easy to find fault with others and harder to look within. However, we cannot correct our flaws unless we find them. To get to the truth about ourselves, we need to get past our ego and self-righteousness. We can do this when we use our pain to find out the truth, not just about others but also about ourselves. Even as the ego tries to hide our faults by blaming others, the truth seeking soul will guide us to the deeper truths within.

Through a process of fearless introspection, we can use our pain to find our mistakes and flaws. As the ego and emotions tell their story and finally wind down, shift toward introspection. As you look inward, remain gentle and compassionate with yourself. Ask your soul and Higher Power to guide you to the truth, whatever it might be. In the light of soul truth, acknowledge your strengths and accomplishments as well as your problems. Create a list of problems including flaws, mistakes, bad habits, attachments, and distorted ideas.

4. SPIRITUALIZE THE STORY

When you finish letting the story unfold, you should have a good idea of your strengths and accomplishments, as well as your weaknesses. Now it is time to spiritualize the story. Here, we recognize the purpose of pain: the expansion of the soul by replacing flaws with spiritual qualities. Guided by these qualities, the story unfolds in the direction of the Spirit.

Consult your problem list and the spiritual alphabet. In response to each problem, choose one or a combination of spiritual qualities. If angry and self-righteous, you may need more understanding, compassion, and forgiveness. If anxious and insecure, you might need courage, strength, and perseverance. If guilty and ashamed, you may need acceptance and forgiveness for yourself.

Remember not to focus on the problem, which will only strengthen its grip. Instead, place all of your attention on the chosen spiritual quality. Let these qualities be your guide.

Bring all of your thoughts, feelings, and actions into alignment with spiritual qualities. As we replace our imperfections with spiritual qualities, the soul expands. Know that you are in the presence of truth when you experience peace, compassion, Love, patience, kindness, forgiveness, courage, and humility.

SPEAKING TRUTH

When we tell ourselves the truth, we gain self-knowledge. We also need to speak the truth in our relationships. The goal of communication is the welfare and benefit of all. This is difficult when there is conflict and emotions run high. When distraught, our words may be true but are often unnecessarily forceful and destructive. We have great power to create harm or good with the spoken word.

To combat negative communications, we can align our intent with the truth of the spoken word. However, truth spoken without kindness may be destructive. Sweetness of speech buffers the potential harshness of truth. The spoken word laced with truth and tempered with kindness incites effective communication and skillful problem-solving.

Following is an exercise combining impeccable truth and sweetness of speech.

1. Avoid gossip, criticism, judgment, debate, and harsh words.
2. Align all of your thoughts and speech with the soul qualities listed in the spiritual alphabet.
3. Speak truth with compassion and kindness.
4. Practice opened-minded discussion.
5. Listen, listen, listen … and then listen some more.
6. Be aware that your word has the vibratory power to spread truth, healing, and Love.

Our speech is a reflection of who we are. When we cultivate Love, our thoughts, words, and actions naturally follow suit.

TRUTH IS LOVE

In this chapter, we reviewed four pathways to truth:

1. Scientific truth: using research methods to discover the immutable laws of nature with measurable certainty;

2. Metaphysical truth: using the laboratory of human experience to discover higher laws through the practice of spiritual disciplines;

3. Personal truth: using fearless introspection to gain self-knowledge;

4. The truth of the spoken word: speaking truth guided by sweetness of speech.

These four distinct routes to truth are connected. They work together. In each of the four methods, we can study ourselves to learn about the ultimate nature of reality. We can do this because the design of a human being reflects the design of the universe. We are a microcosm of the macrocosm. Our mind is a reflection of the Universal Mind. Our soul is a droplet of the great ocean of Spirit. We are made of the same powerful intelligence that creates, operates, and sustains the universe.

Whether we follow the path of science, metaphysics, our personal story, or the spoken word, we discover the same truth: pain management and spiritual practice lead to the realization of our soul and Spirit as the peace, Love, and joy we crave. When we manage our pain skillfully and practice spiritual discipline, we shall know the truth, and it shall make us free. That truth is Love.

All paths lead to Love. Love is the solution to all of our problems. Physical science will prove it. Metaphysicians already know it. We can verify it in our personal story. We can demonstrate it with the power of our word. Love is the law. Love is the answer to the cosmic puzzle. Love is God.

POINTS TO REMEMBER

- The universe operates by law.
- We can study ourselves to understand the laws that govern the universe.
- All of the spiritual methods described in this work lead to the discovery that our soul and Spirit are comprised of the unlimited peace, Love, and joy we crave. We can know this through direct personal experience. The pursuit of truth leads to the experience of these qualities.
- God is Love. We can know Love in silence and express it in words and deeds as service. Then we know the peace that surpasses understanding. This is the law. This is the truth.
- "Truth is not to be found by anybody who has not got an abundant sense of humility. If you would swim on the bosom of the ocean of Truth, you must reduce yourself to zero." Mahatma Gandhi
- Dishonesty is a barrier to spiritual growth. Telling the truth to ourselves, however difficult, is liberating.
- Personal truth reflects metaphysical truth. Our personal story fits into the cosmic story. In discovering meaning in our personal life, we can discover the meaning of life. Follow Love and keep your eyes open. Everything will fall into place.

AFFIRMATIONS

- I establish myself as a center of truth.
- Truth heals.
- I take time daily to reflect upon the power of my word.
- I am true to myself.
- I am true to others.
- My word has the power to carry the truth.
- My word is powerful, positive, and passionate.
- I speak truth guided by sweetness of speech.
- I only speak what is true, necessary, and kind.
- I perceive truth when I am equal to all others.

- I live in truth when I am in Love.
- I live in truth when I am compassionate.
- I live in truth when I am of service.
- I live in truth when I am at peace.
- I live in truth when I recognize beauty.
- I live in truth when I am good.
- The intentions of my words are Love qualities. Otherwise, I do not speak.
- The discovery of truth is the driving force of my life.

EXERCISES

1. Ultimately, it is up to you to decide what truth is at both the individual and cosmic levels. Describe the four methods for discovering truth identified in this chapter. How might these methods help you discern for yourself the nature of truth?
2. What is the greatest barrier to self-knowledge?
3. How does the ego interfere with our ability to discover truth?
4. Can you think of a time when your thinking was incorrect, and how you came to know the truth later?
5. Describe a time when you used denial to avoid a painful truth. What helped you discover the truth?
6. Describe the method for discovering personal truth through introspection.
7. How does the soul guide us to truth during introspection?
8. Describe how you can use the light of your soul qualities to discover and eliminate false or destructive thoughts.
9. Describe the battle between the self-righteous ego and fearless introspection of the soul.
10. Describe how speaking truth guided by sweetness of speech helps us communicate and solve problems?
11. How do the four types of truth work together to help us discover the spiritual laws that govern the universe?

CHAPTER 30

INTUITION

A Higher Order of Intelligence

Omniscience is the intelligent power that creates, operates, and sustains the cosmos, from the tiniest particle to the grandest stellar system. Omniscience is Omnipresent. It occupies every millimeter of space. Omniscient Power organizes and expresses itself on Earth in a seemingly endless parade of spectacular forms, and in galaxies and solar systems in ways that exceed the imagination. This power operates every particle, molecule, cell, tissue, organ, and system within our body so we can hear, see, feel, think, and Love. We can use this Supreme Intelligence to help us solve our problems by cultivating the soul quality of intuition.

In ordinary problem solving, we use reason to determine the best course of action. To get additional help, we can seek guidance from Omniscience through intuition. Intuition, a faculty of the soul, is a sixth sense. It is a higher order of intelligence beyond reason and the five senses. Intuition is the direct, infallible knowledge of the truth gleaned from our connection to God. Omniscient Wisdom is God's will, what He wants to happen, the choices He wants us to make, and the knowledge He wants us to have.

Reason, associated with ordinary consciousness, works with the data collected through the five senses. Intuition works directly with Omniscient Wisdom within. Reason without intuition is unreliable, since it is subject to the whims of desire, emotion, and the ego. Reason guided by intuition approaches wisdom, and pure intuition is wisdom itself.

Reason is a marvelous tool that helps us solve problems and achieve goals. However, the mind, under the influence of the ego, is subject to bias, emotion, likes, and dislikes. Within the consciousness of the ego, we defend our current positions even if based on false convictions. We resist new ideas. We are afraid to be wrong and afraid to change.

Many seemingly spiritual people think they have intuition when in fact they are under the influence of ego, selfishness, and fixed false convictions. Unspeakable destruction occurs in the name of God, under the guise of intuition.

Intuition does not just happen. It does not come by being a member of a particular faith or following certain spiritual leaders. On the contrary, to be intuitive, we must transfer power from organized religion and its leaders to ourselves, for it is within each one of us that the direct connection to Omniscience exists.

Intuition is direct knowledge of the truth, beyond the information accessible to ordinary intellect and the senses. We cannot be intuitive in ordinary states of consciousness. To do so we must go beyond reason, the senses, emotion, desires, and the ego.

The subtle and powerful ego needs to be right all of the time. To grow past it, we must not be afraid to change. We need to stop reacting, defending, and fighting for our current position when we are wrong. We must extricate ourselves from prejudice, bias, and false conviction. We need to reduce mental restlessness and high emotional reactivity. We need to eliminate bad habits, excessive material desire, and dependency on attachments. We must be fearlessly introspective to find our flaws and correct them. We must face all of our fears, including fear of the unknown and death. When we do this, we prepare the soil of our consciousness for the growth of intuition.

Intuition manifests when we are still, humble, empty, and receptive. When we empty ourselves of mental and emotional restlessness, ego, selfish desires, and blind obedience to religious dogma, we can receive direction and guidance from the Divine Mind.

Stillness is the bridge between ordinary reason and intuition. We can get ideas and direction from Higher Intelligence when we are at peace with ourselves. When the mind is calm, we can receive guidance from that voice within. The more peace we have inside, the more guidance we receive from God through intuition.

Following is an exercise in problem solving through intuition. We can use our reason, will, and common sense to work on our problems while using our intuitive connection to Omniscience to get additional help. We can do this by cultivating stillness in both meditation and activity.

TECHNIQUE FOR CULTIVATING INTUITION

1. Reason
2. Meditation
3. Guidance
4. Receptivity
5. Action
6. Blessing
7. Mastery

1. REASON
Work to solve your problem with reason, will, and common sense.

2. MEDITATION
To get additional help from your intuitive connection, reduce your restless thoughts, emotions, and desires by cultivating stillness in meditation. With eyes closed, focus on the point just above the eyebrows. This is the center of intuition and spiritual perception. Practice your routine meditation technique. Relax, surrender, and completely let go of thought. Be still and empty. Feel your heart center.

3. GUIDANCE
Invoke the presence of God as the Infallible Intelligence that rules the universe. Present your problem to God and ask for guidance. "What do I need to do in this situation?" "What do I need to know?" "Guide me to the right thing that I should do." "Your will, my Lord, not mine."

4. RECEPTIVITY

Intuition can occur through thought, feeling, or visions. Be open and receptive to the whispers of counsel from within. Be aware of the feeling in your heart. Receive special guidance for your specific problems from the wisdom of your Confidante and Counselor.

5. ACTION

When you come out of meditation, try to remain inwardly calm so you can continuously receive guidance from Omniscience. Perform every act guided by that inner wisdom. When the mind becomes restless, take several slow, deep, abdominal breaths. Reaffirm the presence of God as your Supreme Guide and Friend, taking you to the best course of action. Be prepared to change directions if necessary.

6. BLESSING

Recognize the blessing. Notice the resources, right people, understanding, help, and other solutions that come.

7. MASTERY

In the beginning, it is unreasonable to assume that our actions stem from pure intuition. We are all subject to ego, emotion, personal desire, and bias. We make mistakes. We cannot tell for sure if our actions result from ego, intuition, or a combination of both. However, Love and other spiritual qualities can always guide us to what is good for others and ourselves. Moreover, we are moving in the right direction when we learn how to cultivate progressively greater degrees of stillness in meditation and activity. Our intuition slowly grows as we become more still. At mastery, when we are one with God's Supreme Wisdom, we can use our perfected intuition in the service of humanity.

POINTS TO REMEMBER

- To solve problems, we can work with ordinary reason, feeling, and the senses. We can use our good judgment and common sense. Simultaneously, we can ask for help from the Omniscience of God and receive it through our intuition.

- Intuition is direct knowledge of the truth, beyond the limited information given by ordinary intellect, emotion, the senses, and the ego.
- Intuition does not just happen. We have to work for it. It grows slowly. Intuition grows as we reduce our ego, calm the restless mind, eliminate emotional reactivity, and control excessive material desire.
- We can get to a higher order of intelligence in the stillness of meditation when we contact the intuition of the soul. When we calm our restless minds, emotions, and desires, we can receive guidance from this Higher Wisdom. Intuition is direct knowledge of the truth, which we can attain when we are completely still.
- We can commune with Infinite Intelligence in the stillness of deep meditation. Moreover, we can maintain contact with Omniscience in activity by remembering that this intelligence occupies every millimeter of space. We live in the mind of God. That same wisdom lives within us.

AFFIRMATIONS

- I commune with Infinite Intelligence in the stillness of deep meditation.
- I bring Omniscience into the moments of my life.
- I ask Omniscience for continuous guidance, direction, and support.
- I am in the Omniscient Mind of God.
- The Omniscient Mind of God is in me.
- God's Omniscience guides my thoughts.
- God's Omniscience guides my choices.
- God's Omniscience guides my relationships.
- God's Omniscience guides my work.
- I practice the presence of God as the Infallible Intelligence that rules the universe.
- Omniscience continuously guides me to virtue and peace.

EXERCISES

1. What is Omniscience?
2. Where is Omniscience?
3. What is intuition?
4. What is the relationship between intuition and Omniscience?
5. Have you had intuitive experiences such as thinking of a friend right before s/he called or had a dream that came true?
6. What is the relationship between reason and intuition?
7. What are the barriers to intuition?
8. Describe how the ego can confuse ordinary consciousness with intuition. Has this happened to you?
9. How can intuition help you with your problems?
10. Describe the technique for cultivating intuition.
11. How can we maintain our connection to the Omniscience of God during activity?
12. Get out of your head, into your heart, and be still. There are secrets here. Test it. Go to silence and ask for help, guidance, and healing.

CHAPTER 31

ONENESS

The Sacred Changeless One

*In seemingly empty space there is one link, one life eternal,
one wave of life flowing through everything, animate and
inanimate, unifying everything in the universe, a oneness of
life, a unity and harmony so vast, so perfect, breathtakingly
perfect, that it automatically breeds reverence and humility.*

Yogananda

God is one and changeless. In this chapter, we will learn how to contact the Changeless One, the One who creates, sustains, permeates, and connects all people and all space. We will explore this experience and why it is important.

We live in an infinite ocean of power. When we immerse ourselves in this ocean, we experience unity with all of life. In the stillness of the ocean, we contact the pure, formless consciousness that is at once the source of everything and the link that connects all. This consciousness fills all space. It cannot be born, confined, limited, divided, or destroyed. When we experience this power, we know that we are immortal, indivisible, and connected to all.

We are always in the Changeless One, even as a wave is part of the ocean. However, because of maya, we experience ourselves as isolated waves, separate from the ocean. Maya refers to the power inherent in ordinary consciousness that makes us think we are separate from the Creator, creation, and other creatures.

Maya is powerful and seductive. It is responsible for our hook to the physical plane. It tricks us into thinking we can achieve peace, Love, and joy by focusing on the little wave of our life to the exclusion of the ocean. Under the spell of maya, we focus on our soap opera, possessions, and bodies while we exclude the Changeless One from our consciousness.

We love maya, the physical plane, despite the limitations, impermanence, and suffering it imposes. However, in order to contact God, we must reduce the power of maya, since it and God occupy the same space. The Omnipresent Giver of peace and Love exists just behind the ever-changing world of people, events, and things. When we contact the Giver, we can draw from Her miraculous healing powers and qualities.

However, the shift from maya to God-consciousness is not easy. To find Her behind the veil of maya, we need help. This work describes a variety of methods designed to help us do this work. With persistent practice of these techniques, we can experience our little wave as a part of the Eternal Ocean. This results in a profound shift of consciousness from separation to oneness with creation. Then we know that we are eternally safe. Following is a review of how two methods, meditation and practicing the presence of God, can help us experience the Sacred One.

MEDITATION

Think of life as an ocean. The waves represent the physical plane where all things are in a state of flux. At times, the waves of the ocean are calm. However, it is only a question of time before the waves become stormy. We spend most of our lives on the surface, riding the waves of change. Their power is great. They command our attention and dominate our consciousness. The waves of the ocean are akin to maya.

Under the surface, the ocean is vast, still, one, and changeless. The goal of meditation is to shift our consciousness from the transient surface of the ocean to its depths; for it is only there that we can experience the eternal peace and safety of changelessness.

To get beneath the waves and benefit from the stillness, we must stop the world, body, senses, and mind. In meditation, we retreat from the world by sitting in a quiet place, closing our eyes, and keeping our body still. Then we discover the most difficult challenge: stopping the waves of the mind. Like the waves of the ocean, one thought after another pounds the shores of our consciousness. With practice, however, we can slowly reduce the intensity and frequency of our thoughts.

As the mind slows, we become increasingly aware of the underlying ocean and its deep healing power of stillness. Immersed, we may still see the changing waves above. However, we care less about their variance, enjoying the peaceful gentle power of the ocean underneath.

With consistent and regular practice of meditation, our identity slowly shifts. We are not the ever-changing surface waves. Rather, we are the changeless peace of the ocean below. Though the small waves, with a beginning, middle, and end do define our lives, we are ever a part of the vast permanent ocean just underneath the wave. When we realize we are always one with the Changeless One, we are at peace no matter what the world does.

PRACTICING THE PRESENCE OF GOD AS THE CHANGELESS ONE

We can experience the Changeless One in activity as well as in meditation. Spirit and matter are two sides of the same coin. On the material side is maya, the physical world of change. On the spiritual side is the Giver, always offering peace, Love, wisdom, and safety. In ordinary consciousness, we focus on the physical world to the exclusion of the Spirit. This is unfortunate; the physical world, however entertaining, ultimately makes us feel separate, insecure, and afraid.

When feeling this way, we can practice the presence of God. Everything we do, even routine activity, can serve as a reminder that the Changeless One is always present. A student returns from a visit with her spiritual teacher, a master. A friend asked her what secrets she learned. She said, "I learned how to tie my shoes."

For one who can see, even the most mundane routine is a window to, and a manifestation of, the Eternal One. Infinite peace, Love, wisdom, and safety are manifested through us at this very moment. We are one wave of the infinite ocean, made of the substance of that ocean. God is One and Changeless when we tie our shoes or experience an earthquake.

To practice the presence of God as such a unifying force, try the following exercise. We can practice this exercise whether we are involved in routine or stressful activities. The endgame is unity with the Great One underneath all, a unity that can never be severed.

TECHNIQUE

1. Stop
2. Breathe
3. Affirm
4. Act

1. STOP
When you become aware that your mind is unfocused or restless, stop and breathe.

2. BREATHE
Take several slow, deep abdominal breaths.

3. AFFIRM
Choose one or several of the affirmations below. Maintain this thought of unity throughout the day.
- All opposing forces merge in the One.
- Unity and harmony permeate my thoughts and actions.
- The Changeless One is in every person, house, flower, and blade of grass.
- All in One and One in all.
- My awareness of unity creates unity.

- My yearning for unity creates unity.
- I keep the unity of the many worlds before me.
- My world is broken. I heal it with oneness.
- The world is broken. I heal it with oneness.
- We are family.
- We are one.
- All of humanity is in the same boat.
- I am peace. I make peace. I am friend to all.
- I honor diversity.
- am a part of one Great Body.
- I am a part of One Person.
- The infinite universe is One Being.
- One Omniscient Power permeates and governs all things.
- I see everything in Her, and Her in everything.
- I see everything in Him, and Him in everything.
- Spirit and matter exist in the same space. I focus on Spirit.
- God and maya exist in the same space. I focus on God.
- The Changeless One is in everything.
- Everything is in the Changeless One.
- The Changeless One is everywhere.
- Every moment is an aspect of and a window to the Infinite One.

4. ACT

God is always right here, offering peace, Love, wisdom, and safety. Whether eating, driving, walking, sleeping, working, dressing, cleaning, socializing, exercising, sitting, thinking, feeling, or dreaming, know you are in the mind of God. Perform every action with the awareness that One Power connects all people, all objects, and all events.

We can learn how to move from the surface of the ocean to its deeper waters. When we learn to be in that place of oneness in both meditation and in activity, we experience peace, safety, and unity with all beings. What a joy it is to experience even a sliver of this beauty within our self! What other response could there be but humility, gratitude, and awe? What other action could we take but gentle, compassionate service to humanity?

POINTS TO REMEMBER

- God is One. All of creation is One. All life is in One Life. All minds are in the One Mind. All hearts are in One Heart. All bodies are in One Body. When we feel our life, mind, heart, and body as separate, we suffer. When we experience unity with all life, we soar.

- The universe is one system through the law of interconnection. Everything is connected to everything else. Maya would have us believe we are isolated. We cannot separate any part from the whole, despite the delusive power of maya.

- Our problems stem from our feeling of separation. We can counter this by developing a spiritual practice. For example, when we practice unconditional Love and service to humanity, we see the unity and connection that rule the cosmic order. When we help one person, we help the universe.

- The Intelligent Power that runs the universe organizes every millimeter of space, from particle to galaxy. The human body is composed of atoms, cells, organs, and systems, each necessary for the body to work. Each of us is part of the greater system of family, city, nation, and Earth. The Earth is a member of the family of planets, which form solar systems, which form galaxies. Each part, from particle to galaxy, is necessary for the whole to function correctly.

- Our consciousness exists as part of a vastly complex universe. We are a part of the whole and have a rightful place in it.

- Every individual, group, and nation of this earth has a unique, necessary role to play in the stupendous human drama.

- The Teacher of Oneness presents life to us as a puzzle. Every circumstance we encounter reveals something. There are clues and lessons. We can put the pieces of the puzzle together to make a coherent whole. When we do the work, we discover how the pieces fit together in a unique way to create our personal story, which in turn fits into the grand story of life.

- Find the Changeless One in your own consciousness. Then even the simplest most mundane action holds the key to the universe. You can know Him when you do the laundry or brew a pot of tea. Intelligent Power is in every nook and cranny.

- When we know the Changeless One within, we need not fear any condition of the body or the world. It takes time to get to this advanced state. On the way, we need courage, faith, patience, and perseverance.

- The Changeless One unites everything, inside and outside, you and I, and all creation. Despite the apparent separation, we are all one.

EXERCISES

The following exercises help us achieve peace of mind and oneness with humanity.

1. The true test of religion is Love. Does your path help you connect with others, or does it separate you?

2. Judgment of others creates separation. Acceptance and support bring us closer. What thoughts, feelings, and activities are you engaged in that separate you from others?

3. Finding the faults of others is easy. Instead, focus on their positive qualities. Give them support for their psychological and spiritual growth. What thoughts, feelings, and activities are you engaged in that bring you closer to others?

4. The basis of all spirituality is morality and goodness. We must learn how to behave. First, do no harm to others in thought or word. Stop judging, criticizing, and gossiping. Then practice compassionate service. Notice the peace of mind and strength you kindle as a result. Keep going, and you will experience solidarity with humanity and creation.

5. In ordinary consciousness, under the direction of the ego, we often feel superior or inferior to others. With spiritual consciousness, we are equal and one. No matter what your ego tells you, practice equality and unity with all others. Notice the harmony and rhythm that come to you as a result.

6. We can use the consciousness of One to help us when we are in conflict with others. Think of someone who provokes you. Visualize the healing light of Love melting his or her imperfections. Visualize the healing light of Love melting your own imperfections. Picture yourself in harmony with this person.

CHAPTER 32

HEALING

The Infinite Intelligent Healing Power

Healing power is unfathomable! To contemplate even a tiny aspect of this Omniscient Power breeds awe and respect. Reflect on its brilliance. A cut heals. In response to bacteria or viruses, the body creates precisely designed antibodies which hunt down and destroy the invaders. The body knows how to transform food into energy and materials for repair of damaged cells. Cells in the body are like construction workers with specialized jobs. Some build. Others tear down. Some transport. Still others eliminate debris. We can trust the infinitely intelligent healing power to do its work as the process of life unfolds. Moreover, we can tap into this power to help us manage our problems.

This chapter outlines two healing processes for transformation of the inevitable suffering of life into Love qualities. The processes are "The Ocean" and "The House." In "The Ocean," we learn how to get help in meditation for any pain or problem from the Great Healer. In "The House," we learn how to expand our space to receive the problems of life with equanimity.

THE OCEAN

We live in an infinite ocean of Love. The ocean has unlimited quantities of compassion, understanding, peace, forgiveness, courage, wisdom and other spiritual qualities. Each one of us is a drop of that ocean, made of the same qualities, but when we are separate from the ocean, these qualities remain limited. In ordinary states of consciousness, our droplet exists within but remains separate from the ocean. In advanced meditation, when separation dissolves, we join the ocean and absorb Her powers and qualities. This is contacting God in Her aspect as the Great Healer. In this role, She is the keeper of the ocean of Love.

We can bathe in the ocean of Love. In meditation, when we calm the waves, we enter the deep part of the ocean and absorb Her nature. In the stillness and silence of meditation, Love and her sister qualities slowly expand and replace our ego and problems. Love is the greatest healing force in the universe. It is more powerful than any pain or problem. Armed with this knowledge, we can go to the Great Healer in meditation and ask for help.

However, we must remember that healing is a slow process of purification, sometimes by fire. Although some problems dissolve easily, others are deeply embedded and take years of work. Often we think we have eliminated a problem, only to find additional layers later in life. Moreover, during crisis, we may experience immersion in the ocean of suffering rather than the ocean of Love. Immersed in suffering, we feel as though we might drown in the pain waves.

With long-term practice, however, we can learn how to ride out any wave of pain. When we stay with our pain, we come to the other side of the crisis where we find ourselves with more Love.

Love burns up problems one layer at a time, until Love is all there is. At mastery, we are always deep in the ocean of Love, no matter what the waves are doing. We come to know Love as the foundation of the universe. We feel safe, secure, and immortal. We are Love, and give only that.

TECHNIQUE

We can expand any one or a combination of the qualities listed in the spiritual alphabet by entering the ocean of Love in meditation. To get help with problems, try the following exercise.

1. Introspection
2. Spiritual alphabet
3. Prayer

4. Meditation
5. Action
6. Repetition
7. Mastery

1. INTROSPECTION

Make a problem list. For example, your problem might be fear of dying.

2. SPIRITUAL ALPHABET

Consult the spiritual alphabet and decide which qualities you would like to expand in response to your problem. You might choose safety, security, and immortality.

3. PRAYER

Ask for help from the Keeper of the ocean of Love. "Great Healer, I am drowning in waves of fear and pain. I need Your help. I need more of Your Love manifest as the safety, security, and immortality of my soul."

4. MEDITATION

With your will and concentration, eliminate all thoughts except those of safety, security, and immortality. In the increasing stillness of meditation, feel these qualities permeate and saturate your entire being, slowly melting your fear. Bathe in the healing ocean as long as you can.

5. ACTION

When you come out of meditation, bring your expanded feeling of safety, security, and immortality to all your experiences.

6. REPETITION

Repeat this process as often as possible.

7. MASTERY

In time, with your effort and God's grace, your little droplet of ocean completely merges with the ocean of Love. Then you will know you are safe, secure, and immortal.

Go to the healing ocean as often as possible. Bring all of your painful problems to the Great Healer. Consult the spiritual alphabet. Choose one or any combination of qualities you need in response to your problems. Focus on these qualities in the stillness of meditation. Repeat this process of purification until your Love is perfect.

POINTS TO REMEMBER

- We can turn the tables on our pain and make it work for us. Bring any problem to the stillness of deep meditation. Invoke God as the Great Healer. Ask for help. In the stillness of deep meditation, through the grace of the Keeper of the Ocean, Love qualities slowly replace our ego and problems.
- Love is more powerful than even the most brutal reality. We can go to the ocean of Love in deep meditation and absorb its unlimited supply of healing spiritual qualities as often as necessary, until we achieve mastery. At mastery, we experience our consciousness as a part of the vast ocean below. Then we know we are safe, secure, and immortal.

THE HOUSE

Imagine you live in a bi-level house. On the first floor is the physical plane, with all its tests and trials. Here we struggle with issues, problems, flaws, and symptoms. Sometimes we react well, other times, poorly. We need help. On the second floor are soul qualities. The atmosphere on the second floor is serene and spacious. Here is perfect Love. The goal is to bring Love qualities to the first floor, to help us manage our painful problems.

The steps to the second floor are spiritual practices such as affirmations, mindfulness, meditation, and loving service. When we practice these and other spiritual disciplines, we climb to the second floor where we absorb the qualities needed to manage whatever difficulties we must face on the first floor.

All of us have problems that take up residence on the first floor of our home against our will. Some of these we can fix. Others do not respond so easily. We do everything we can to eliminate them. However, no matter what we try, some problems will not budge. We cannot fix them or evict them. On the contrary, the more we struggle, the more upset and agitated we become.

When we find ourselves in this dilemma, we can accept the problem in our home as a resident instructor. Until this time, the problem has been treated as an uninvited guest. When agitated, it is often because we have not created enough space for the problem. Now we give the guest a room with plenty of space, and an atmosphere graced with acceptance.

We turn the table on the problem by going up to the second floor, where there is unlimited space. We take a portion of this space to the first floor and create a guestroom for the problem. We can create as many rooms as we need; there is an infinite supply of space on the second floor of this magical house. We can do this with all of our problems so that on the first floor, all we have are invited guests, our teachers in the school of life.

TECHNIQUE

In this exercise, we transfer the magical healing powers of the soul qualities on the second floor to the first floor to help us with our homework.

1. Introspection
2. Guest-teachers
3. Healing and purification
4. Action
5. Repetition
6. Mastery

1. INTROSPECTION

Make a list of problems that you are unable to eliminate from the first floor of your house: for example, highly reactive emotions.

2. CONVERT PROBLEMS TO INVITED GUEST-TEACHERS

Practice meditation, mindfulness, service to humanity, or any other set of spiritual practices that you enjoy. These disciplines will help you climb to the second floor where you can draw from an unlimited supply of space. With your expanded space from the second floor, create a room for your problem. Fill the atmosphere of the room with acceptance, thus making the uninvited problem a guest. This sets the stage for healing and purification.

3. HEALING AND PURIFICATION

When we respond to our painful problems with soul qualities, we heal and purify our consciousness. All our problems are teachers with the goal of helping us expand spiritual qualities until these qualities are unconditional. Go back up to the second floor to get whatever spiritual qualities you need to manage your problem. We have an army of 100 qualities to choose from up there! For highly reactive emotions, you might choose peace, gratitude, and patience. You can cultivate these qualities by practicing any one or combination of spiritual methods.

4. ACTION

Bring your expanded peace, gratitude, and patience to all of your actions.

5. REPETITION

Repeat this process of healing and purification until the spiritual qualities become unconditional.

6. MASTERY

In the end, we become unconditionally peaceful, grateful, and patient. Then we can give these qualities to all we meet.

POINTS TO REMEMBER

- An uninvited problem that we cannot eliminate creates agitation. We can reduce this agitation by giving the problem a spacious room filled with stillness, silence, and serenity.

- When life does not change, our response to it can. We can accept all problems with serenity. When we practice the spiritual methods described in this work, we create an increasingly serene space to hold our problems.

- We can bring the spiritual qualities down to the first floor in response to the tests and trials of our lives. When we focus on these qualities instead of our problems, we slowly spiritualize the entire first floor of our home. Eventually, Love, compassion, understanding, humor, cheerfulness, and strength permeate our atmosphere.

- In the beginning, in ordinary consciousness, a problem like a big fish creates many ripples in a small pond. In higher states of consciousness, the same fish has little or no effect, as our consciousness has expanded. We have the space inside to handle anything, including death.

- Whenever we have problems with difficult people, we can give each of them a room with plenty of space. We can then permeate that room with understanding, patience, tolerance, and kindness.

- Do not try to escape your problems. They are invited guest-teachers, but they do not own the house. Welcome these guests into your home but not as permanent residents. And always remember: you have the help of an army of 100 spiritual qualities!

AFFIRMATIONS

- I add Love to every moment.
- I entertain every guest-teacher.
- I accept all problems with serenity.
- I am serene no matter what happens.
- I manifest unflinching peace no matter what the world does.

- I manifest unflinching peace no matter what state my body is in.
- I stay deep in the ocean of Love no matter what happens on the surface.
- I am safe, secure, and immortal.
- I hold all of my problems in a compassionate space.
- I hold all of your problems in a compassionate space.
- I burn karmic problems with Love.
- Love burns karma: mine, yours, and ours.
- I surround, feed, permeate, and saturate all of my problems with Love.

EXERCISES

1. Describe the seven steps of the healing process called "The Ocean."

2. Do you use meditation to help you work with your pain and problems?

3. How might you use "The Ocean" to help you contain your problems?

4. Describe the six steps of the healing process called "The House."

5. What happens if you do not have enough space in your house to hold your problems?

6. When you practice spiritual disciplines, you expand the space in your house so it will be big enough to hold your problems. When you have a lot of space, problems can show up with barely a ripple. Is your house big enough? What will you do to create more space?

7. Make a list of the people who provoke you. In a meditative state, visualize each one of them in a room with plenty of space. Then permeate the room with understanding, patience, tolerance, and kindness. Picture yourself with each of these people in harmony and peace.

8. When you feel ashamed because of your mistakes, visualize yourself in a spacious room filled with understanding, compassion, and forgiveness. Absorb these qualities.

PART SEVEN
CONCLUSION

CHAPTER 33: A BALANCED HEALING PROGRAM

CHAPTER 33

A BALANCED HEALING PROGRAM

Putting It All Together

In this chapter, you will learn how to create a personal, balanced healing program to use for any painful condition, including major life crises or longstanding problems.

Our most basic instinct is to be happy and avoid suffering. Yet, physical, mental and emotional pain always slips past our best defenses. Our natural impulse is to do whatever it takes to rid ourselves of the discomfort. However, there is no escape from these trials of life.

We lock all of the doors of our body-home, trying to keep the peace by warding off uninvited guests. All too often our attempts to avoid suffering compound our problems, as explained in Chapter 4. When we persist in trying to escape our problems, our pain increases to the point of despair, physical and mental illness, disrupted relationships, reduced functioning, and potential danger to ourselves and others.

On the other hand, stepping into the pain and managing our problems wisely leads to healing, peace of mind, strength, and ultimately, joy. In step 8, pain management, we see pain as a directional signal pointing the way to our internal powers. When we learn to use suffering as a stimulant for the growth of spiritual qualities, the result is a shift in the locus of control from outside to inside. From this position of inner peace and strength, we can handle whatever comes our way.

Following is a complete list of the pain management techniques described in this book. These techniques help us mobilize our resources so that we can work through our problems, realize our spiritual power, and avoid unnecessary suffering. In this chapter, we will review how these methods work together to help us meet challenges head-on.

PAIN MANAGEMENT OPTIONS

To help you manage problems and pain, you can choose any one or combination of the following:

1. People
2. Activities
3. Belief system
4. Affirmations
5. Habit transformation
6. Progressive muscle relaxation
7. Breathwork
8. Contemplation
9. Meditation
10. Prayer
11. Mindfulness
12. Practicing the presence of God
13. Service
14. Yoga
15. Transformation of emotion

1. PEOPLE

When we suffer, we turn to trusted friends and family. We tell our story seeking understanding, support, and solace. At times, we seek advice, but more often, we just need to be heard and accepted. Just getting the story out brings relief and healing.

Often, however, we experience emotional pain that does not go away after talking it out. And sometimes our relationships make things worse because we are misunderstood or poorly treated. Even if we have a strong, loving support network filled with understanding, humor, and forgiveness, we will have emotional pain requiring management by other methods. In fact, one of the mistakes many of us make is looking to others for emotional pain relief when it is not possible. This leads to codependency, which is in effect addiction to people. We become codependent when we look to others to solve problems that can only be solved by ourselves.

2. ACTIVITIES

Constructive, meaningful activities are powerful pain managers. School, work, the arts, sports, recreation, and hobbies provide us with opportunities for growth and healing. We need a list of activities to turn to when pain arrives. It is helpful to have activities performed alone and with others.

3. BELIEF SYSTEM

Belief systems reduce and contain human suffering and emotion. We experience relief when we discover the meaning of life and of suffering. When we find our metaphor or story, we can survive even the worst conditions.

In addition to providing meaning and story, spiritual belief systems give us powerful methods (pain management options 4-15 above) to help us manage suffering.

CREATING A PERSONAL BALANCED HEALING PROGRAM

Review the pain management options listed above. Through trial and error, we can discover which option or combination will work for any given problem. For some problems, good friends and activities will suffice. On other days, contemplation, reading sacred texts, and meditation are most effective.

Some techniques, such as meditation or the transformation of emotion, may be more difficult for some people. If a technique causes too much pain, you can turn to another less invasive method. For example, if processing emotions causes you to feel frightened, and you are tempted to turn to an unhealthy painkiller such as alcohol, you can turn to a method, such as support from your friends or going to the gym, to restore your balance. When you feel stronger, you can return to the transformation of emotion. You can move from emotional processing to being with a friend for dinner, to emotional processing, to watching television, to prayer and meditation, to physical exercise, to emotional processing ....

The combination of methods used on any particular day may vary. As our experience grows, our ability to match techniques to problems improves. We become more effective pain managers. Eventually, we reach the point where we can handle anything, including the unknown and death.

CONCLUSION

Buddha and Christ discovered the secret connection between skillful pain management and healing. Recognizing pain as a law of life, the Buddha teaches us how to transform personal suffering into compassion for others. Christ on the cross demonstrated masterful skill in pain management when he forgave his tormentors at a time of excruciating suffering. We can follow their lead if we experience our pain and learn from it.

The ultimate goal of pain management is Love. When we stop running and accept pain as our teacher, we learn the necessary lessons which inevitably have to do with expansion of Love. There is a powerful narrative embedded in our feelings having to do with unconditional Love, friendship, and service. When we understand and forgive others and ourselves, the way is opened for healing and purification.

With Love as your tool, dig deep. Eliminate all traces of negativity. Get rid of your bad habits. Practice affirmation, mindfulness, the presence of God, and meditation. Contemplate the great sacred texts. Transform emotion to self-knowledge. Learn how to spiritualize your story. Serve all of humanity.

With people, activities, a strong belief system, and the 12 spiritual practices described in this work, you can field whatever life throws. Design a pain management program for yourself. Work with these practices for the rest of your life. Arrange and rearrange the methods to find the combinations that best suit you.

Accept pain as your teacher and allow the healing power to do its work. And remember, you can play hooky from school and go to the movies, but eventually you have to return to class. You need to do your homework first. You need to learn how to be a good pain manager. Then you can enjoy the show.

The Great Physician prescribes Love as the medication for all our ills. Follow Love and keep your eyes open. It will take you where you need to go. Even if you must pass through the cave of darkness, Love will light the way. Let your pain take you to the next level of higher consciousness. For every problem you navigate, you rise. When you complete all of your problems, you will rise above all of creation. Then you will know the foundation of the universe is Eternal Peace, Omniscient Love and Ecstatic Joy.

"May you find the peace, Love, and joy that are your soul."

POINTS TO REMEMBER

- Many of us have longstanding problems that may take years of work. We should not be discouraged if these problems do not respond immediately. Effort is progress. If we do the work, our problems slowly burn up. We stop attracting the same negative circumstances and people. The positive experiences in our lives increase. Peace, courage, strength, and wisdom grow.

- There are times in all of our lives when there are too many problems to handle at once. Problems compound. Our pain grows from moderate to severe. We go into crisis. There may be symptoms, impaired functioning, and danger. We can get discouraged or frightened. This may be a time to seek professional help. Some are reluctant to do this, thinking it to be failure. However, life is painful. At times, suffering is great. Getting help is a sign of strength and wisdom.

- We want to avoid pain and be happy. We have an aversion to suffering. We are afraid that our pain may cause us to lose control. We choose all kinds of behavior to avoid suffering, but pain is a part of reality. Eventually we must face it. If your life is focused only on feeling good, you are vulnerable to bad habits. Go deeper. Face your pain, fears, and problems. If you manage your pain wisely by practicing the spiritual disciplines described in this work, you will find out who you really are: peace, Love, joy, power, and wisdom.

AFFIRMATIONS

- I am a stronger and wiser because of my tests and challenges.
- Better to have pain than to remain the same.
- I see all problems as opportunities in disguise.
- Rather than seek pleasure and avoid pain, I accept both as having benefit.
- I develop spiritual muscles by working through my painful problems.
- I accept the difficulties of life as necessary for spiritual growth.
- I am strong and calm in any outer condition.
- Time and Love heal all of my wounds.
- I thank Spirit for providing me with opportunities to grow and transform.
- My suffering leads to compassion, strength, and wisdom.

EXERCISES

1. Review the list of pain management options described in this lesson. Which of these methods are you currently using? Which of these methods might you add to your program?
2. Discuss how people, activities, a belief system, and the 12 spiritual methods work together to help manage pain and suffering.
3. What is the nature of a balanced healing program?

APPENDIX A

Group Guidelines

I use this book for teaching in a group setting. We follow these guidelines. If there is a new member in the group, we read these guidelines before we start.

- Introduction and names

- This is a class on spiritual concepts, methods, and practices taught by the world's great religious traditions. We do not promote a particular religion. We do promote the development of your individual approach to spirituality.

- We have respect and tolerance for the great variety of ways to understand and practice spirituality.

- We are here to listen and share, learn and grow, study and practice.

- We do not proselytize.

- We engage in discussion without debate.

- We are not here to change others. We are here to figure out how to change ourselves.

- Although active participation is encouraged, it is perfectly okay to remain silent throughout the meeting.

- During the class, we take turns reading. If you don't wish to read, you are welcome to pass.

- Take what you need and leave the rest.

- We begin and end each class with a period of silent meditation for two minutes. The best meditation position is with the eyes closed, focused on the point just above the eyebrows, feet flat on the floor, hands resting in your lap with palms upward, spine straight, and slightly bent as a bow. You may repeat your focus word, mantra, or a favorite affirmation. You might also just focus on your breath.

- The term "Higher Power" is used to describe the God of your understanding, your higher self, higher states of consciousness, or your higher meaning and purpose.

- The group is 90 minutes. Usually, we read and discuss one chapter a week. Each person reads about 1/2 -1 page. We read the chapter first, then discuss the material.

- We avoid giving advice or trying to fix other people's problems. We focus on our personal experience using the spiritual methods for cultivating soul qualities in response to life's problems.

- When we finish the book, we return to the beginning and read it again.

- This is an open group. You can come and go as you please.

PERMISSIONS

I gratefully acknowledge permission from these sources to reprint the following:

The Guest House, from *The Essential Rumi,* Translations by Coleman Barks, 1995, reprinted by permission of Coleman Barks

Two Frogs in Trouble, From the teachings of Paramahansa Yogananda, reprinted with permission of Self-Realization Fellowship

REFERENCES

Alter, R. (2000). *The transformative power of crisis*. New York Harper-Collins.

Anandamoy. (2001, Spring). Converting what you read into personal realization, *Self-Realization Magazine*, 44-50.

Benson, H. (1996). *Timeless healing: The power and biology of belief.* New York: Fireside.

Benson, H. (1975). *The relaxation response.* New York: Morrow.

Birkedahl, N. (1990). *The habit control workbook.* Oakland: New Harbinger Publications.

Bloch, D. (1998). *Words that heal: Affirmations for daily living.* New York: Bantam Books.

Bloch, D. (1992). *I am with you always.* New York: Bantam Books.

Cooper, D. (1999). *A heart of stillness.* Woodstock: Skylight Paths Publishing.

Cooper, D. (1999). *Silence, simplicity, and solitude.* Woodstock: Skylight Paths Publishing.

Courage to change. (1992). New York: Al-Anon Family Group Headquarters.

Dass, R. & Mirabai, B. (1992). *Compassion in action.* New York: Bell Tower.

Dass, R. & Gorman, P. (1985). *How can I help?* New York: Alfred A. Knopf.

Dossey, L. (1992). *Healing words: The power of prayer and the practice of medicine.* New York: Harper-Collins.

Enright, R. (2001). *Forgiveness is a choice.* Washington D.C.: American Psychological Association.

Firestone, T. (1998). *With roots in heaven.* New York: Penguin.

Frankl, V. (1984). *Man's search for meaning.* New York: Washington Square Press.

Gibran, K. (1955). *The prophet.* New York: Alfred A. Knopf.

Hanh, T. N. (1992). *Peace is every step.* New York: Bantam.

Hendricks, G. (1995). *Conscious breathing.* New York: Bantam.

Herrmann, R. (2000). *God, science, and humility.* Philadelphia: Templeton Foundation Press.

Jackson, E. (1974). *Progressive relaxation.* Chicago: University of Chicago Press.

Kabat-Zinn, J. (1994). *Wherever you go, there you are.* New York: Hyperion.

Kabat-Zinn, J. (1990). *Full catastrophe living.* New York: Delta.

Kamala. (1969). *Priceless precepts.* Oakland: Kamala.

Keating, T. (2002). *Intimacy with God.* New York: The Crossroad Publishing Company.

Keating, T. (2001). *Open mind, open heart.* New York: Continuum.

Keating, T. (1997). *Active meditations for contemplative prayer.* New York: Continuum.

Khalsa, G. S. & Bhajan. (2000). *Breathwalk.* New York: Broadway Books.

Kornfield, J. (2000). *After the ecstasy, the laundry.* New York: Bantam Books.

Kushner, L. (1995). *Honey from the rock.* Woodstock: Jewish Lights Publishing.

Lawrence, B. & Laubach, F. (1973). *Practicing His presence.* Beaumont, Texas: The SeedSowers.

Lawrence, B. (1982). *The practice of the presence of God.* Springdale, Pennsylvania: Whitaker House.

Luskin, F. (2002). *Forgive for good.* San Francisco: Harper.

Mata, D. (2003). *Intuition: Soul-guidance for life's decisions.* Los Angeles: Self-Realization Fellowship.

Mata, D. (1990). *Finding the joy within you.* Los Angeles: Self-Realization Fellowship.

Mata, D. (1971). *Only love.* Los Angeles: Self-Realization Fellowship.

May, G. (1991). *The awakened heart.* San Francisco: Harper.

May, G. (1982). *Care of mind, care of spirit.* San Francisco: Harper.

Moffit, P. (2002, February). Forgiving the unforgivable. *Yoga Journal.*

Mosley, G. & Hill, J. (2000). *The power of prayer around the world.* Philadelphia: Templeton Foundation Press.

Prabhavananda, S. (1953). *How to know God.* Hollywood: Vedanta Press.

Rinpoche, S. (1993). *The Tibetan book of living and dying.* San Francisco: Harper.

Ruiz, D. M. (2001). *Prayers: Communions with our creator.* San Rafael: Amber-Allen Publishing.

Ruiz, D. M. (2000). *The four agreements companion book.* San Rafael: Amber-Allen Publishing.

Ruiz, D. M. (1997). *The four agreements: A Toltec wisdom book*. San Rafael: Amber-Allen Publishing.

Ruskan, J. (2000). *Emotional clearing*. New York: Broadway Books.

Salzberg, S. (2002). *Faith*. New York: Riverhead Books.

Segal, Z. (2002). *Mindfulness-based cognitive therapy for depression*. New York: Guilford Press.

Smith, H. (1999). *The world's religions*. San Francisco: Harper.

Sobel, D. & Ornstein, R. (1996). *The healthy mind, healthy body handbook*. New York: Patient Education Media.

Sorokin, P. (2002). *The ways and power of love*. Philadelphia: Templeton Foundation Press.

Templeton, J. (2002). *Wisdom from world religions*. Philadelphia: Templeton Foundation Press.

Templeton, J. (1999). *Agape love: A tradition found in eight world religions*. Philadelphia: Templeton Foundation Press.

Templeton, J. (1997). *Worldwide laws of life*. Philadelphia: Templeton Foundation Press.

The big book. (1983). New York: Alcoholics Anonymous World Services.

Vanzant, I. (1998). *One day my soul just opened up*. New York: Simon and Schuster.

Walsh, R. (1999). *Essential spirituality*. New York: John Wiley and Sons.

Walter, D. (1990). *The essence of self-realization*. Nevada City: Crystal Clarity Publishers.

Weil, A. (1999). *Breathing, the master key to self-healing*. Boulder: Sounds True, Inc.

Yogananda, P. (2003, Spring). Faith. *Self-Realization Magazine*, 4-15.

Yogananda, P. (2003). *Living fearlessly*. Los Angeles: Self-Realization Fellowship.

Yogananda, P. (1999). *Inner peace*. Los Angeles: Self-Realization Fellowship.

Yogananda, P. (1997). *Journey to self-realization*. Los Angeles: Self-Realization Fellowship.

Yogananda, P. (1997). *Autobiography of a yogi*. Los Angeles: Self Realization Fellowship.

Yogananda, P. (1995). *The Bhagavad Gita*. Los Angeles: Self-Realization Fellowship.

Yogananda, P. (1986). *The divine romance*. Los Angeles: Self Realization Fellowship.

Yogananda, P. (1984). *Worldwide prayer circle*. Los Angeles: Self-Realization Fellowship.

Yogananda, P. (1982). *Man's eternal quest*. Los Angeles: Self-Realization Fellowship.

Yogananda, P. (1981). *Scientific healing affirmations*. Los Angeles: Self Realization Fellowship.

Yogananda, P. (1968). *Spiritual diary*. Los Angeles: Self Realization Fellowship.

Zubko, A. (1998). *Treasury of spiritual wisdom*. San Diego: Blue Dove Press.

INDEX

ABOUT THE AUTHOR

Dr. Phil Shapiro has had a 30-year career as a clinician, teacher, and administrator in public psychiatry. Work has taken him from the inner city to the Alaska bush, from holistic to addiction medicine, and from the head office of a state mental health division to 100-year-old state hospital wards.

Dr. Shapiro has worked with a variety of people including African-American and Hispanic people in Harlem and Bedford-Stuyvesant, Native Alaskans, retired military and postal workers in Maine, among others. In 1974, he worked in one of the first interdisciplinary holistic clinics in New York City. In 1983, he became the Director of Mental Health and Developmental Disabilities for the State of Alaska. Following that, he was the Chief Medical Officer at Oregon State Hospital and then Clinical Director of Forensic Psychiatry at Western State Hospital. He has been a surveyor, reviewing quality of care in hospitals and clinics throughout the country.

Dr. Shapiro received his medical degree in 1969 from the University of Illinois Medical School, where he was a member of the medical honor society, Alpha Omega Alpha. He trained in psychiatry at Albert Einstein College of Medicine, Downstate and Kings County Hospital in New York City, and received a Masters Degree in Public Health from Columbia University. Dr. Shapiro has been on the faculty of the Department of Psychiatry at Columbia University, and is currently an Associate Clinical Professor in the Department of Psychiatry at Oregon Health and Sciences University.

While he has studied the nature of disease and suffering with many of the masters of psychiatry and psychology, his greatest teachers have been his patients who are the carriers of the devastating aspects of life: racism, poverty, mental and physical illness, homelessness, child sex abuse, rape, domestic violence, and addiction. These courageous people and the mean streets they walk continue to be his teachers of the brutal realities of life.

Dr. Shapiro lives in Portland, Oregon happily married to Sharon Whitney, author and playwright. They have two sons and five grandchildren. He works for a community mental health center where his understanding of suffering and the magnificence of the healing power continues to evolve.

Printed in the United States
69109LVS00003B/25